THE
BRANDMINDSET®

THE
BRANDMINDSET®

DUANE E. KNAPP

McGraw-Hill

New York   Chicago   San Francisco   Lisbon   London
Madrid   Mexico City   Milan   New Delhi   San Juan
Seoul   Singapore   Sydney   Toronto

Library of Congress Catalog Number: 99-074659

McGraw-Hill

A Division of The McGraw-Hill Companies

For readability and ease of reference, the BrandPromise™ methodology will be referred to alternatively as the *promise*.

FutureBrand℠ is a registered service mark of The FutureBrand Company and is used with permission.

"Living our Brand's Promise," the Leader's Culturalization Guide in Chapter 9, is an approved adaptation of "Building Quality Customer Relations," © 1994 Competitive Dynamics, Inc.

     6 7 8 9 0   AGM/AGM   0 9 8 7 6 5 4 3

ISBN 0-07-134795-X

Set in New Century Schoolbook by Lisa Hernandez of Editorial and Production Services.

Printed and bound by Quebecor.

To the memory of my grandmother and father, and in honor of my mother who gave me love and inspiration

CONTENTS

Chapter 3

Chapter 4

FOREWORD

Defining a brand is one thing. How to build one is another. In the BrandMindset®, Duane Knapp clearly outlines what a genuine brand is and how to build one. His book adds practical perspective to the fast-growing body of knowledge about branding as a corporate strategy and provides a detailed "how to do it" process for any organization.

Branding is not the exclusive domain of worldwide products, such as Coca-Cola soft drinks, McDonald's fast food, or Maytag household appliances. Every corporate leader needs to ask the questions: "How can we create a genuine brand? What, in our situation, would be an ideal strategy for our brand? What kind of effort will it take, and will the payoff be worth it?"

These questions encompass a myriad of issues for organizations to consider: What is distinctive about our product and service? Whose perception is important to us—who are our customers? What do we want them to think about us? How do we achieve our desired perception? How do we inform them about who we are, and how do we get them to believe and trust in our products and services?

The questions don't stop there. Do we want to be perceived as high-priced and exclusive, or is our target market price-sensitive, in which case we need to offer "value pricing"? Hard-nosed internal assessments, competitive analysis, and market research are the tools to answer these questions and build a strong brand foundation.

Even if an ideal strategy for the brand is conceived, though, the work has just started. The tough part is building the brand, making it work, and making it last.

At first glance, branding might be seen as something created by a marketing department. Nothing could be farther from the truth. I have done quite a bit of work with organizations wanting to become "customercentric." That's very much what branding is about. A customercentric culture starts with pervasive focus throughout an organization to identify, understand, and satisfy customers' needs—both external and internal customers.

Genuine brands focus on their functional and emotional benefits for the consumer, i.e., their BrandPromise™.

Every action that impacts people's perceptions of a product or service requires attention. Everything. Most significant is senior management's demonstration of their commitment to creating and sustaining the brand. Brand creation begins with a passionate leader. Ray Kroc, L. L. Bean, and Sam Walton—none of whom was formally schooled in the concept of branding—all started small, but they had the vision, passion, and leadership ability to build groups of employees into customer-focused teams who created brands that have become successful far beyond what they could possibly have imagined.

What measures a brand's success? One sign is that customers, in effect, "take themselves out of the market." They need look no further for a similar product or service. The brand offers all they want, and they know that the company producing it will stand behind it—period.

Building a brand-driven culture is not an event. It's a lifelong commitment to a mindset and a way of life that takes time, planning, and perseverance. I think of it as investing in the construction of a factory—one that produces *intangible outputs*. The outputs include greater customer satisfaction, reduced price sensitivity, fewer customer defections, a greater share of customers' wallets, more referrals, and a higher percentage of repeat business. At the same time, this factory produces internal benefits, such as lower costs, higher morale, and greater productivity.

Today, it is not enough to provide a service or a product. Success comes when the product and service are created and delivered through a BrandMindset—the system of leadership, team spirit, innovation, and customer sensitivity described in the following chapters.

Christopher W. Hart, Ph.D.
President, Spire Group, Ltd.
and Adjunct Professor of Marketing,
The University of Michigan

PREFACE

Brand. What is it? Why is it important? How do you get one? Everybody's using the word; it's the hot topic of the day. As a colleague of mine used to say, "What does it all mean?" Indeed, that is the right question and that is the reason for this book.

Brand is becoming one of the most popular words used in the press today, from the nightly news to business publications. The public in general is becoming more aware of the implications, benefits, and the power of a well-managed brand. *Brand* is no longer a word to be associated only with products or packaged goods but now also with a thought process and a key business strategy.

In fact, when people use the word *brand*, they usually are thinking about a *brand name* or a product or service bearing a widely known brand name. *Brand* can be defined as a variety of something that is characterized by some *distinctive* attribute. Many brands are really just brand names because they either have lost their distinctive characteristic or are not perceived to be unique.

WHAT IS A GENUINE BRAND?

We define *genuine brand* as the internalized sum of all impressions received by customers and consumers resulting in a distinctive position in their mind's eye based on perceived emotional and functional benefits.

Distinctive is the key word to understanding the real meaning of a brand. It's not an organization that gets to decide whether or not its brand is distinctive. A brand is only distinctive if the consumer perceives and believes that it truly is.

In order for an organization to have a genuine brand, it must meet several expectations:

1. Is it truly distinctive or different in a manner that is important or valued by its consumers?
2. Is it committed to providing certain emotional and functional benefits to the consumer?
3. Does it consistently fulfill its promise and deliver on its commitment?

It would appear that the concept of a real or genuine brand is not intuitive. People who used to be responsible for "sales" over time became "marketing" executives and now have added "brand" to their titles. Generic products become "private labels" and now they are called "private brands." Brand has become synonymous with marketing and advertising.

An organization that has a BrandPromise that is understood and lived by every single person in the organization has the right stuff to become a genuine brand. A genuine brand occupies a distinctive and valued position in the consumer's mind. It's not just an image created by the marketing department or advertising agency. It is the customer's perception, a sum total of every person, experience, product, and service that an organization provides and that the customer experiences.

BRANDSTRATEGY™ DOCTRINE

A genuine brand is a "way of life." It's not just about a word, its about passion, commitment, and a unique promise that gets fulfilled every day. We have identified five strategies to create, manage, or enhance a genuine brand:

- "Think like a Brand"
- Make a BrandPromise
- Communicate the optimum Brand message
- Live the Brand
- Leverage the Brand

The BrandStrategy Doctrine Process is the roadmap through the thought process. It consists of five steps:

- Completion of a Brand Assessment
- Developing the BrandPromise
- Creating the Brand Blueprint
- Brand Culturalization
- Enhancing the Brand Advantage

The BrandMindset consists of eight key concepts that parallel and support the BrandStrategy Doctrine Process outlined above.

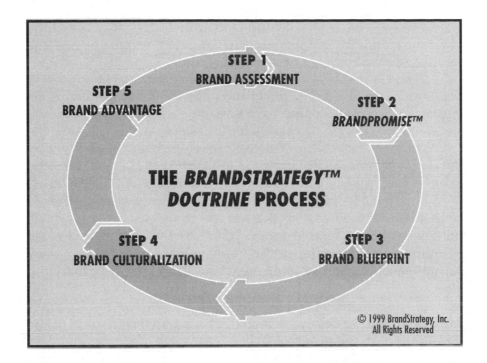

First, as a precursor to the process of creating a genuine brand, the BrandMindset introduces a "point of view," a way of thinking about the subject of brand and its related components.

Second, the BrandStrategy Doctrine Process is explained in more detail as it relates to the entire book. We also address the importance of a brand's requirement to be perceived as distinctive.

The Brand Assessment can be described as a compass for a brand. It outlines the procedures that can be utilized to evaluate a brand's position as well as its current and future equity.

The fourth concept is the BrandPromise, which is the foundation for a customer's expectation of how the brand will perform. The process for developing a BrandPromise is discussed in detail. Any organization, large or small, can apply this methodology to create a genuine brand.

Next, the Brand Blueprint chapter explains the benefits of developing an architecture to maximize a brand's messages and communications.

The sixth concept is Brand Culturalization, which explains the importance of customer service as a key requirement, "the heart and soul," of a genuine brand.

Brand Advantage is detailed in three approaches (private brands, FutureBrands^SM, and brand alliances) that organizations can utilize to create competitive advantage, increase distinctiveness, and position their brands for long-term success.

The last concept, brandstrategy.com, outlines the philosophy for creating genuine brands on the Internet. It also includes the criteria for evaluating brands in the virtual world of the Internet.

Finally, the Brand Tools chapter provides readers a chance to test their "brand I.Q." with a variety of self-scoring appraisals on several brand-related topics. This chapter also includes six sample reports, training guides, and evaluations to make it easy for any organization to implement the BrandStrategy Doctrine Process.

At the conclusion of most chapters, we have profiled a genuine brand that we believe demonstrates an understanding of the BrandMindset and deserves to be an example. Each chapter also has an Action Guide, which outlines ideas to remember as you are building your own brand.

In an attempt to make the book easier to read, please note that we will use the following italicized words to sometimes represent our core concepts throughout the book:

- BrandPromise   *promise*
- BrandStrategy Doctrine   *doctrine*
- Brand Assessment   *assessment*
- Brand Blueprint   *blueprint*

Following the Acknowledgments, we have provided a Brandictionary that explains the terms listed above as well as a variety of brand-related terms and definitions to assist in understanding the concepts behind *The BrandMindset*. Please take a few minutes to review them prior to reading the book.

ACKNOWLEDGMENTS

For most of my life I have been involved in the pursuit of brand excellence, knowingly and unknowingly. In retrospect, I am sure the seeds for *The BrandMindset* were planted while growing up on my grandmother's farm in Michigan. She required that our asparagus be truly unique; i.e., the freshest, always moist, and a taste so good you could eat it right in the field. We snapped every stem by hand to preserve its freshness for our customers.

I am thankful for the opportunities provided to me and feel that I have "stood on the shoulders of so many giants," beginning with my mentor and graduate school advisor at the University of Toledo School of Business, Dr. Douglas Austin. My early career began with one of the most successful Chevrolet automobile dealership organizations in the United States. The founder's dedication to quality, integrity, and service—offering only the finest used cars (never an adjusted speedometer, even though it was popular at the time)—and the power of the Chevrolet brand in the 1970s reinforced my appreciation for genuine differentiation and quality.

The opportunity to be influenced by two CEOs of Westin Hotels, Lynn Himmelman and Eddie Carlson, as well as Dan McClaskey, Larry Magnan, and Jack Gaines, gave me a unique opportunity to experience the culture and passion of a true dedication to quality and excellent service.

The light really came on for me when I joined Holiday Corporation and worked for Michael Rose. His understanding of the importance of a brand "thought process" and his personal leadership was fundamental to my brand education. The opportunity to study strategic marketing at Stanford's Graduate School of Business had a huge impact on my belief in the discipline required to have a successful brand.

And thanks would not be complete without a tribute to David Aaker, the Et Grether Professor of Marketing at the Haas School of Business of the University of California, Berkeley, and perhaps the most revered brand thinker today. His advice and friendship have been extraordinary and greatly appreciated.

One of my primary beliefs about genuine brands is that an organization's culture must support and energize the brand. My thanks to Elyse Kaplan, who has been a pioneer in what we have referred to as the "science of brand culturalization," which we believe should replace the traditional "training for behavior" approach.

I am also indebted to many exceptional executives for their insight, expertise, and friendship, including: Gwen Baum, Joe Feczko, and Carol Sanger of Federated Department Stores; David Evans of Starwood Hotels and Resorts; Roy Evans, Jr., of the Professional Convention Management Association; Chris Hart, Adjunct Professor of Marketing at the University of Michigan, President of The Spire Group, and author of five books including *Extraordinary Guarantees: A New Way to Build Quality Throughout Your Company and Ensure Satisfaction for Your Customers*; Michael Gould and Tony Spring of Bloomingdales; Ted Leonhardt of the Leonhardt Group; Paul Marth of Quality Food Centers; Rich Komen of Restaurants Unlimited, Inc.; Roger McClung of Acosta; John Melin of Coinstar; Don Morgan of GMA Research; Ray Schultz, Founder of Hampton Inn; Carey Watson of Burdines; Gary Yiatchos of The Bon Marché; Tim Carter of Bell Carter Foods; Sheila Field and Martine Reardon of Macy's; Kent Anderson of macys.com; Lee Richardson of Rich's, Lazarus, Goldsmith's; Susan Mesec of Stern's; and Andrea T. Goeglein, Ph.D., of ConServ International.

This book would not have been possible without the support and assistance of Rachel Bolton of Hallmark Cards Inc.; Brian Ruder of Citigroup; Michael J. Lacorazza of Lexus; Kevin Carothers of Starbucks Coffee Company; John Elkins of The FutureBrand Company; Retha Martin of Whirlpool Corporation; Tom Keltner of Promus Companies; and Mary Glenn and Jane Palmieri of McGraw-Hill.

On a personal note, I am indebted to my colleagues: Blaine Becker for his excellent thinking, Katie McKenna for her significant contribution, and Dana Kirschbaum. I would also like to express my appreciation to Victoria Morgan for her conceptualization and writing contributions, and to Jim Bessent for his exceptional editing and professional expertise.

Duane E. Knapp

BRANDICTIONARY™
Definitions to Help You Think Like a Genuine Brand

Throughout this book, we have used a variety of brand-related terminology, our own definitions, and other terms that are indicated by their source. We thought it might be helpful to utilize the *Brandictionary* as a summary of the book's concepts and a ready-reference for your convenience as you read the book. BrandMindset™, BrandPromise™, Brandictionary™, and BrandStrategy™ are trademarks of BrandStrategy, Inc. All other trademarks are the property of their respective companies. In addition, other easily recognizable brands and brand names are used for illustrative purposes and are not associated with BrandStrategy, Inc.

BrandMindset™: The ability to think like a brand.

BrandPromise™: The essence of the brand's benefits—functional and emotional—that current and potential customers should expect to receive when experiencing a brand's products and services, a brand value proposition.

BrandStrategy™ Doctrine: The comprehensive action plan (roadmap) used by an organization to define its essence (the BrandPromise), the purpose of which is to create a paradigm shift and a "position of privilege" (sustainable competitive advantage) and to optimize overall brand equity.

Brand Advantage: The result of consistent enhancing, nurturing, and innovating a brand.

Brand Alliances: Utilizing other appropriate brands to enhance an organization's brand equity.

Brand Assessment: An objective analysis of a brand's image and perception.

Brand Blueprint: 1. The disciplined action and process required to create, plan, design, and build brands. 2. The character and structure of a brand's representations, i.e., the architecture of a brand (brand name, byline, tag line, brand promise, and graphic representation).

Brand Bribery: The practice of "buying loyalty" by some brands, especially those perceived as commodities, when they are unable or unwilling to offer a distinctive BrandPromise.

Brand Byline: A short phrase or descriptive words that accompany a brand name to clearly communicate to customers and potential customers where to place the brand's products and services in their mind's eye, e.g., Whirlpool's brand byline: "Home Appliances."

Brand Culturalization: **1.** To expose all current and future employees and associates to the sum total of beliefs, behaviors, and ways characteristic of a particular brand. **2.** To raise the level of awareness with a view toward improvement (self and organizational). **3.** To Live the BrandPromise.

Brand Discipline: Making decisions like a brand: utilizing business facts, consumer and market research, and brand expertise.

Brand Drivers: Key ways brands communicate their benefits to build and enhance their brand equity.[1] They include perceived quality, brand associations, name awareness, brand loyalty, and other proprietary assets.

Brand Equity: A brand's valuation based on the totality of its perception, including the relative quality of its products and services, financial performance, customer loyalty, satisfaction, esteem, and so forth.

Brand Focus: A concentrated thought process that holds the BrandStrategy Doctrine as the primary focus of an organization's business plans and budgets, and not the other way around.

Brand Leverage: Developing a conscious plan for optimizing a brand's perceived size and value relative to the scope of its business.

Brand Loyalty: When customers have positive feelings regarding a brand and they use the brand's products and services on a regular basis; the expected result when a brand establishes as a priority to be perceived first and foremost as a "friend" to consumers.

Brand Name: A product, line of products, or service bearing a widely known brand name. (*Random House Dictionary of the English Language*)

Brand Paradigm Shift: **1.** A fundamental change in a business or strategic model. **2.** A fundamental and significant change in a brand's perceived distinctiveness.

Brand Playing Field: The competitive environment in which organizations, by utilizing all of the aspects—people, products, services, etc.—vie to create a distinctive brand perception.

Brand Tag Line: An expressive series of words or a short phrase used to communicate or dramatize the brand's emotional and functional benefits to customers and potential customers in an effort to influence how consumers feel about the brand; e.g., Nike's "Just Do It."

Brand Value: The feeling consumers take away from their experience with a brand.

D.R.E.A.M.: Acronym for the determinants of genuine brand building: **D**ifferentiation, **R**elevance, **E**steem, **A**wareness, and **M**ind's eye.

FutureBrand[SM]**:** The creative expression of a compelling branded idea that represents the aspirations of the business strategy in a truly differentiated way today and in the future.

Generic Brands: A term used to describe products that are sold in a package without a brand name; e.g., a *generic* drug.

Genuine Brand: The internalized sum of all impressions received by customers and consumers, which results in a distinctive position in their mind's eye based on perceived emotional and functional benefits.

Higher Motives: Term describing a heightened state of aspiration, emotion, or inspiration resulting from the intentional design and implementation of a brand's appeal; e.g., Disney World.

Icon (Iconographic Mark): An image or graphic representation associated with a product or business; e.g., the Starbucks Siren or mermaid image.

Logo (Logotype): A graphic representation or symbol of a company name, trademark, abbreviation, etc., often uniquely designed for ease of recognition.

Mind's Eye: The position in the consumer's mind that a brand occupies.

National Brand: A widely known brand within a product category; e.g., Del Monte in canned vegetables or Ralph Lauren in sweaters.

Position of Privilege: A sustainable distinctive competitive advantage.

Private Brand: Description used to refer to types of products that retailers create for their exclusive or private use; e.g., Charter Club.

Private Label: A description used to refer to types of products provided by suppliers to the retail industry which bear the name of the respective retailer's store brand or another created name; e.g., Safeway Select or President's Choice.

® (Registered Trademark): Symbol used with trademarks that have been registered with the U.S. Patent and Trademark Office. Also may be used with registered service marks.

ˢᴹ(Service Mark): Similar to a trademark (registered with the U.S. Patent and Trademark Office), except that service marks promote services and events, whereas trademarks promote products.

™ (Trademark): Symbol identifying trademarks that have not been issued a registration by the U.S. Patent and Trademark Office.

Trade Dress: The distinctive visual appearance of a brand's products, packaging, building, etc.

Visual Vocabulary®: The visual translation of a brand into a flexible set of images, symbols, colors, typography, overall style, and ownable messages.

1

The BrandMindset®

Thinking like a Genuine Brand
with a Brand Profile of Hallmark Cards

I am a brand.[1]
—Martha Stewart

BRANDING IS A MINDSET

The BrandMindset concept is dedicated to the proposition that each person and every activity in any organization should be focused daily on the question: "How am I building our brand's equity?" This question is universally applicable. Enterprises of all sizes, from home-based professionals, new ventures, and small corporations to "not for profit" associations and large global conglomerates, are challenged not only to answer this fundamental question but also to deliver tangible results.

While most employees can easily describe their functional job tasks—"I answer the phone"; "I am the vice president of marketing"; "I fill orders"; "I execute retail promotions"; or "I sell more pharmaceuticals..."—they may not be clear as to how they enhance their organization's brand equity.

Our brand advisory experience with all types of organizations (corporations, associations, and new startup ventures), from Belgium to Singapore and New York to Seattle, has led to the conclusion that if a brand is to be genuine and truly successful, the organization must learn to "think like a brand." It is not enough to think only in terms of providing the best of something in a category or industry. Merely innovating products and services won't necessarily achieve a long-term, sustainable "position of privilege" with consumers. Everyone in an organization must have a personal understanding of what their brand stands for and how they deliver the brand's essence.

In order to convey how to think like a brand and have fun along the way, we have endeavored to introduce the concepts and methodologies of the BrandMindset in a clear, concise, and direct manner, similar to a Microsoft PowerPoint® presentation. At the conclusion of this chapter, we profile Hallmark Cards because we believe that Hallmark is an outstanding example of an organization that thinks like a brand. The concepts introduced in this chapter are explained in greater detail in later chapters. So let's begin to see what it means to think like a brand.

WHAT IS BRAND EQUITY?

As indicated in the introduction, it's everyone's job to build an organization's brand equity, from the voicemail recording to the chief executive officer. You would think the one person in the or-

FIGURE 1–1

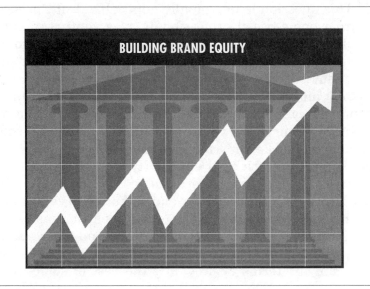

BUILDING BRAND EQUITY

ganization who would know the most about brand equity would be the chief executive officer. The fact is, just the opposite is sometimes true. In *Marketing Myths That Are Killing Business,* Kevin Clancy and Robert Shulman write that in truth, "many chief executive officers know very little about marketing and much of what they know is wrong."[2]

We believe—and define—*brand equity* as the totality of the brand's perception, including the relative quality of products and services, financial performance, customer loyalty, satisfaction, and overall esteem toward the brand. It's all about how consumers, customers, employees, and all stakeholders *feel* about a brand. All too often, running the daily rat race gets in the way of making customers or clients happy, i.e., enhancing their perception of the brand.

BRANDS ARE IGNORED AS STRATEGIC ASSETS

Our research indicates that organizations rarely optimize brand equity. When chief executive officers are asked who's responsible for their brand, a frequent answer is "the advertising agency" or "someone in marketing."

However, if you ask chief executive officers such questions as:

- Who determines what products and services to offer?
- Who decides which customer service employees to hire?
- Who is responsible for formulating pricing for products and services?

they do not answer that it is the advertising agency.

The fallacy entertained in many organizations is that the brand has to do primarily with advertising, promotions or messages that the marketing department or advertising agency creates, as opposed to the firm's total strategy. Or as John Bissell put it in a *BrandWeek* magazine article, "It is clear that a big marketing budget is no substitute for a lack of a marketing strategy. That's a fact that's too often ignored."[3]

Enormous opportunity exists for most organizations to enhance their brand equity if all stakeholders (employees, agents, vendors, and outside professionals) who work for the entity could

FIGURE 1–2

BRANDS IGNORED AS STRATEGIC ASSETS

Brands are not being treated as strategic corporate assets,
according to results from a study by Kuczmarski & Associates, Chicago.

**"The brand mismanagement among all companies
was a surprise even to us."**

— More than 60% of the companies had no contingency plans.

— 56% said they did not measure brand value.

— 33% did not have formal, long-term brand strategies.

---

truly understand the BrandMindset. When organizations embrace the concept of thinking like a brand, everything they do—every product, service, and customer interaction—is analyzed to determine whether it is fulfilling the brand's goal. As indicated in Figure 1-3, the idea is to harness a brand's energy so that it adds to overall equity. Brands like Starbucks, Hard Rock Cafe, and Tiffany provide good examples of this. Historically, Starbucks, as a business, has not been a big player in the overall world production of coffee; however, its brand arguably makes a bigger contribution to its overall corporate equity than any other coffee brand.

It's important to avoid confusing size with brand equity. Although size can be important, the Starbucks brand has been a significant factor in its success from the beginning of Howard Schultz's leadership. The ability to leverage a brand relates directly to its distinctiveness from other competitors in the mind of the consumer. Also, brand leverage does not necessarily depend on a large media budget. Tiffany, Starbucks, and Hard Rock Cafe have all built national and international brands with relatively

FIGURE 1–3

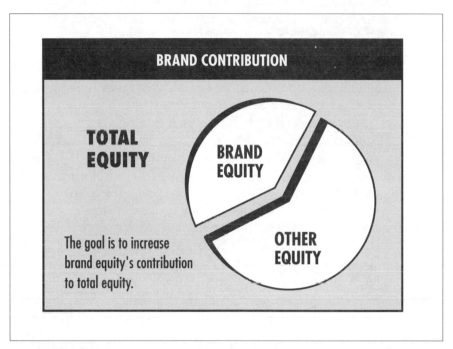

little media advertising. In Chapter 7, the section called Brand Alliances, we will discuss in greater detail how Starbucks has leveraged its brand equity.

The real question is: Are you ready to leverage *your* brand and significantly grow your total equity?

WHAT IS A BRAND?

It seems that everyone is talking about brand this and brand that. *Brand* is becoming one of the most popular words used today. But when you ask any group of people what a brand is, the answers vary widely. Some think a brand is a name or a trademark. Some think it is a product, or even a commitment. Essentially, all of these could be correct.

Our interviews and discussions with thousands of executives, employees, entrepreneurs, and the general public reveal that when most people use the word *brand*, they are thinking brand *name*.

The *Random House Dictionary of the English Language* defines brand name as a "product or service bearing a widely <u>known</u> brand name." Brand names are really the most familiar representations of brands. We see them on a daily basis. As the definitions in Figure 1-4 indicate, the key aspect regarding brand names is familiarity.

But as you can also see, just because a brand name is familiar does not ensure that it will be *distinctive*. A brand name is not necessarily a brand! As Stephen Dunphy, business editor for *The Seattle Times*, says, "Brand does not mean the same thing to everybody; some organizations get the concept and many don't." According to Dunphy, the key is whether an organization "walks the talk" and really understands the necessity for a brand to be distinctive in a manner that's beneficial to its customer. In fact, it could be argued that many brand names might be well-known, yet not all that distinctive in the consumer's mind when com-

FIGURE 1–4

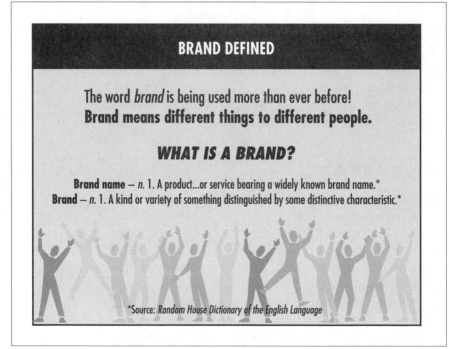

BRAND DEFINED

The word *brand* is being used more than ever before!
Brand means different things to different people.

WHAT IS A BRAND?

Brand name – *n.* 1. A product...or service bearing a widely known brand name.*
Brand – *n.* 1. A kind or variety of something distinguished by some distinctive characteristic.*

*Source: *Random House Dictionary of the English Language*

parcd to other brand names in their industry. Examine the following brand names and consider whether any of them are perceived as unique:

- Merrill Lynch, T. Rowe Price, Piper Jaffrey—securities firms
- Prudential, New York Life, Metlife—life insurance
- Blue Cross, Blue Shield, Principal—health insurance
- Florsheim, Johnston & Murphy—shoes
- MCI, Sprint, WorldCom – long distance providers

In order to be a brand, a product or service must be characterized by a distinctive attribute in the consumer's mind.

WHAT IS A GENUINE BRAND?

As explained in Figure 1-5, there are three fundamental traits that differentiate a *genuine brand* in consumers' minds:

- The *internalized* sum of impressions
- A *distinctive* position in their mind's eye
- Perceived *functional* and *emotional* benefits

It is critical to understand that brands are not simply the result of the advertising or messages that an organization places in the marketplace. At the end of the day, a brand is only that which is perceived in the consumer's mind, or what we denote as the mind's eye. The consumer's mind's eye is influenced by thousands of impressions daily and changes just as often. Not only must a brand monitor its impressions constantly, it also has to occupy a distinctive position in the consumer's mind to really be a brand.

The less distinctive or different a brand is in the consumer's mind, the more room for competitors to occupy a position in the mind's eye, and the less genuine a brand becomes. The easiest way to visualize the difference between brand names, brands, and genuine brands is to look at them on a continuum that compares relative distinctiveness (see Figure 1-6). The more distinctive a brand becomes in the consumer's mind, the closer it approaches the definition of a genuine brand.

FIGURE 1–5

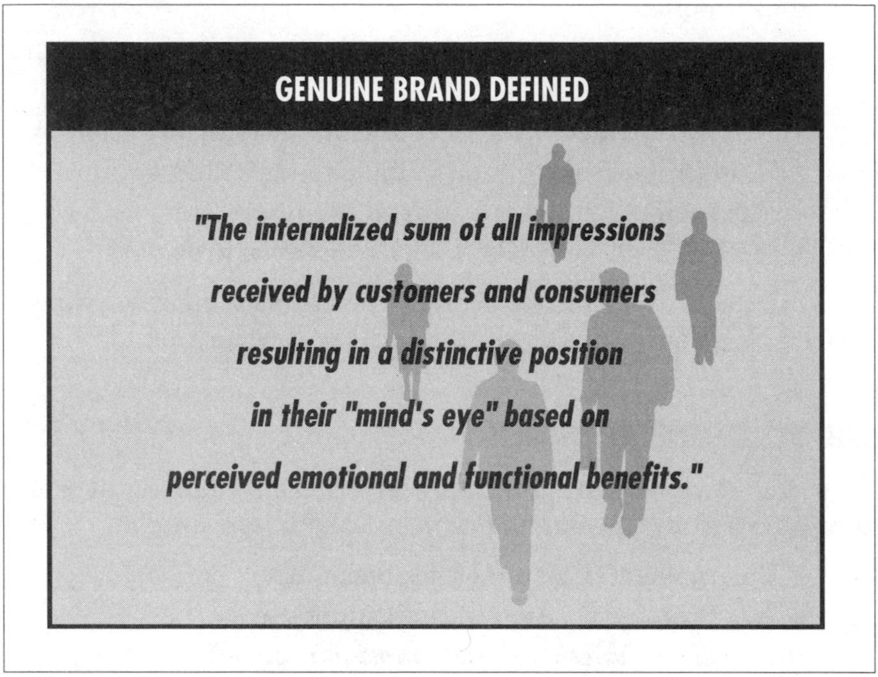

GENUINE BRAND DEFINED

"The internalized sum of all impressions
received by customers and consumers
resulting in a distinctive position
in their "mind's eye" based on
perceived emotional and functional benefits."

FIGURE 1–6

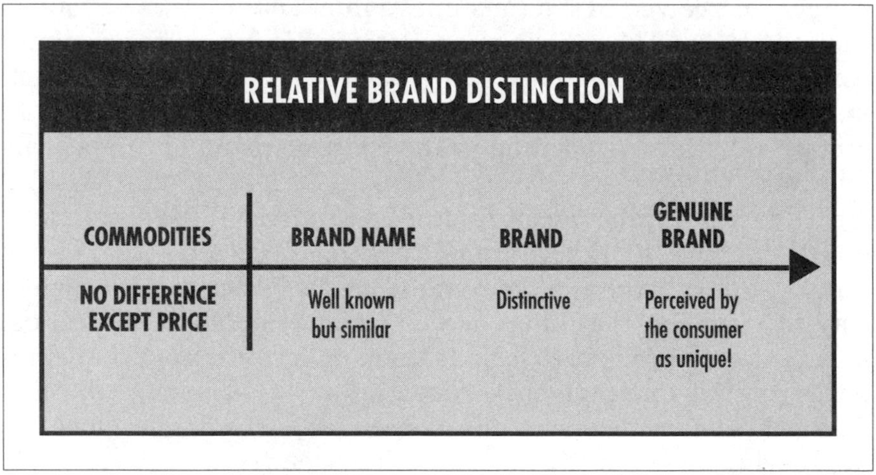

RELATIVE BRAND DISTINCTION

COMMODITIES	BRAND NAME	BRAND	GENUINE BRAND
NO DIFFERENCE EXCEPT PRICE	Well known but similar	Distinctive	Perceived by the consumer as unique!

Genuine Brands Exist to Add Value

The primary objective of genuine brands should be to add value to people's lives. A genuine brand is about benefiting the customer, and the more differentiated a brand is, the easier it is to communicate efficiently with the consumer.

Hence, differentiation needs to be focused on the benefits to consumers, as opposed to the production process related to the product or service. All too often, an organization focuses the majority of its attention on getting the sale instead of on inspiring confidence in the purchase decision and delivering use satisfaction from the enjoyment of the product or service. However, a genuine brand provides value or positive brand equity to its customers, as Figure 1-7 indicates.

Consider the last time you returned a product to a store for a refund or called your telephone company or software company to get help. Did you enjoy the experience, or did you experience anxiety? Did you feel as good about the return experience as you felt about the initial purchase? Did you feel welcomed by the service associate? Was that person interested in your problem or his?

It's always interesting how quickly a purchase charge appears on a credit card statement and how slowly (or not at all) the refund credit appears. As T. Scott Gross aptly observed in a recent *Design Forum / Ideations* newsletter article, "No one likes to be sold, but everyone likes to feel served."[4]

The primary concern of consumers today is "What's in it for me?" The processes involved and the size of the brand mean nothing to a consumer unless it communicates a clear benefit that the consumer deems important. It seems so obvious that consumers want to know what's in it for them, yet every day, hundreds of millions of dollars are wasted on advertising that doesn't communicate a distinctive benefit that is important to consumers.

It appears that many brand names, when compared to their competition, suffer from a lack of a distinctive position. They float along in a "sea of sameness." Next time you visit an antique shop, look at some of the old signs or posters for brands. You'll discover that a brand's value used to be synonymous with its unique and distinctive characteristics. Take Eagle Claw Hooks as an example, depicted in Figure 1-8. From the clawlike graphic design of the

FIGURE 1–7

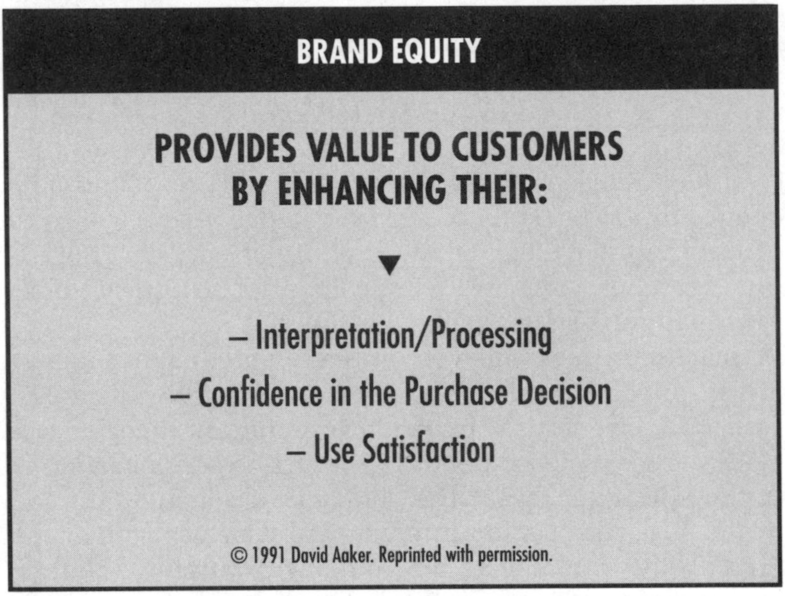

BRAND EQUITY

PROVIDES VALUE TO CUSTOMERS BY ENHANCING THEIR:

▼

– Interpretation/Processing

– Confidence in the Purchase Decision

– Use Satisfaction

© 1991 David Aaker. Reprinted with permission.

brand name to the tagline, "They hook and hold," every Eagle Claw package communicates the distinctive benefit to the consumer: catching fish. Eagle Claw has been communicating this distinct brand benefit since 1937.

THE BEST WAY TO BUILD A BRAND

It has long been believed that the way to build brands was to follow the F.R.E.D. model—(**F**amiliarity, **R**elevance, **E**steem, and **D**ifferentiation). The most important part of the F.R.E.D. concept was to make consumers familiar with a brand's product and service offering. While no one would argue that awareness is important, the F.R.E.D. theory reflects the World War II mentality of shortages. Hence, many organizations' preoccupation with awareness has led to a reliance on advertising as their primary market-

ing activity. In sharp contrast, we now live in an era characterized by an overabundance of choices. Thus the critical issue for
organizations today is to differentiate their products and services
in ways that consumers will appreciate and value.

Advertising agencies are paid to create messages, and they
get paid a substantial portion of their fees based on the "media
spend." Therefore, one would expect them to have certain media
biases. This is not to say that advertising is not important, but to
be effective, it should address three questions:

FIGURE 1–8

Used with permission.

FIGURE 1–9

- What are the best ways to build a specific brand's image?
- How is the marketing budget directed to optimize brand equity?
- What is the distinctive benefit to be communicated to the target audience?

A brand has to do with customers' perceptions of the business and the type of service they expect. An international study by Young & Rubicam provides solid proof of how this can work. Y&R conducted a survey of 13,000 brands among 95,000 consumers around the world, the largest and most complete survey of its kind. The research study, called BrandAsset® Valuator (BVA), which began in 1993, gives Y&R strategic insight into the strengths and weaknesses of a client's brand. This research tool demonstrates that a brand's strength is primarily built through differentiation and relevance. In lay terms, that means a brand needs to be different from other similar products and relevant to consumers' lives. Knowing this, companies differentiate their brands even if they exist in a commodity market: by providing better quality, value, and most important, customer service.[5]

In today's global marketplace, companies with successful brands understand what business they are in. They know that first and foremost, they are in the service business. Meeting customer service expectations will be the defining factor in distinguishing their brand from the competitors' in the eyes and minds of consumers.

Instead of F.R.E.D., the brand-building mindset should be D.R.E.A.M., as indicated in Figure 1-10. Differentiation should be the first step if a brand is to cut through the clutter in the marketplace and occupy a distinctive position in a target audience's mind. We substituted awareness for familiarity since most experts recognize "unaided/aided" awareness as one of the strengths of a brand's equity. We also believe these attributes are

FIGURE 1–10

only as good as the consumer's perception of them, and how firmly positioned they are in what we call the consumer's mind's eye, the mental equivalent of a Rolodex® file.

Creating and building awareness, contrary to traditional marketing practices, does not necessarily require a multimillion-dollar advertising campaign. In today's business environment, media channels are becoming more fragmented and costly. In order to be considered and eventually chosen, a brand must be effective at communicating its uniquely differentiated attributes in a wide variety of applications.

In a 1997 *Harvard Business Review* article, "Building Brands Without Mass Media," it was stated that for U.S.-based companies to build strong brands, they could take a lesson from their European counterparts who have faced similar "post mass-media era realities." According to the authors, the bottom line is that "managers of brands in Europe found that communication through traditional mass media has been ineffective, inefficient, and costly. As a result, many European companies have long relied on alternative communication channels to create product awareness, convey brand associations, and develop loyal customer bases."[6]

Our experience with clients reveals that when an organization has significantly differentiated its brand's products and services, public relations and other third-party endorsements can be powerful tools for building genuine brands. Not only are these methodologies less costly than media advertising, but they build a much higher level of credibility for a brand.

DRIVERS OF BRAND EQUITY

There are many ways for a brand to communicate its benefits. In *Managing Brand Equity*, David Aaker summarizes them well as perceived quality, name awareness, brand associations, brand loyalty, and other proprietary assets. These are the drivers of brand equity, and they are outlined in Figure 1-11.

There is no question that perceived quality is essential, as evidenced by the tremendous attention given to the Baldrige Awards for quality management and the J.D. Power and Associates Satisfaction Research. Regardless of how one chooses to rate perceived quality, ultimately it is only as good as the consumer perceives it.

FIGURE 1–11

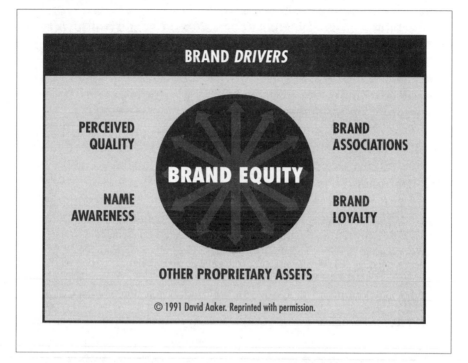

BRAND *DRIVERS*

PERCEIVED QUALITY

BRAND ASSOCIATIONS

BRAND EQUITY

NAME AWARENESS

BRAND LOYALTY

OTHER PROPRIETARY ASSETS

© 1991 David Aaker. Reprinted with permission.

Name awareness or familiarity is also a driver of overall brand equity; however, the more differentiated the better. Awareness without differentiation produces well-known commodity brand names that can become marginally profitable, exhibit little loyalty, and become vulnerable to extinction.

Organizations are discovering the benefits of associating their brand with other images, icons, and especially other brands. Brand associations can be very helpful to consumers in their processing of information about a brand. Starbucks associated with Marriott, Nike with Michael Jordan, McDonald's with Disney, and Intel uses a distinctive audible tone to help consumers relate to their brands' products and services. The old saying, "you can tell a person by the company she keeps" applies here.

The most often forgotten driver in building brand equity is brand loyalty. There is nothing like a satisfied customer to tell a brand's story and influence others. Other proprietary assets such

as patents, trademarks, and unique attributes can be very helpful as well when consumers must sift through the clutter of choices
that exists in today's marketplace.

Customers can be characterized by a variety of loyalty de-
scriptions. On any given day, a brand will likely have customers
in each of the four primary loyalty segments outlined in Figure
1-12. How does a brand create *absolute* loyalty? The key is to
exceed customers' expectations and pleasantly surprise them
whenever possible.

One of the common misperceptions is that the way to build
loyalty is to focus on future sales. Frequent flyer and customer
loyalty programs are tools some brands utilize in an attempt to
lock customers into future purchases.

Genuine brands, however, set as a priority to be perceived
first and foremost as a "friend" to the consumers. An overwhelming focus on future sales can become a distraction for brands,

FIGURE 1–12

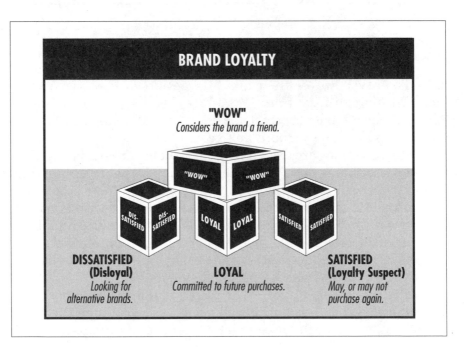

because they are buying their way to loyalty through what might be referred to as *brand bribery*.

Brand bribery exists when a particular industry becomes perceived as a commodity (i.e., relatively undifferentiated among brand choices) and characterized by lack of outstanding service or quality. Two prime examples are large domestic airlines and supermarket chains. Many brands in these industries have resorted to brand bribery in the form of "frequent customer" incentives and other promotional tactics because they have not been able to differentiate their offerings or have not become perceived as "real friends" to consumers. Brand bribery can backfire if customers feel that the "deal" may not really be a bargain or that the process is a hassle. Consumers become very unhappy when they can't use their benefits (such as free airline tickets or coupons) because of restrictions, fine print, or changes in the rules. Regarding supermarkets, privacy concerns can also become a concern for consumers. Insurance companies are all too eager to learn who's purchasing which medications, alcoholic beverages, and over-the-counter vitamins or health supplements, such as St. John's wort. Rewarding customer loyalty is a wonderful strategy, but it should not be the only reason customers return.

THE BRANDSTRATEGY™ DOCTRINE PROCESS*

Our process for developing a genuine brand is called the BrandStrategy™ Doctrine and is shown in Figure 1-13. The BrandStrategy Doctrine (*doctrine*) is the comprehensive action plan utilized by an organization to:

- Define its essence, or BrandPromise™
- Create a brand paradigm shift, i.e., become distinctive
- Gain a sustainable competitive advantage

The overall result of this doctrine should be to optimize the organization's brand equity. The *doctrine* process is further explained in Chapter 2, and each step in the process is developed in significant detail in subsequent chapters.

---

*For readability and case of reference, the BrandStrategy™ Doctrine is sometimes referred to as the *doctrine*.

FIGURE 1–13

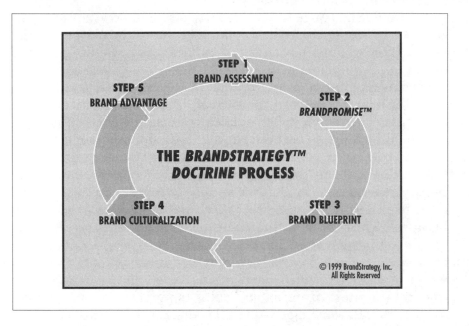

FIGURE 1–14

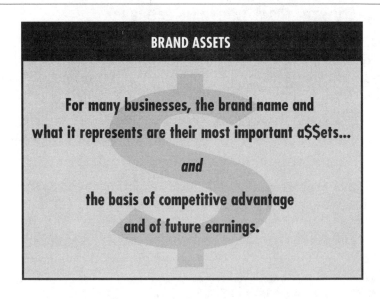

Now that we understand the fundamentals of thinking like a brand and the imperative need to focus on brand equity, how does an organization measure brand equity? There are many ways to measure brand equity, and it seems there are as many methods as there are organizations that calculate brand equity. A consistent methodology can be applied to determine, measure, and monitor brand equity, based on the cumulative results gathered from a number of relevant core factors, such as:

- Price leadership
- Perceived quality
- Visual imagery (personality)
- Trust (admiration and esteem)
- Awareness
- Market share
- Intent to purchase (conversion)
- Satisfaction

Once an organization has decided which brand equity measurements to track, it is equally important to decide how to communicate them. For instance, some very successful brands internally report their brand equity results on the monthly financial statements, with a prominence equal to net earnings. Chapter 6, under the heading Establishing Brand Equity Goals, provides more insight into this subject.

BRAND PARADIGM SHIFTS

A significant part of the BrandMindset concept is understanding the idea of a paradigm shift. A paradigm is a model or formula for how something operates or works. When an organization can create or "brand" a paradigm shift in its business, the result can be a more distinctive brand perception and enormous competitive advantage. The first step in the paradigm shift approach is to understand what we call the "winning combination."

A brand has a much better chance for success if it can embrace two concepts: (1) doing things right and (2) doing the right things as indicated in Figure 1-15. Many excellent businesses do things right, i.e., execute the fundamentals of their business well.

FIGURE 1–15

However, unless they also understand the right things to do, i.e., understand and execute a BrandMindset, they may not achieve genuine brand status over the long term. There are five fundamental brand paradigm shifts that can be utilized by organizations to develop a more distinctive perception and enhance their brand equity. They include brand leverage, brand discipline, brand playing field, brand focus, and brand value.

Brand Leverage

The traditional point of view is that if you're good at what you do, that's enough. Every organization buys and sells some combination of products and services and "doing it right" is required, but that may not be enough to become a genuine brand. Your competition may run their business as well as you do and also utilize the brand leveraging depicted in Figure 1-16.

At the beginning of every day, CEOs who practice the BrandMindset lead their organizations with two primary objectives: exceptional operation of the business and maximum leverage of brand equity.

FIGURE 1–16

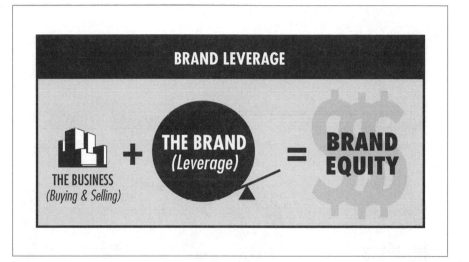

Brand Discipline

Most decisions on a daily basis are made based on the "O" word: opinions. If business opinions are well informed, the organization may, with hope, succeed. All too often, however, decisions are based on opinions that do not accurately reflect an objective evaluation of the brand's situation at hand.

The marketplace changes so rapidly that it is essential to have information that is accurate, current, relevant, and objective in order to reach correct conclusions. In addition, it is all important to have consumer and customer input. Ask yourself, "Who sits in the consumer's chair and represents the customer's viewpoint during every meeting?" Especially when important decisions are made, it is essential to test proposed changes with customers to fully understand the impact on a brand.

Why do airline pilots run through a preflight checklist *every single time* before they depart? It's because there is no room for error. Lives are at stake. It is essential to the success of the flight that everything be in proper working order and "done by the book." The same rigor should be applied to every brand decision. A brand discipline checklist should be completed for every decision in which the life of a brand is at stake.

FIGURE 1–17

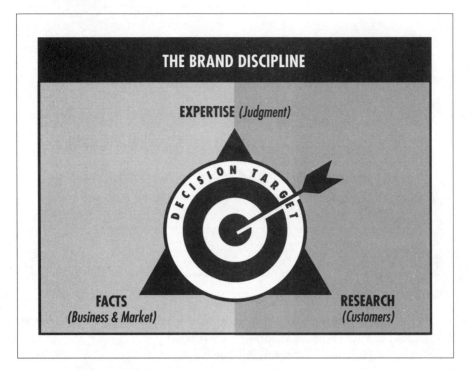

Brand Playing Field

The majority of most organizations' time is involved discussing or analyzing the product or process part of the business. This narrow focus is the reason genuine brands can upset and capture a marketplace so rapidly. Consider Federal Express; they have been so successful they have even changed their name to FedEx. They have utilized the BrandMindset by focusing their brand on the entire playing field, not just products or processes. Most organizations pay the lowest wage to their associates who service the customers. By design, this was not how FedEx built its brand. Prior to the existence of FedEx, the place to go for shipping packages overnight was the nearest airport. FedEx turned the tables and changed the playing field. It brought the "airport" to the customer. Today, you can find a FedEx drop-box in thousands of loca-

FIGURE 1–18

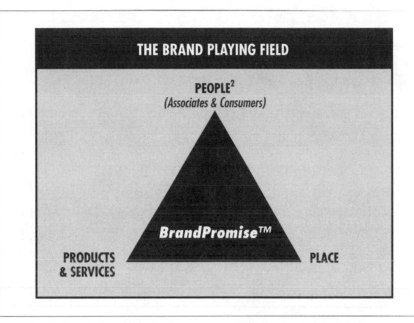

tions, from street corners and office buildings to hotels and, yes, every Kinko's®. FedEx picks up and delivers! Moreover, some 18,000 customers a day navigate their own way via FedEx's Website. FedEx believes a good line of products is the entry fee to compete, but their service, i.e., "immediate gratification," is what their brand is all about. FedEx is more than just a business with a brand name. FedEx has become synonymous with overnight satisfaction. When consumers really want to be sure a package is going to be received, they say, "FedEx it."

Brand Focus

The traditional business approach has been to create a business plan or even a strategic plan that drives the budgets, which in turn fund an organization's activities. On the contrary, it is essential for the BrandStrategy doctrine to drive all the organization's activities as well as the business plan and then the budgets, not the other way around (see Figure 1-19). In too many

FIGURE 1–19

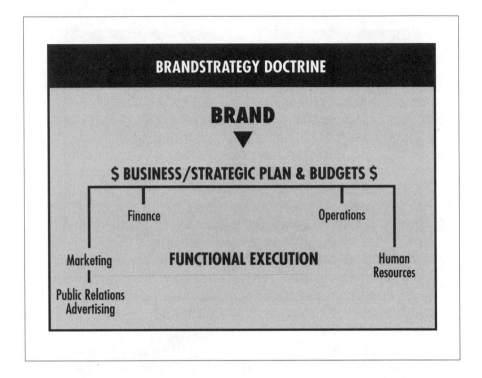

cases, anything that has to do with brand has been relegated to marketing or advertising.

An organization's leadership and executive team must direct and own this *doctrine*. Marketing's primary function, among other responsibilities, is to communicate the desired brand perception using the appropriate messages and mediums.

Brand Value

When the subject of value comes up today, *price* always seems to be the term at the forefront of the conversation. Traditional marketing methods have examined the price/value relationship in terms of dollars paid. Many marketers believe that customers perceive value to mean lowest price. Lowest price is also interpreted to mean frequent sales and promotional discounts. But a marketing position of lowest price is the most difficult to sustain, and it usually is an indication that the brand or organization has become a commodity in the minds of consumers. Commodities generally have no distinct point of differentiation except price. Customers looking for the lowest price tend to be loyal to the price, not the brand.

Consumers perceive that they pay in three important ways: time, money, and feelings, as shown in Figure 1-20. Many consumers today are saying their most precious resource is time. Brands that understand this concept are careful to develop and deliver *promises* that reflect what consumers value. As a result, genuine brands enjoy increased profitability, more customer loyalty, and enhanced brand equity when customers perceive that a brand consistently delivers value.

The following profile features Hallmark Cards, one of the really great organizations that thinks like a brand. It's interesting to note that J.C. Hall, the founder of Hallmark, and Walt Disney became friends and business associates during Disney's early career in Kansas City. These visionaries clearly understood the fundamentals of creating genuine brands.

FIGURE 1–20

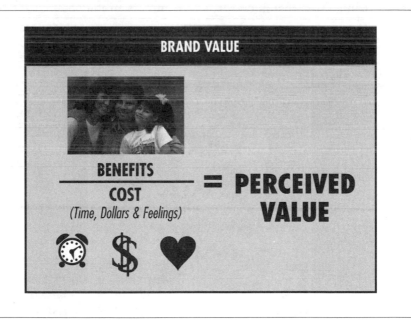

HALLMARK*
"When You Care Enough" to Expect the Best, You Become a Genuine Brand

The Hallmark brand phenomenon began in 1910 when company founder Joyce C. Hall started selling postcards out of a Kansas City, Missouri, YMCA room. From the company's inception through today, Hallmark has consistently stood for two things: *helping people show they care* and *excellence*. In 1928, Hall was intrigued by something he read: A fourteenth-century London goldsmith named Hall used a "hall mark" to guarantee the purity of every gold and silver article made. To better connote quality, this led Hall to change the name of his company from Hall Brothers to Hallmark.

Despite a lack of enthusiasm from advertising agencies, Hallmark was the first company to brand greeting cards. In 1938, the Tony Wons radio shows urged listeners to look for the Hallmark name on the back of the card. Interestingly, Hallmark returned to that brand insistence campaign in the late 1990s with its EFFIE-winning print and television ad campaign that invited consumers to "sneak a peek" at the back of the cards they receive, looking for the Hallmark logo.

Hallmark president and CEO Irv Hockaday stated in a 1998 *BrandWeek* magazine interview, "You have to decide what your promise and deliverable can be... once a key connection with consumers is made, brands can go from being ones that consumers prefer to one that they *insist* on."

FIGURE 1–21

---

*Information provided by Hallmark Cards, Inc. and used with permission.

In 1944, Hall introduced a slogan that would promote the brand name and emphasize quality. Since then, Hallmark's slogan has been *When you care enough to send the very best*. Today, it is one of the nation's most recognized slogans as well as a business commitment.

In 1951, Hallmark created the *Hallmark Hall of Fame* television series. It is the longest-running television series in history, with approximately 200 dramatic presentations by the end of 1998. Again, this was done to associate the Hallmark name with quality. Hall said, "We wanted shows that would not only be top entertainment but top quality as well."

The formula worked and the shows have received nearly 80 Emmys. With 34 percent of the viewing audience, the 1997 *Hallmark Hall of Fame* presentation "What the Deaf Man Heard" became the most-watched original drama on television since the 1991 *Hallmark Hall of Fame* presentation of "Sarah Plain and Tall."

A recent Conference Board study, "Managing the Corporate Brand," indicates that a distinctive corporate culture serving as a foundation for the brand promise is a key success factor for companies with strong brands.

Hallmark's Beliefs and Values statement delineates standards for the organization and can be seen at almost every desk and workstation throughout the company. It begins by asserting, "We believe that our products and services must enrich people's lives and enhance their relationships." It continues by declaring that one of the values that guides the company is "excellence in all we do."

Hallmark's creative community of more than 700 people is further guided by the Product Concept statement, which says "At Hallmark, we create products that help people capture their emotions and share them with one another. After a century, this is what we do best; and we are still dedicated to creating the very best." In addition, Hallmark employees are given a daily planner page finder with Hallmark's brand promise on it along with a list of those actions that drive Hallmark's brand equity.

Brad VanAuken, Hallmark's director of brand management and marketing from 1995 to 1998, indicates that Hallmark "builds a brand strategy component into virtually every employee training program and integrates the brand essence and promise throughout internal communication vehicles." Furthermore, he says, "Hallmark has adopted a brand equity model that helps focus the organization's efforts on those activities that can best create consumer insistence for the Hallmark brand."

Total Research Corporation of Princeton, New Jersey, studies brand equity performance among the major brands in the United States. Through its EquiTrend ranking of brand equity, it has surveyed consumer perceptions of the quality associated with America's primary brands since 1990. Each brand's "quality score" is measured on a 10-point scale. Hallmark achieved a score of 8.33 in the 1997 survey, one of only 21 companies of the 282 brands studied to achieve a score of 8.0 or higher. The ranking places Hallmark alongside such elite brands as Kodak and Disney. According to VanAuken, the EquiTrend study is "a measure of not only how well consumers recognize a brand, but also of their positive feelings about the brand's quality."

Consistently communicating and delivering upon Hallmark's promise of helping people show they care through the very best quality products not only translates to strong brand equity but also to exceptional retail sales performance. The Hallmark Gold Crown network of stores has achieved a consistent month-to-month sales increase for well over four years.

By consistently living its original brand promise and enjoying an inherent knack for how to build genuine brand equity, Hallmark has created a deeply embedded positive impression in the collective mind of the American consumer. Like a coat of arms passed down from generation to generation, current Hallmark personnel have inherited a valuable symbol—the Hallmark crown—and a brand that carries a clear, uniquely differentiated, and consistently positive meaning to the consumer.

This is no small legacy. If Hallmark continues to "live the brand" and execute its communications consistent with its established values and proven formula, the future success of its brand is indisputable.

ACTION GUIDE

THE BRANDMINDSET®

- Most of the time, an organization's brand is not contributing as much as it could to overall brand equity for an organization.
- Brand names are not necessarily brands because they may not be perceived as truly distinctive in the mind's eye of the customer.
- A genuine brand is the internalized sum of all impressions received by customers and consumers, which results in a *distinctive* position in their mind's eye based on perceived emotional and functional benefits.
- If a brand is to be *genuine* and truly successful, the organization must learn to "think like a brand." It is not enough to just have good products or innovative services.

- When organizations embrace the concept of thinking like a brand, everything they do—every product, service, and customer interaction—is analyzed to determine whether it is fulfilling the brand's promise.
- A brand may not achieve success unless it embraces the twin principles of doing things right (business expertise) and doing the right thing (brand expertise).
- The pursuit of awareness by traditional marketing managers has caused organizations to overlook the fundamental brand requirement to be perceived as different or distinctive in the mind's eye of the target audience.
- A genuine brand creates paradigm shifts by:

  Leveraging the brand

  Following a disciplined brand process

  Utilizing the entire brand playing field

  Creating brand value for the customer

  Using the BrandStrategy Doctrine to drive the business and budgets

  Consistently focusing on the brand

CHAPTER **2**

An Introduction to the BrandStrategy™ Doctrine Process

The Roadmap for a Genuine Brand

Discipline is the soul of an army. It makes small numbers formidable, procures success to the weak, and esteem to all.
—George Washington

THE BRANDSTRATEGY DOCTRINE PHILOSOPHY

In Chapter 1, we introduced the approach of thinking like a brand and our recommended process for developing a genuine brand. The BrandStrategy Doctrine Process as outlined in Figure 2-1 results in a written brand action guide and includes five primary steps:

- Assessing the brand's current situation and future prospects
- Developing the BrandPromise
- Creating the Brand Blueprint
- Finalizing a Brand Culturalization plan and the written BrandStrategy Doctrine
- Establishing Brand Advantages

FIGURE 2–1

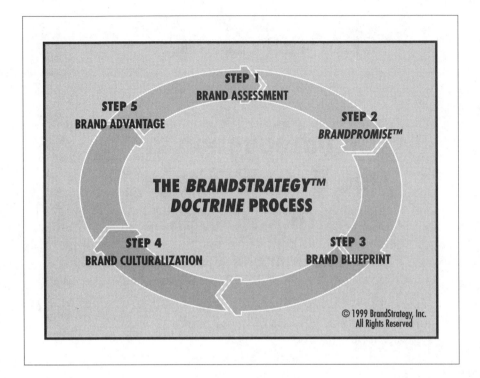

Our fundamental philosophy suggests that everything related to creating the BrandStrategy Doctrine (*doctrine*) must include the customer's point of view and represent an objective
viewpoint. Perhaps the biggest challenge within organizations
today, in their desire to have a successful brand, is the lack of an
objective point of view based on consumer realities.

In observing hundreds of strategic planning sessions it would
seem that most key decisions in organizations are based on the
"O," or opinions, theory. Everyone seems to have an opinion. If
their judgment is well-informed, up-to-date, and reflects consumer
feelings and desires, then it is possible to make good brand decisions. The value of the BrandStrategy Doctrine is that it forces
discipline and provides a roadmap for all to follow.

If you have ever taken a long road trip and tried to plot your
course by following large state maps, you know how difficult and

sometimes confusing the task can be. On the other hand, if you are a member of the American Automobile Association, you probably have experienced the joy of the AAA Triptik® shortcut maps. The Triptik provides you with "current" road information, best routes, and expertise to make your trip more enjoyable and efficient. The BrandStrategy Doctrine works the same way: a current, relevant, fact-based, easy to use, roadmap for the development of a genuine brand.

You may be wondering why we use the term *doctrine*. A doctrine is something to be taken seriously. It is based on policy, principles, and a system of teachings. A genuine brand requires a serious doctrine based on specific principles that an organization believes are fundamental and which in turn determine the key policies and actions that govern a genuine brand.

THE BRANDSTRATEGY DOCTRINE METHODOLOGY

The initial step in the process is the assessment of a brand's current position; an independent "situation analysis" of the marketplace, customers, competitors, and relevant economic and industry conditions supported by demographic and pyschographic data and trends.

Once the Brand Assessment is completed, then the BrandPromise, or value proposition, can be formulated and tested with the target audience (see Figure 2-2). The BrandPromise (*promise*) is defined as the essence of the benefits (both functional and emotional) that current and potential customers can expect to receive from experiencing a brand's products and services. The BrandPromise incorporates the consumer's point of view and is intended to reflect the heart, soul, and spirit of the brand. It's intended as an internal directive, not as an advertising message, although it should drive an organization's activities and messages.

Any strategic process usually involves determining what business a company is in. In the Starbucks case, it is obviously coffee. However, the fundamental distinction of the *promise* is that it should determine what business the brand is in from the consumer's point of view. The Starbucks brand is focused on the "third place." The first place is home, the second place is the office, and the third place is a relaxing oasis, a comforting, stimu-

FIGURE 2–2

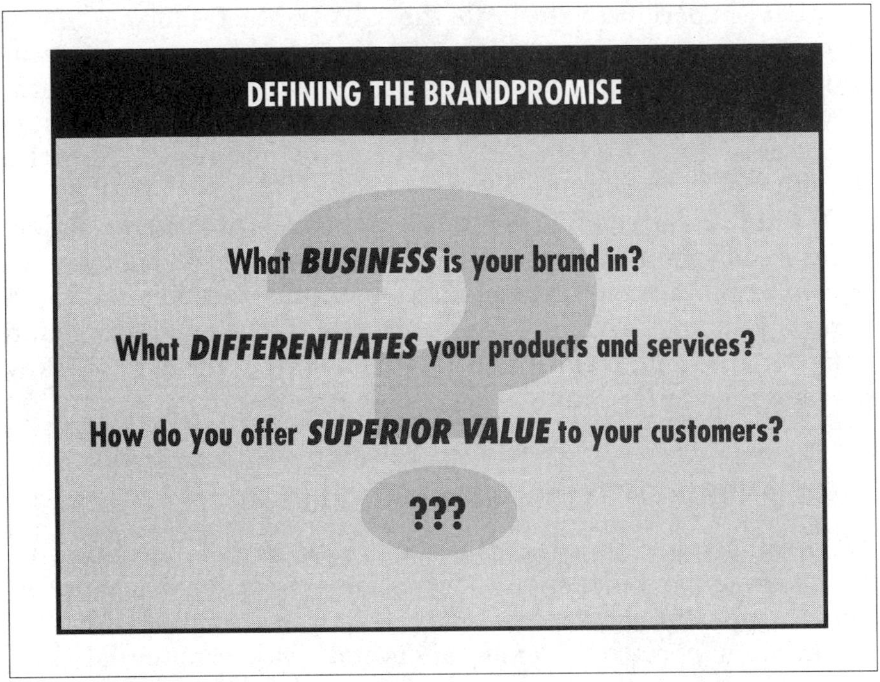

DEFINING THE BRANDPROMISE

What *BUSINESS* is your brand in?

What *DIFFERENTIATES* your products and services?

How do you offer *SUPERIOR VALUE* to your customers?

???

lating place to indulge oneself and feel good. While FedEx is in the overnight delivery business, the brand is in the business of immediate gratification. Successful brands become focused on the consumer benefits, which results in delighted customers and enormous competitive advantage.

If differentiation is the key to building genuine brands, then the *promise* must express the unique benefits a brand offers its customers. Surprisingly, people still attempt to classify businesses as *product* or *service*. That no longer applies. There is no such thing as a product business *or* a service business. Every business should view itself as being in both the product and service sectors. A large domestic U.S. automobile company executive was recently quoted as saying, "Product is 99% of the game." When an organization focuses only on the product or process for competitive advantage, they significantly limit their ability to effectively gain a "position of privilege" and perceived brand differentiation.

All too often, organizations focus solely on product innovation only to lose out to a new competing brand that leverages both service and product advantages.

A perfect example of a message that succinctly communicates a promise is the historic Coca-Cola advertisement (see Figure 2-3). Recently, Coca-Cola returned to their original promise

FIGURE 2–3

of "refreshing." It is now on every can, bottle, and package. This has helped the Coca-Cola Company to increase market share, sustain their position of privilege, and enhance overall brand equity. Coca-Cola is a model of consistency; every message, each advertisement and promotion, reflects their *promise*.

As we have discussed, the *promise* is the foundation of a brand. An organization's level of commitment and dedication to superior value, meaningful differentiation, and executional excellence will determine its ability to become or continue as a genuine brand.

Genuine brands are generally viewed as *the* source of expertise in their respective market or business. This expertise provides consistent reinforcement of a brand's perceived value. As a result, consumers' expectations are compared to the level of the leading brand's ability to communicate and ultimately deliver on its *promise*.

After the *promise* has been finalized, the Brand Blueprint (*blueprint*) for the architecture of the brand can be developed. The Brand Blueprint outlines the various types of messages that will be used to communicate the *promise*. These include the name, brand representation, byline, tagline, story, etc. The actual messages will then be created by creative experts such as advertising agencies or graphic design firms. The purpose of the *blueprint* is to call out or set forth the types of messages to be used to communicate the brand's essence, not dictate the messages themselves.

The next step is prepare a written action guide that outlines the *doctrine,* including the Brand Principles and the culturalization plan that will guide a brand for the next year. The *doctrine* should be updated annually and should provide the discipline for an effective and consistent nurturing of the brand, resulting in Brand Advantage. Each aspect of this process will be discussed in further detail in each of the following chapters.

GETTING THE PROCESS STARTED

With the right point of view, ample free time, appropriate information, dedication, discipline, the correct leadership, and the desire to become a genuine brand, any organization can develop a strategy for their brand. However, having observed the process hundreds of times over the past 20 years, I can say that it is easier said than done, especially if the organization does not have a disciplined process and some outside influence or expertise. Experience indicates that all too often an internal approach falls short in three areas: lack of objectivity, difficulty in gaining a real consensus, and the absence of significant results.

The *doctrine* process has been successful for a wide variety of organizations that have demonstrated the required dedication and commitment. Here's how it works. First, the guidelines for the process include the following:

- One of the senior level officers (the chief executive officer, president, chairman, or chief operating officer) must buy in and be involved in the process on a reasonable basis.
- One executive, designated by the executive team, must take responsibility for the development of the *doctrine*.
- A small cross-functional brand team should be assembled to participate in the development of the *doctrine*. Throughout this book the brand team will be referred to as the focal point of the *doctrine* process.
- An outside brand advisor should be retained to participate or guide the development process and ensure objectivity.
- A timetable and workplan should be established for the project, with monthly updates and progress reports. A *doctrine* overview and a detailed workplan are included in Chapter 9, Brand Tools.
- Progress presentations should be made to the organization's executive team on a regular basis.
- The *doctrine* should be completed, in writing, by the conclusion of the process. It should direct all of the organization's activities and be reviewed and updated annually prior to the strategic planning or budgeting process. Again, an example of a completed written *doctrine* is included in Chapter 9, Brand Tools.

If an organization is small, with limited resources, or is a new startup venture, then an outside advisor can be a friend, board member, or other reasonably available resource. Everything about the *doctrine* process is relative to the size, sophistication, and resources of an organization. However, any organization that develops a *doctrine* can benefit from the disciplined objectivity and required focus toward building brand equity.

Let's review the reasons for the above guidelines. If the CEO, COO, or president is not involved in the process, chances are slim that the work will ever go anywhere. There are so many initiatives in organizations today and so intense are the time pressures that only a few ideas can survive. Someone within the organization must own and champion the *doctrine* process as the primary driver to achieve desired results and be responsible for its development and execution. A consultant cannot and should not "own" an organization's brand. The reason for this methodology and process is for everyone in an organization to understand the importance of building a brand and learning to think like a customer. The cross-functional brand team provides a variety of perspectives, and its members communicate with their respective disciplines, groups, or divisions. An outside advisor can be invaluable when it comes time to face the facts about a brand's specific situation or challenge. Executives may play down the aspects of politics and fear within their organizations. In reality, however, the "truth" is not always welcome. It's similar to parents not wanting to hear that their kids may be bad. The real value of a brand advisor is to keep the process on track, maintain an independent point of view, and add intellectual horsepower to enhance the quality of decisions.

How long should it take to complete a *doctrine*? It takes anywhere from 90 days to a year, depending on the complexity of the situation and organization, the availability of internal resources, and the level of organizational commitment. Typically, midsize organizations take six to nine months and larger organizations need nine to twelve months. One of the interesting benefits of this methodology is that it is not necessary to complete the entire process before beginning implementation of certain specific recommendations. Unlike many strategic projects where everything has to wait for the report to be finalized, the *doctrine* process encourages early execution as appropriate. Generally, meetings should be held every two to three weeks, or as is reasonable, pursuant to the availability of resources and the completion of assignments. An overview of the *doctrine* process and a detailed workplan are outlined in Chapter 9 as tools to organize this process for any organization. We have also provided a sample of what a completed written *doctrine* might look like.

Once an organization has decided to develop a *doctrine*, a leader should be selected and a brand team recruited to work together. Typically, a group of between three and ten members is optimal, and it should represent a cross section of the company's activities—marketing, operations, engineering, research and development, human resources, finance, and so forth. As the project progresses through the five primary stages, some members of the team may exit and new ones may join the effort as required. Outside external resources, such as representatives of the organization's market research, advertising, public relations, and investment banking firms, may also join the process as appropriate.

BRANDS ARE SUPPOSED TO BE DISTINCTIVE

As we discussed earlier in Chapter 1, the key to thinking like a genuine brand is understanding the requirement to be distinctive. It's not an optional kind of idea. It's not possible to have a genuine brand without achieving the perception of being distinctive. The purpose of the *doctrine* process is to identify, develop, maintain, or enhance a brand's distinctive characteristics, which are intended to be translated into a distinctive perception in the minds of the brand's target audience. Figure 2-4 provides an image of a distinctive landmark.

In understanding the meaning of *distinct, distinctive,* and *distinction*, the following attributes take on primary importance:

- Separateness—not being the same
- Difference in nature or quality
- Prominence, clarity to the senses
- Special quality, style, attractiveness
- Superiority, notableness
- Conspicuousness, eminence, excellence

FIGURE 2–4

First of all, it's clear that the word *distinctive* is intended to possess positive connotation. Note the consistency of such descriptors as notableness, attractiveness, and excellence. This is consistent with the concept that a brand should be aspirational and invoke a positive feeling as well as a sense of pride. The *doctrine* process should be focused on identifying, communicating, and delivering a brand's distinctive characteristics, those that are important to its stakeholders and especially to the customer.

As we have pointed out previously, it's imperative for a brand to identify its current or desired distinctive characteristics during the first step in the *doctrine* process, i.e., in developing its *promise*. It's interesting to note that many organizations do not seem to be able to create the required distinction for their brands. While there may be other possible explanations for the lack of distinction among brands, that lack tends to be the result of one or more of the following:

- Not understanding the need to be distinctive.
- Difficulty in identifying their distinctive characteristics.
- Failing to create the perception of distinctiveness.
- Lack of continuous innovations or enhancements to reinforce distinctive characteristics.
- Choosing or communicating the wrong characteristics, i.e., those that are not beneficial, valued, or desired by the target audience.

It's not enough to just create distinctive characteristics; it's essential that they be beneficial to the customer. As John Bissell recently wrote in *BrandWeek*, "Little of what the industry [high-tech] regards as differentiation is relevant to the typical consumer."[1] In order to be a genuine brand, the target audience must perceive the characteristics to be beneficial and indeed distinctive. Building a genuine brand is difficult enough in today's quickly changing markets. In the retail footwear business, it takes a minimum of three to five years to build brand recognition, owing to production cycles, development lead times, and delivery to the retail market.

According to Bill Baum, president of the Intershoe Group (Via Spiga branded footwear), "Brand extensions only work when the new product offers a unique or distinctive concept and gives the customer a compelling reason to buy something they don't already own."

While working with a supermarket client to create a distinctive brand of milk, we faced a typical brand challenge. The supermarket had already decided which dairy would produce their new brand of milk, but I wanted to meet with the dairy executives to review their commitment to quality and identify their distinctive attributes.

During a meeting with the owner of the dairy, he indicated that basically, all brands of milk are the same because they are so closely regulated. While he was very proud of the quality of his milk, he really was convinced there was no difference between brands. So I followed the milk trucks, toured the dairies and farms, talked to the farmers, visited the milk processing plant, and examined the process from top to bottom. Surprisingly enough, several distinctive characteristics were identified that would be valued by customers. This particular dairy had the only state-certified laboratory actually located within the dairy plant, a real assurance of safety. The dairy's absolute commitment to quality, combined with their rigorous on-site testing process and proprietary safety methodology, made it possible to detect the slightest chemical or bacteria impurities before the milk was packaged. Most important, their farmers were individually selected by the dairy to provide milk on an exclusive basis. Selection was based on a long list of criteria, including consistent feeding, grazing requirements, and sanitary and humanitarian conditions. At the farms, the cows were really treated well, and the milk was chilled to the optimum temperature from the moment it left the cows. Not only does this provide a health advantage, but their meticulous monitoring of the optimum temperature allowed a longer and more convenient shelf life for their customers.

All too often, quality conscious organizations overlook some of their best brand benefits and sources of distinctiveness because the customer is not included in the brand process. Because of the entrepreneurial nature of our economy today, the pressure to keep brands fresh and innovative has never been greater. Hence, organizations that wish to develop or maintain genuine brands must ask themselves, "How have we enhanced our brand's perception of distinction today?"

CREATING A DISTINCTIVE BRAND PERCEPTION

The options available to brands to become truly distinctive are mind-boggling when you think of the various attributes and the limitless combinations. Figure 2-5 outlines various brand characteristics and attributes that could be utilized to develop distinctive brand perceptions.

The secret to harnessing the power of these unlimited attributes is to perform a brand analysis that approaches the issue of distinction from three angles:

- From our customer's perspective, determining which of these attributes (if any), presently apply to our brand?

FIGURE 2-5

Distinctive Brand Attributes

Sensory
- Visual
- Smell, aroma, scent
- Touch
- Sound
- Comfort
- Sense of arrival

Understanding/ Education

Authoritative/Expertise
- The leader
- The innovator

Access

Endurance, dependability

Craftsmanship

Quality

Packaging

Size

Relevant

Healthy
- "Good for you"
- Natural
- Pure
- Wholesome
- Preventative

Special/Personal
- Customized
- Personalized

Service
- Speed
- Fast
- Personal
- Knowledgeable
- Hassle-free
- Convenience

Guarantee
- Unconditional
- 100% satisfaction
- Hassle-free

Source of Origin

Consistency

Functionality
- Versatility
- Utilization

Ingredients

Scarcity (uniqueness)
- One of a kind
- The original
- The first one
- The last one

Communications
- Advertising/Marketing

Value
- Price
- Time
- Feelings

Personality, emotion (feelings)
- Self-esteem
- Ego
- Sense of humor
- Sexuality

Design (aesthetics)
- Color
- Fabric
- Texture
- Style
- Typeface (font)
- Symbol
- "Look"

Place
- "Its own"
- Position (mind's eye)

- Selecting five of these attributes that would be most valued by our brand's customers.
- Selecting five attributes that our brand could reasonably be expected to deliver to our customers if we decided they should become a priority.

The next step is to examine where the attributes listed above coincide, then ultimately to select one primary attribute around which to build the brand's distinctiveness. It also is helpful to identify two secondary distinctive attributes that could become defensive attributes for the brand. The reality is that most genuine brands can only develop and ultimately occupy one distinctive offensive brand position in the mind's eye of the target audience. However, defensive attribute positions are helpful in strengthening the brand's ultimate performance over the long term. As an example, Nike's primary distinctive attribute (offensively) since its beginning has been performance, i.e., run faster, run easier, jump higher, etc. However, Nike has a distinctive secondary attribute (defensive) focused around the "Just Do It" theme, i.e., the independent, nonconventional athlete free spirit. The primary distinctive attribute (offensive) of Kinko's is successful presentations. However, its secondary distinctive attribute is "your office," i.e., a place for job interviews, live video conferences, and computer workstations to complete various office tasks.

In summary, if a brand desires to be distinctive, there is a virtually unlimited selection of distinctive options. The secret is to have the desire and passion to become a distinctive brand and select or develop distinctive attributes that the brand's customers will value.

ACTION GUIDE
_____

THE BRANDSTRATEGY™ DOCTRINE

- Everything related to creating the BrandStrategy Doctrine must include the consumers' and customers' point of view and represent an objective viewpoint.

- The BrandStrategy Doctrine process is utilized to:
  Define the brand's essence, i.e., the BrandPromise.
  Create a paradigm shift, i.e., become distinctive.
  Gain a sustainable competitive advantage, i.e., a position of privilege.
- Every genuine brand that occupies the leadership position in its respective market, is viewed as *the* source of expertise in its business.
- The key to thinking like a genuine brand is understanding the requirement of distinctiveness. It's not optional. You cannot have a genuine brand without achieving a perception of being distinctive.
- In understanding the meaning of *distinct, distinctive,* and *distinction,* the following attributes take on primary importance:

  Separateness—not being the same
  Difference in nature or quality
  Prominence, clarity to the senses
  Special quality, style, attractiveness
  Superiority, notableness
  Conspicuousness, eminence, excellence

3

The Brand Assessment

The Process to Evaluate Current and
Future Brand Equity

with a Brand Profile of Citibank

*Without a yardstick, there is no measurement. And without
measurement, there is no control.*
—Pravin M. Shah, management consultant

THE BRAND ASSESSMENT PHILOSOPHY

The concept of a Brand Assessment (*assessment*)* is all about
objectivity, which is why it is the first step in the BrandStrategy
Doctrine Process (*doctrine*), as indicated in Figure 3-1. The *assessment* process is designed to characterize the current perceptions of a brand based on factual and observable conclusions and
material in a manner that attempts to preclude unwanted subjective prejudice. Just as an audit is required to verify the financial condition of an organization, an assessment of the brand is
required to verify and examine a brand's image and perception.

If you have ever been lost and called the place you're supposed to be, the first and most obvious question you're asked is:

---

*For readability and ease of reference, the Brand Assessment concept will sometimes be
    referred to as the *assessment*.

FIGURE 3–1

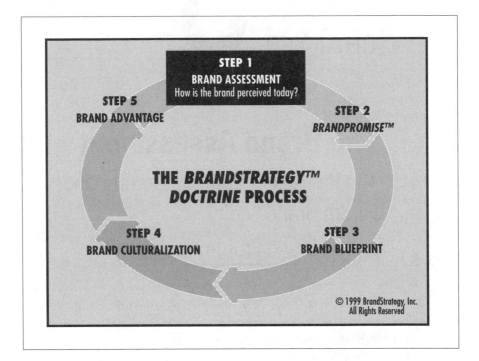

"Where are you?" It's the same for a brand. It is pretty hard to decide what a brand's position should be if you don't know where the brand is today! Sometimes when people are lost, they are asked to describe their surroundings, perhaps identify a landmark, in the hope that it will provide clues as to their current location. If it wants to map out a strategy to become or continue to be a genuine brand, it's vital for an organization to know where its brand currently is in the minds of its target audience, to know its "landmarks" and understand its surroundings.

Many organizations regularly make significant decisions or implement important changes without the benefit of the perspectives of their various stakeholders. An easy way to remedy this is to make permanent signs listing each of a brand's typical stakeholders, such as customers or employees. Then every time a meeting is held to discuss an important subject, each of the participants can be assigned the responsibility of representing a respective stakeholder for that decision. If more information is required, the appropriate representative can be responsible for getting that information in order to make an informed brand decision.

This exercise helps decision-makers think like a brand by taking into account the input from stakeholders as a tool to make the best-informed brand decisions. Of course, this exercise is no substitute for actual input from various stakeholders or objective market research.

THE BRAND ASSESSMENT METHODOLOGY

The *assessment* process will objectively assess a brand's perceived position and build consensus in the organization consistent with a brand's reality. The methodology (see Figure 3-2) has been designed to assess key aspects of the brand's image, current business, industry trends (current and future), and to identify all of the relevant critical success factors, strengths, and weaknesses

FIGURE 3–2

BRAND ASSESSMENT OVERVIEW

1. PURPOSE
- Correctly identify current brand perception.
- Gain executive team consensus on current brand position.

2. PROCESS
- Conduct customer research.
- Review the business environment.
- Review current marketing strategy.
- Evaluate customer transaction analysis.
- Market research and competitive trends.
- Analyze technological migration.
- Create written brand assessment and present to executive team.

3. RESULTS
- Determine how a brand is perceived today.
- Understand the importance of building a brand and learn to think like a customer.

that may affect the brand's performance. These include, but are not limited to:

- Business environmental review
- Competitive trends and competing brands positions
- Comparative industry data
- Product and service offerings
- Technological migration
- Consumer transaction analysis
- Brand relationships and associations (current and potential)
- Current marketing plans
- Communication research
- Customer and consumer research

Figure 3-3 outlines a sample *assessment* workplan and time-table. The time frames are flexible and usually can be customized (compressed or expanded) to meet the organization's needs, resources, and desired results.

FIGURE 3–3

Brand Assessment Workplan Steps

Step 1	Step 2	Step 3
• Review all brand communications (internal and external) and existing market and consumer research and marketing plan. • Prepare written summary and index.	• Complete the transaction, technology, competitive, and market analyses as well as the consumer research.	• Complete preliminary assessment and review with selected senior executives. • Finalize assessment and completion of report.
• Initial project kickoff meeting and begin field research.	• Second team meeting.	• Third team meeting. • Presentation to executive team.

Brand Assessment Questions

The objective of the *assessment* is to provide answers to critical brand issues. The following list provides a representative sampling of the kinds of questions that should be answered:

- Does the brand currently have a BrandPromise (value proposition)?
- What does the brand stand for in the minds of the executive team?
- What BrandPromise is being communicated by the brand's representatives to current and potential customers, partners, vendors, employees, and the like?
- What do various stakeholders perceive *the promise* to be?
- Do different departments communicate an identical *promise* and messages to their respective audiences?
- What brand identity does the current customer service reflect?
- Who are the brand's current and future customers?
- How do current customers do business with the brand?
- What are the key statistics that drive the business?
- Who are the highest potential customers, based on sales, by segment?
- What are the current media messages?
- How is the brand currently positioned?
- What is the consensus of opinion regarding the brand's business, image, and future position?
- What companies and/or brands would be appropriate and potential brand alliance candidates?
- What is the most effective way to use marketing, promotions, and so forth, to increase sales, profits, and brand equity?
- What is the first word to come to mind when customers and noncustomers think of the brand?
- What are the brand's strengths and weaknesses (internal and external perceptions)?
- What are the brand's strongest positive benefits (attributes) to customers and consumers?

We are now going to turn our attention to examining the work involved in the key areas of the *assessment,* including:

- Consumer research
- Business environment review
- Customer transaction analysis
- Market research and competitive trends
- Technology migration

Consumer Research

The consumer research should provide insight into how a brand's customers and the general public perceive the brand and its competitors across five broad parameters:

- Differentiation between competing brands
- Trust (esteem)
- Relevance
- Awareness
- Use satisfaction and future intent

Collecting consumer information of this nature often requires the expertise of a third party research company that has the necessary resources and technology. The right type of information is essential to an objective assessment.

It is important to understand consumers' and customers' perceptions of a brand relative to the competitive marketplace. Primary research should be compared from three perspectives:

- In an *absolute* sense
- In a *relative* sense compared to key competitors
- From a *best-demonstrated-practices* perspective

It is important to understand customer satisfaction from an absolute standpoint. "How satisfied are customers with our service?" It is also important to understand customer satisfaction compared to other competitors and from a macro point of view. In other words, what's reasonable, acceptable, or the norm in a particular industry or segment? The best-demonstrated-practices approach is to identify the industry's "gold standard" or top performance (inside or outside the industry) in order to establish benchmarking targets.

In order to establish brand trends, measurement, and reasonable goals, it is equally important to establish an ongoing research timetable with scheduled intervals. The purpose of consumer and customer research is to create a perceptual map (a comparison of important product and service attributes) that illustrates a brand's position relative to its competitive set in the consumer's mind. (An example is provided in the Citibank Brand Profile at the end of this chapter.) Professional research firms are generally retained to collect consumer data using a variety of interview techniques, such as targeted telephone calls, direct mail, focus groups, or personal intercepts at locations such as shopping malls.

Small companies or new ventures can interview representatives of their target audience themselves, although the lack of objectivity may present a risk to the desired outcome and results. The Internet has proven to be a robust secondary source for consumer, competitive, market, and industry data. Secondary research of this type is a useful tool to supplement primary research and internal opinions. It provides an added element of comparative data to the process.

An essential step in the *assessment* process is to gain insight from all stakeholders in the brand. These include:

- Customers (current)
- Consumers (potential customers)
- Influencers (intermediaries such as distributors or dealers)
- Suppliers (vendors, professional services, accounting, strategic, etc.)
- Employees
- Stockholders

Any group of individuals that has a stake in a brand's success should be regularly researched to understand their point of view. For some organizations, this would include their members. For others, it might be agents or franchisees.

The unprecedented entrepreneurial growth and robust economy we are experiencing has funded more research than ever before by investment bankers and venture capitalists on just about every topic imaginable. Industry analyst reports are also a great source of reliable research and trend identification that can be accessed at a fraction of the cost of customized primary research. The Internet has become a phenomenal tool to access all kinds of research sources and information.

It isn't necessary, and it could even be considered unwise, to "boil the ocean" searching for every possible piece of information in order to assess a brand's situation. The key when obtaining information is to attempt at all times to triangulate or confirm the information from at least one or two other sources. Genuine brands are committed to understanding their customers' (demographic and psychographic) perceptions and behavior (past, present, and future).

The Current Marketing Strategy

The purpose of examining the brand's current marketing is to gain insights into the consistency, commitment, and effectiveness of the current and proposed programs. Questions that should be answered include:

- What channels of distribution and communication are being utilized?
- Who are the target customers and why?
- Who are the most feared competitors today as well as in the future?
- Which organizations are likely to be the future competitors?
- What is the concise positioning statement that summarizes the marketing goals?
- What are the major expenditures and measured results for each over the past three years? (list)
- What is the pricing strategy for each product and service?

After all of the information has been collected, a concise summary should be written that captures the key programs for the current year and compares them with past and future plans and performance.

Business Environment Review

An environmental review is a long-range perspective of the business aspects of a brand's marketplace. If you can't see the forest for the trees, it is necessary to step back from the nitty-gritty, day-to-day details of the business to gain a fresh brand perspective. Imagine you're in a high altitude radar plane surveying a brand's business to address questions such as:

- How has the industry developed historically and how is it likely to develop in the future?
- What kinds of people (employees) are attracted to a specific segment or industry?
- How have customers' needs and expectations developed over time?
- Who are the competitors, what part of the business did they come from, and where are they likely to go in the future?
- What role does government play in the business and how are they likely to be involved in the future?
- What brands have come and gone in the business, category, or industry and why?

The purpose of this exercise is to characterize a brand's business situation in order to gain insight into the forces at work in a given industry or market. By providing a written summary of each of the assessment findings a brand can gain consensus among its management team with regard to how it fares in the larger environment. It is crucial to gain consensus on a brand's situation and perception during the assessment phase. Otherwise, it will be difficult to agree on a *doctrine* and more specifically, the right action plan.

Customer Transaction Analysis

The old saying goes: "Don't criticize someone unless you have walked in their shoes for a day." It's amazing how little organizations sometimes know about the details of activities affecting their brand. How often have you called someone to find out he or she is not in, the recording says to press zero for immediate assistance.

But the next thing you hear is, "This mailbox is not accepting messages right now, please call back at another time." Yet when someone points this out to an organization, they seem surprised.

The idea behind a transaction analysis is to assign brand team members the task of experiencing all the steps a customer might go through to see how the system makes the customer feel. Brand team members should conduct their transaction analyses in pairs so that experiences and conclusions can be compared among all the team members.

The exercise begins with a pad of paper on which the team member writes down each reaction to each experience along the way. Let's assume an organization is in the restaurant business and has eight locations. The first step is to check out the telephone brand image by calling the restaurant and noting:

- How many times did the phone ring?
- How do they answer the phone? (writing down exact words)
- The attitude of the person answering the phone
- What was said and how you were made to feel when booking a reservation, asking how a certain kind of food is prepared, and inquiring about the hours of operation. (write down what is said)
- Next, follow up in person. If possible, when you visit the restaurant, keep your identity secret. It is important that the people not know you. Visit the restaurant at night. Initially, park on the street to take note of the building's exterior, entry way, and sign. How would you characterize it? (Is it easy to read, well lit, and clean? What impression do you get from the sign?)
- Now enter the parking lot and make further observations. (Is it easy to navigate, well lit? clean? Is it easy to tell where the entrance to the restaurant is?) Add them to your notes.
- From the time you approach the restaurant, note everything you see, hear, smell, and feel. (How are you greeted? Do you feel special?)

The key is to operate in this kind of retentive mode and capture every piece of information, no matter how small or seemingly unimportant. It is important to "stage" a problem with part of the food order. Be sure to ask the server what happens if you don't like a certain food item. It is important to observe how employees and associates react to a variety of "real world" customer experiences. Observe and take note of how you feel when you have a problem. It is the same for an organization in the retail business. Try returning a purchased item to see how the return policy and process works.

A very successful restaurant organization conducted a transaction analysis for its new Palomino brand. After a second location opened, it was discovered that while the food was excellent, there was an opportunity to improve the service experience after customers were served their entrée. As a result, they took specific measures to be sure that their "team members" returned regularly to check on the customers' satisfaction with their dining experience. They also changed how the bill was presented. And to make the experience more memorable and positive (and different from competitors), each guest is now presented a small personal card with the final check, as illustrated in Figure 3-4. Opening the card reveals an enjoyable quote or positive message, a sort of Americanized version of the Chinese fortune cookie.

The results were impressive. Customer service and satisfaction increased throughout the dining experience, and the Palomino brand has grown to 17 locations in major cities throughout the United States.

The transactional analysis is then compared to other team member's experiences for highlights, similarities, and differences. An individual is then assigned the task of preparing an executive summary of the entire transaction analysis, complete with recommendations for further research and changes to benefit the brand. This summary provides another source of information to the overall assessment process, which will be compared to the other research before overall brand conclusions are reached.

Market Research and Competitive Trends

The object of this analysis is to find out as much as possible about the segment or category in which a brand does business. The same questions to be answered for a specific market should also be ad-

FIGURE 3–4

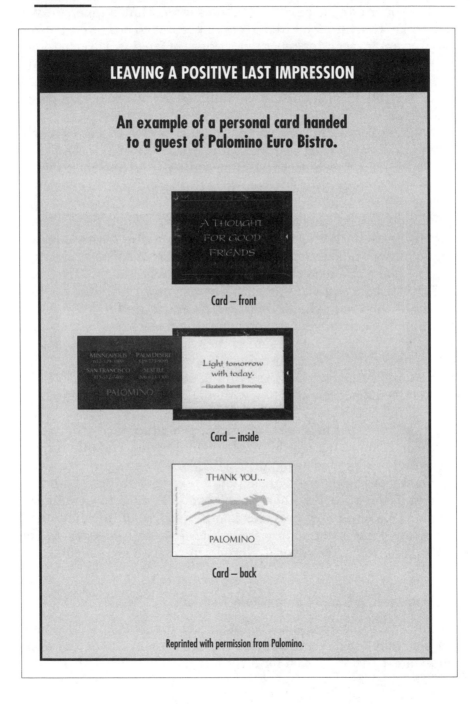

LEAVING A POSITIVE LAST IMPRESSION

An example of a personal card handed to a guest of Palomino Euro Bistro.

Card – front

Card – inside

Card – back

Reprinted with permission from Palomino.

dressed for a brand's top two to three competitors. Let's assume a brand is a small retailer of office equipment supplies with three local area locations. Because of national chain competition from companies like Office Max, Staples, and Office Depot, the small local retailer wants to assess its brand in order to position it for future success.

The market research and competitive analysis should answer all the questions an investor might ask. A great outline to follow is a new initial public offering prospectus. A sample can be obtained from any broker or investment firm. The key headings for this analysis include:

- Description of the business
- Risk factors
- Competitors: strengths and weaknesses
- Government regulations and restrictions
- Management experience and expertise
- Unique attributes, technologies, solutions, proprietary rights, and applications that the brand utilizes
- Growth strategy
- Customer identification analysis
- Economic forecast for the business segment and related sectors of the economy

The market research and competitive analysis is designed to answer key questions regarding the current brand situation. Selected questions would include:

- What are our most profitable segments of business?
- What products and services are growing the fastest?
- What new products and services are likely to enter the market?
- How can we better serve our customers?
- What differentiates our brand, our stores, and our business from those of competitors?
- What are the projections for future sales and profits in our category of business?

The competitive analysis should select one to three competitors that are believed to be the biggest threats to the brand's success, or they should be determined by asking customers which competing brands they do business with most often. A matrix should be prepared that compares all aspects of the market research and competitive information by topic or attribute across the brand and its competitors. A method of scoring or analyzing the positive and negative attributes of each competitor is determined and utilized throughout the matrix. A simple method is merely to use symbols, such as a plus sign (+) for an advantage, a minus sign (–) for a disadvantage, and a zero (Ø) from status quo, to compare an organization's brand with the competitive research. It is also a good idea to include a brief written description supporting the rating.

Sources for the information are widespread and include industry journal reports, annual forecasts, annual reports (of public companies), the Internet, investment analysts' reports, local newspaper articles, Dun & Bradstreet reports, and conversations with vendors, suppliers, employees of competitors, and competitors' newsletters.

Once the information has been compiled into a report similar to a prospectus, it should be shared and presented to various executives within the brand for review, revisions, and to gain a consensus around the fundamental conclusions.

Technology Migration Analysis

There isn't any brand today that will not be affected by technological change. It isn't a question of whether or not a brand *will* change due to automation, computerization, or high-tech applications. It's only a question of *how* the brand will change or be affected as a result of competitors embracing new technologies and racing to apply them strategically to their businesses and brands.

Brands that embrace technology and employ the correct applications have an opportunity to change the competitive paradigm. For example, when Amazon.com's Internet retail model is compared to traditional "bricks and mortar" retail booksellers, it would appear that Amazon.com literally and forever altered the course for many retail businesses and accomplished it "overnight." Similarly, if a brand's sales presentations are being made to customers and potential customers using manual transparencies individually placed on overhead projectors, look out for the competitor who shows up with a laptop computer and dynamic graphics software that presents expert analysis of the customer's business in a more compelling presentation format.

Even the most fundamental and taken-for-granted technologies, like voicemail, can be brand equity boosters or customer turn-offs. Let's examine the choices for a typical customer service operation. Recently, a digital cellular brand was running full page advertisements daily in *The Wall Street Journal,* yet upon attempting to contact this major cellular brand on a dozen different occasions, I was never able to "connect" with a real person. It is obvious that this particular brand does not have a BrandPromise or completely lacks understanding about the importance of providing acceptable levels of service. Even more surprising was their recording, which said, "We're experiencing unusually high levels of call volume." I find it ironic; doesn't their whole business revolve around answering the phone?

The idea is this: Assess what impact current technology is having on a brand's image and how future technology is likely to impact the brand. Be sure that the analysis begins with the applications that are important to the customer today, such as:

- How long do customers have to wait before the phone is answered?
- Can the customer always reach a real person?
- How long does it take to access the customer's account information?
- What is the average amount of time spent by an employee and the total cost to respond to a typical customer request?
- Have new proposed technologies that will affect customers been tested with real customers first?

While technology issues may all sound high-tech, the relevant aspect for the *assessment* is gauging how technology affects a brand's perception by its customers as well as competitors for those customers. In other words, "How does the technology we employ make our customers feel, and for that matter, other stakeholders too?"

In summary, the *assessment* should capture all of the relevant information necessary to correctly establish a brand's current position in the marketplace, its image in the customer's mind, and it should identify the appropriate trends that will impact the brand in the future.

Concluding the Brand Assessment

Once the various research efforts have been completed, a written report on each subject should be prepared following a common outline:

- Background (purpose, methodology, sources, etc.)
- Brand conclusions (each one supported by fact or reference)
- Brand recommendations
- Quotes to consider (stakeholder quotes noted during research or brand-related quotes that are relevant)
- Exhibits (copies of reports, sources, and articles to support findings)

The *assessment* team should then meet and present their findings as a draft report. The team should recommend revisions and additions to each subject as preparation for a final written report on each subject. A written executive summary of the *assessment* research should be prepared by one person and circulated to other team members for comments. In Chapter 9 we provide a sample of a generic *assessment* report. When the brand team has reached general consensus, a formal assessment presentation should be scheduled with senior management to present the findings. At the conclusion of the presentation, but prior to a question and answer discussion, the written brand assessment executive summary should be distributed. Usually, a follow-up meeting is scheduled to gain consensus on the assessment before the second phase of the *doctrine* process is activated.

Citibank (now a part of Citigroup) believes in the value of an objective assessment of an organization's brand. The following brand profile demonstrates the analysis that is a necessary step in the process of creating a genuine brand.

BRAND PROFILE

CITIBANK*
A Lesson from the Real World of Branding

City Bank of New York opened for business on June 16, 1812, with $2 million of capital under the direction of the bank's cofounder and first president, Samuel Osgood. Originally founded to provide badly needed financial services to the underserviced local merchants of New York, City Bank of New York has grown into a dominant global brand. Citibank (it officially changed its name in 1976 under the parent company name of Citicorp) changed the face of U.S. retail banking in 1977 with its Citicard Banking Centers, anchored by customer-friendly and versatile ATMs. At the same time, in conjunction with the rollout of its 24-hour ATMs, Citibank launched its legendary "The CITI never sleeps" ad campaign. Citibank continued its legacy of providing technological innovation in consumer banking services into the 1980s with the introduction of unique touch-screen automated teller machines. To ensure its place as a global dominant banking and financial services brand for the future, Citicorp and Travelers Group merged to form Citigroup, the merger announced April 6, 1998. The merger positions Citigroup, with combined assets of $700 billion, to become one of the first trillion-dollar financial institutions.

FIGURE 3–5

*Information provided by Citigroup and used with permission.

FIGURE 3–6

Brian Ruder, executive vice president in charge of all of Citibank's branding activities as well as Global Marketing for Citibank's consumer businesses, sees an appealing opportunity for Citibank to build its strong image into a brand the likes of Disney, Coke, or Nike. In Ruder's words, "Branding is an emotional bond between retailer and customer. Disney means fun in people's minds. Nike is athleticism, and Coke is refreshment. Citibank is *aspirations*." Citibank aspires to be more than a bank; it wants to transform itself into a brand. The reason is, as Ruder explains, "Not necessarily so people will pay a premium price, but to enhance and deepen the relationship that people have with our service and with our product." In addition to their desire to be a brand, Citibank aspires to be an "indestructible brand." Ruder agrees that branding is "clearly the hot idea," but he views most of the approaches employed by other organizations as "one-dimensional, even simplistic." Ruder says that branding is a dynamic process, not a static idea, and it encompasses every dimension of a business. Building successful brands is a long-term process.

With core earnings growth in the 10 to 12 percent range annually, return on investments in excess of 18 percent, and free capital of $2 billion yearly, Citibank can certainly be classified a successful brand insofar as the numbers are concerned. Even with that sort of track record, how does Citibank plan to make the transition from bank to brand? By implementing a *BrandStrategy Doctrine*. What does the brand mean to everyone at Citibank? Bill Campbell, co-chief executive officer of the Citigroup Consumer Business, articulates their vision this way: "It is a promise that we'll be there consistently, providing customers with products relevant to their needs that serve them where and when they want. Customers will use your product over and over again when they are confident that you continuously keep your promise." Genuine brands deliver on their promises to customers. Coca-Cola delivers superior refreshment, Boeing promises high-performance aircraft, and Starbucks provides the best fresh-roasted coffee in a truly unique setting.

BUILDING CITIBANK INTO A BRAND

The banking and financial services industries have not developed their brands to attain or maximize brand equity the same way other genuinely great brands have done. Genuine brands have developed distinctive products and services. "All I have to say is 'Big Mac' in just about any country where Citibank does business and everyone knows I'm talking about McDonald's," says Ruder. What happens when I say the word 'loans?' This brings to mind only the word 'banks.' In order for banks to establish a brand identity, they must establish products that are relevant to the customer and have unique product attributes," he adds.

When you look at the banking industry that Citibank is a part of, you begin to understand why Brian Ruder sees tremendous opportunities for Citibank to become a genuine brand. According to Young & Rubicam, Inc., Citibank's global advertising partner, there are no big brands among banks that are based on performance in each of the four major categories of differentiation, relevance, esteem, and knowledge. Highly successful brands reside in the upper right quadrant of the Brand Asset Valuator, Young & Rubicam's proprietary measurement tool that tracks how brands develop and grow and graphically represents how brands measure up relative to one another. No banking institution comes close to the positions held by Disney, General Electric, Coca-Cola, or Home Depot. "Comparing what powerful brands have done and what bank or

FIGURE 3–7

FIGURE 3–8

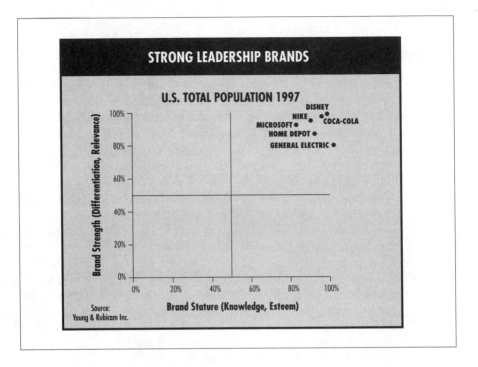

financial services companies have not done illustrates the necessities of brand building," says Ruder. In order for a bank—or any organization—to build a successful brand, Ruder believes they must:

- Establish distinctive products and services
- Provide consistent, convenient delivery, anywhere, always
- Deliver a quality customer experience
- Consistently communicate the BrandPromise

INTEGRATING THE BRANDPROMISE

As Ruder explains, "The brand is a promise. And that promise is delivered daily by and through Citibankers [Citibank's internal term for its employees]. So to ensure that we live up to our promise, we have to integrate living up to our brand standards, which means that we must integrate quality into every single interaction with our customers. We have a corporatewide quality program under way to educate every

Citibanker on how we can integrate quality into everything we do." Citibank is working with companies such as Motorola and Disney to design their training programs and services.

The brand is a living entity and the organization's people are its lifeblood. Citibank understands that it cannot build a brand in the same class as Coca-Cola without raising the employee's level of awareness to branding and the need to integrate branding into everything they do. Citibank has a *Brand Book*, which was given to all Citibankers so there would be a consistent presentation of their brand, both internally and externally. In this way, every Citibanker becomes a brand manager and an ambassador of the Citibank brand. It takes understanding and commitment on the part of employees; it takes a BrandStrategy Doctrine to outline the details of how the brand will remain relevant, distinct, offer superior quality, and earn the esteem of customers and consumers.

Indeed, the Citibank brand will "never sleep"—or rest on its laurels— if they continue to work on the development, implementation, and integration of their vision and BrandStrategy Doctrine.

FIGURE 3–9

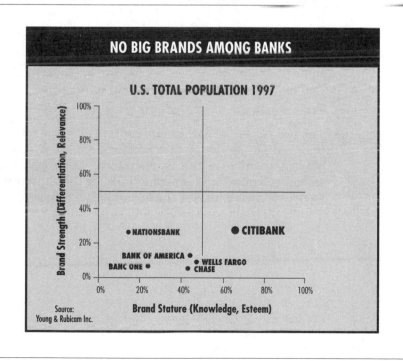

THE BRAND ASSESSMENT

- If you don't know where your brand currently is, then you cannot successfully determine how to get it to where it needs to be in the future. A disciplined assessment process is necessary to find the answers to these fundamental questions.

- You need to walk in your customers' shoes to understand how your brand measures up in their minds. A consumer transaction analysis is necessary to capture this all-important data from your customers' and consumers' perspectives.

- The concept of a Brand Assessment is all about objectivity. The Brand Assessment process is designed to characterize the current perceptions of a brand based on factual and observable conclusions and material in a manner that attempts to preclude unwanted subjective prejudice.

- Primary research should be compared from three perspectives:

  In an *absolute* sense

  In a *relative* sense compared to key competitors

  From a *best-demonstrated-practices* perspective

- The Brand Assessment should capture all of the relevant information necessary to correctly establish a brand's current position in the marketplace, its image in the customer's mind, and it should identify the appropriate trends that may impact the brand in the future.

4

The BrandPromise™

The "Guiding Star" for Genuine Brands with a Brand Profile of Lexus

Never promise more than you can perform.
—Publilius Syrus, first century Roman author

THE PHILOSOPHY OF A BRANDPROMISE

As we discussed in Chapter 1, in order to have a truly genuine brand, it is fundamental to understand how to think like a brand. Thinking like a brand is quite different from thinking like a business. It is kind of like the difference between being at work and being on vacation. In order to really enjoy a vacation, it is necessary to think differently from how you would at the office. Thinking like a brand requires a different perspective and approach than business as usual. The key to this different approach is the BrandPromise (the *promise*),* and as indicated in Figure 4-1, it is the next step in the BrandStrategy Doctrine Process after the completion of the Brand Assessment.

The BrandPromise is absolutely fundamental to creating, developing, or enhancing a new or existing genuine brand. The BrandPromise is the rallying cry of a Genuine Brand and the crux of its differentiation. A BrandPromise communicates three inherent attributes:

---

*For readability and ease of reference, the BrandPromise™ methodology is sometimes
 referred to as the *promise*.

FIGURE 4–1

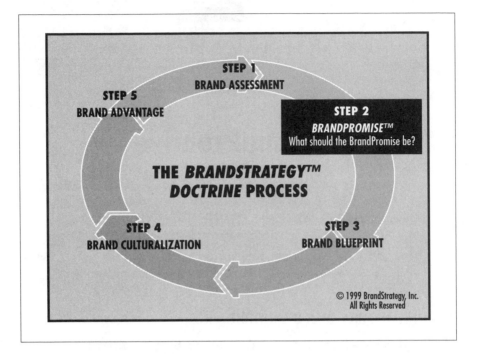

1. Something will be done
2. An expressed assurance
3. A perception of future excellence and achievement

The *promise* is a short paragraph comprised of two to four sentences. An example of a *promise* is that of Cinnabon world famous cinnamon rolls shown in Figure 4-2. At a glance, it may not seem to be all that special or different. However, after a serious examination of Cinnabon's written BrandStrategy Doctrine, it becomes very apparent what the key distinct drivers of its *promise* are. Let's examine these drivers for the Cinnabon brand as an example of how to think about this concept.

Unique Cinnamon

The Makara cinnamon is unique to Cinnabon. With over 300 percent more volatile oils than the typical cinnamon that is available at a supermarket, Makara, grown in a specific area high in the mountains of Indonesia and processed though a 56-step proprietary temperature-controlled process, is at the heart of the world-famous taste. This extra attention to quality produces a cinnamon which has a rich texture and color and releases its maximum flavor during the baking process.

Emotional Experience

A Cinnabon is not about eating food; it is an indulgence of the senses. Jerilyn Brusseau, Cinnabon's creator, eloquently describes the experience of eating a Cinnabon as "the discovery of essential goodness."

Aroma

The aroma is essential to creating the expectation for delight with the first bite.

Attentive, Cheerful, and Timely Service

Cinnabon's values enhance this promise, as shown in Figure 4-3.

FIGURE 4–2

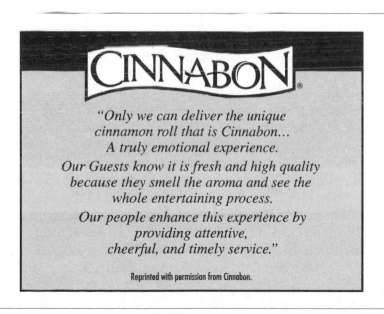

"Only we can deliver the unique cinnamon roll that is Cinnabon... A truly emotional experience. Our Guests know it is fresh and high quality because they smell the aroma and see the whole entertaining process. Our people enhance this experience by providing attentive, cheerful, and timely service."

Reprinted with permission from Cinnabon.

FIGURE 4–3

Living the BrandPromise

If an organization is living its *promise*, every single employee understands the essence of the *promise* and is dedicated to its fulfillment. Every new associate learns the *promise*, each and every employee learns it, from the president through temporary employees, and each person knows what the organization is promising its customers and stakeholders. As we will discuss later, the *promise* is the foundation for developing the Brand Principles, which in turn provide the guidelines for the action plan.

The *promise* is not designed to become the advertising message. However, every advertisement and all internal and external communications should be consistent with the spirit of the *promise*.

FIGURE 4–4

The Unsinkable Legend™

When you examine the meaning of a *promise,* it is clear what it should communicate: an expressed assurance that something will occur with a clear perception of future excellence. Figure 4-4 is an excellent example of how a brand can use its tag line as the vehicle to communicate its *promise.* Boston Whaler's tag line is "the unsinkable legend."

While there is more to Boston Whaler's *promise* than a three-word tag line, it does provide an excellent example of how a brand's messages should reflect its *promise.*

There are many other examples of great communications that have reflected *promises*: FedEx's "absolutely, positively overnight"; LensCrafters' "your glasses in about an hour"; and Intel's "Intel inside." Each of these brands has successfully communicated the essence of their *promises,* i.e., you are assured of a positive outcome and future excellence.

A Real Commitment to a BrandPromise

In 1988, during the process of selling the Holiday Inn brand to the Bass Brewery company of England, Holiday Corporation's chairman, Michael Rose, was thinking about the corporate identity for the new parent company that would own the Hampton Inn, Embassy Suites, Homewood Suites, and Harrah's brands. The concept of a real, *unconditional* 100-percent guarantee was so successful at Hampton Inn that Rose was interested in a corporate name that would reflect his passion for guaranteed satisfaction. (See the brand profile at the end of Chapter 6 for a complete review of Hampton Inn's 100-percent satisfaction guarantee.) As Mike Rose relates the story, "All the obvious names had already been taken, like *promise,* and the derivations of the word *guarantee* all sounded like trust companies." Finally, with the help of Mike Purvis, a brand image consultant and long-time friend, *promus* was offered up, from the Latin root "to serve." Hence, Promus® Companies was born, and as Rose had wanted, it really was "a genuine reflection of our core values."

An excerpt from an early Promus brochure captures the spirit, "Our name says promise representing our commitment to providing excellence to *every customer, every time.*" In fact, the company implemented its 100-percent unconditional guarantee in every Promus® brand. As Figure 4-5 indicates, their promise was not to provide good service occasionally but excellence to *every* customer *all* the time.

FIGURE 4–5

A PROMISE TO OUR CUSTOMERS

We promise
excellent service
to every casino and
hotel customer every time.
Our promise is
unconditional, universal
and backed by
our satisfaction
guarantee.

PROMUS
HOTEL CORPORATION

© Promus® Companies. Reprinted with permission.

A Mission, Vision, or Promise?

As we discussed in the first chapter, if an organization is to become brand-driven, then it must learn to think like a brand. Business planning during the first half of the twentieth century was focused on the development of mission or vision statements to provide strategic direction for an organization. While vision and mission have been important in guiding organizations' activities, they can be worlds apart from a *promise* or value proposition. Mission and vision statements generally represent what a company wants to be or do, as indicated in Figure 4-6. They are usually written from the company's point of view. A *promise* is written to define the intended functional and emotional benefits from the customer's point of view, after experiencing the product and service provided.

Mission and vision statements are usually created by selected groups of an organization's managers or executives and are rarely ever reviewed with customers or consumers until after they are introduced. A *promise* is always reviewed in draft form with customers, consumers, and employees to gain their insight before adoption. This ensures that the *promise* is realistic yet aspirational from a future positioning standpoint. If an organization has a relevant mission or vision statement, or even a list of appropriate values, they may be compatible with a *promise*. Alternatively, key ideas from a mission or vision statement could become part of the *promise* or the brand's principles, thereby eliminating separate missions or visions as organizations embrace the BrandMindset concept.

FIGURE 4-6

Mission, Vision, or BrandPromise

Mission
- The overall goal or reason the organization exists
- A self-imposed duty

Vision
- The overview of a company's purpose from 30,000 feet
- Intelligent foresight

BrandPromise
- The expected emotional and functional benefits of experiencing an organization's products and services, i.e., how an organization wants the customer to feel.

In an existing brand situation, once the *promise* has been decided, it must drive everything an organization does. Hence, mission, vision, values, and any and all corporate statements should be modified to reinforce the *promise* or be eliminated completely. Everyone must "sing from the same hymnal" if an organization expects to become or continue as a genuine brand.

BRANDPROMISE METHODOLOGY

Earlier, we discussed the intent of the *promise* as an expressed assurance that something will occur with a clear perception of future excellence.

To stand the test of time, a brand needs to stand for something larger than just a product benefit. Competitors can copy product benefits, sometimes even more cheaply. However, consumers choose a particular brand because of its intrinsic value. The American Automobile Association's promise to its members is "peace of mind." Wal-Mart is associated with a distinct set of American values, including patriotism and duty to country. Nike stands out not merely for the quality of its athletic shoes but also for the spirit of self-reliance and achievement. Product traits can be copied, but an organization's commitment to brand values provides the foundation for a unique *promise*.

How Is the BrandPromise Used?

The *promise* should serve as the "guiding star" for everything an organization does. Its primary purpose is to communicate clearly to every stakeholder associated with an organization (employees, agents, representatives, etc.) what the brand stands for (see Figure 4-7). A *promise* acts as a compass reading for everyone connected with a brand and also as a constant reality check to evaluate an organization's activities and performance and priorities.

Developing a BrandPromise

The first step in the development of a *promise* is to examine the existing culture of an organization in order to understand what

FIGURE 4–7

The *BrandPromise™* serves as the "Guiding Star."

its beliefs are. An organization's beliefs can be discovered by how it communicates, acts, and decides what direction to take.

In examining an organization's communications, all the messages an organization sends internally and externally need to be analyzed. This can be accomplished by collecting copies of any current or former missions, visions, or strategic plans. It is also necessary to collect a representative sampling of copies of business cards, faxes, invoices, newsletters, and typical correspondence, such as letters, press releases, customer complaint responses, and direct mail pieces. Once these are collected, they should all be displayed on a large wall, on a table, or on the floor to be examined for the following brand clues:

FIGURE 4–8

THE BRANDPROMISE OVERVIEW

1. PURPOSE
- Create and communicate a long-term value proposition with the customer's perspective.

2. PROCESS
- Answer three fundamental questions:
  - What business is our brand in?
  - What differentiates our products and services from competition?
  - What is superior about the value we offer our customers?

3. RESULTS
- Provides the foundation for guidance, direction and expectations of customers, employees and stakeholders.
- Everyone understands how to "*think like a customer.*"

- Strategic direction
- Key messages or themes
- Consistency of image and messages
- Tone or personality

This information should be compared to the data analyzed during the Brand Assessment for similarities and differences. The key to this analysis is the comparison of the organization's beliefs to its messages and the resulting customer perception of the organization and its brand.

Meeting of the Minds

The next step in the development of a *promise* is to meet with a cross section of an organization's executives and employees to gain their point of view on the organization's beliefs. After an employee or representative has elaborated on her view of the organization's beliefs, she should be asked for comments on some of the preliminary ideas surfaced during the discovery process.

At this point, a conclusion should be reached as to the nature of a brand's current beliefs or promise. This conclusion becomes the first "stake in the ground," or point of reference, in an organization's process to develop a *promise*. If an organization is a new venture, then the first step in the process consists primarily of interviews with the founders, etc. Also, it should be noted that in a new venture the name or identity should not be chosen until after the *promise* has been finalized.

Now an organization is ready for a brainstorming session to discuss the "desired" attributes of the brand going forward and possibly some of the brand's current attributes that may need to be disposed of. A representative group of executives and employees should plan to get together for a half-day or a full-day session away from the office to discuss the following aspects of their brand(s):

- What is a brand and what does it mean to be a genuine brand?
- What words come to mind when we think of a brand?
- If you think of a brand as an automobile, celebrity, or animal, what kind of each of these would it be?
- What are examples of other excellent or genuine brands, and why are they successful?

A facilitator should manage the session and record all the input on flipcharts for summarization later. Midway through the session, specific conclusions reached from the previous interviews across the organization should be shared with the group and discussed widely.

At this juncture, it is time to focus on preliminary answers to the three primary questions of the *promise*:

- What business is our brand in?
- What differentiates our products and services from the competition?
- What is superior about the value we offer our customers?

When the *promise* concept was introduced in Chapter 1, the point was made that it must be developed with the customer's point of view. The Brand Assessment conclusions should have clearly revealed the customer point of view. Obviously, the customer point of view should be merged with an organization's strategic direction to create the optimum *promise*. While the questions above may seem straightforward, let's examine them in detail to uncover their value.

What Business Is the Brand In?

The popular question in most strategic processes is, "What business are you in?" The purpose of this question is to get companies focused on the strategic implications and expertise that is relevant for optimum performance. In the mid-1980s most hotel companies were focused on the operations aspect of their business. However, the best strategic thinkers of that time were able to convince the more progressive organizations that they were actually in the real estate business; hence it was important to improve their return on assets. This was very important to the investors but of little immediate consequence or interest to hotel guests.

In contrast, when we ask the question, "What business is your brand in?" we are asking the question in relationship to how a customer will benefit from the brand's products and services. Figure 4-9 illustrates some examples of the difference between understanding the business of the brand and the business itself—from the customer's perspective.

Let's use an imaginary health insurance company, Hardline Health, as an example of an organization that wants to develop a *promise*. Hopefully, they know that they are in the business of selling insurance. Let's assume, however, that they discover that their customers' primary need is to reduce anxiety about their health and the associated costs of health care. Assume that Hardline Health decides that its brand is in the business of "caring for the quality of people's lives, to make them feel healthy and happy" and that they want to change their brand name to Friendly Health. However, when they discuss this internally, they realize that the reality is:

FIGURE 4–9

Company	Business	Brand
Kinko's	Copies and office supplies	Successful presentations or *Your* office
FedEx	Shipping	Immediate gratification
Coca-Cola	Beverages	Refreshing
Starbucks	Coffee	The third place
Walt Disney Companies	Theme parks, movies, etc.	The magic of feeling good

- When customers phone in for assistance, they are always put on hold and have to wait a long time.
- The corporate financial goal as well as the employees' goal is to keep the customers from receiving benefits whenever possible.
- The average time before a benefit is paid to either the customer or a physician is 100 days.

Unless this imaginary insurance company makes a revolutionary change in its practice, it should reconsider what business the brand is really in and should definitely not change its name.

What Differentiates a Brand's Products and Services?

If differentiation or distinctiveness is the key to building genuine brands, then the *promise* must express the unique benefits a brand offers its customers. Surprisingly, people still ask, "Are you in the product or service business?" This question is typical of the way organizations have thought about their businesses. Business has popularly been viewed as either product-driven or service-oriented. Historically, many businesses have not considered service and products as equally important. Today, every organization should view itself as being in both the product *and* service business.

The purpose of developing the *promise* is to create competitive advantages. If an organization views itself too narrowly, then it risks an invitation to a competitor who embraces the combined product-service mindset. It is not enough for an organization to think that its product can stand on its own merits. Customers expect more from products than just performing certain functions. They expect the brands behind the products to back them with service. Genuine brands understand and link products and services together into one mindset.

It is important to ask, "What does the customer think is different about our brand's offering when compared to our competitors?" The answer to this question makes it possible for an organization to consider what it might do to further the perception of differentiation in consumers' minds, keeping in mind that the brand's perceived differentiation is a lifelong quest, not just an idea for the current quarter. Innovation is a requirement for a genuine brand, not an option. Where would Coke be without Diet Coke, Tide without Tide with bleach, and Dow without Ziplocks? And where would we be without Domino's pizza delivery, fax machines, and e-mail? The mistake new brands most often make is to believe that their initial differentiation is enough to last forever.

How Does a Brand Offer Superior Value?

All too often, when organizations see this question, they focus on price. Many marketers believe that customers perceive value to mean lowest price. Lowest price is also translated to mean frequent sales and promotional discounts. A marketing position of lowest price is the most difficult to sustain and generally is an indication that the brand or organization has become a commodity in the minds of consumers. In general, commodities have few distinct differences except price.

Savvy marketers understand that while "low price" operators frequently can influence the purchase decision, this does not necessarily create long-term customer loyalty. Customers looking for the lowest price will only be loyal to the price, not the brand. On the other hand, when customers perceive that a brand *consistently* delivers value, it has the foundation to become a genuine brand. As a result, genuine brands enjoy higher degrees of profitability, customer loyalty, and enhanced brand equity.

Brand value can be defined by identifying, measuring, and analyzing customer needs and interpreting that information into actionable items for creating satisfied customers. Customers develop their perceptions of value through subjective *feeling* as a result of comparing the brand's product and service offerings with those of its competitors, based on his or her own needs, preferences, buying behavior, and characteristics. Thus, the customer's feeling of value will constantly change. The brand's ability to deliver value and delight customers is deeply rooted in the *promise*. Growth comes from serving customers better (not just bigger) and concentrating on the brand's *distinctive competence*.

When an organization is thinking like a brand, they understand that customers are buying more than just products or services. Genuine brands rarely focus on product alone; they are committed to their brand as both product and service. To concentrate on product alone is to assume that the customer doesn't care about time, convenience, feelings, and overall satisfaction. As illustrated in Figure 4-10, the formula for brand value is:

Value = "what you get" ÷ "how much you paid"

FIGURE 4–10

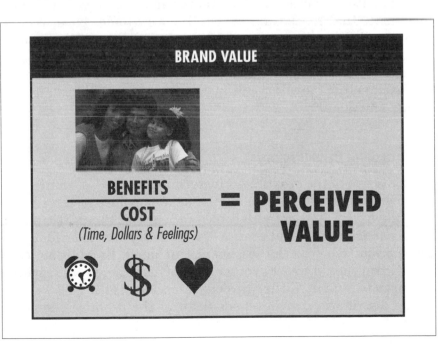

In the brand value formula, the perceived "get" should exceed the amount paid. The degree to which the get exceeds the amount paid will be the consumer's ultimate assessment of a brand's ability to deliver value.

The term *gestalt* aptly describes the phenomenon brands can use to deliver exceptional *perceived* value. The theory of gestalt suggests that nothing is simply the sum of its individual parts. A symphony, for example, is so much more than just the aggregate of its individual notes. The gestalt (or configuration) of anything has new and unique properties that are not derivable from the mere summation of its components. Psychologists use the concept of gestalt to describe our process of perception—how we interpret and assign meaning to sensory input. Genuine brands understand that their products *and* services are not simply a set of attributes or just a "thing." They understand that consumers are moved by the gestalt of the brand—all of its tangible and intangible (functional and emotional) benefits—integrated into the consumer's consciousness. This is why Tiffany, Godiva, and Nordstrom are special; they are more than just a turquoise colored box, a chocolate, or a department store. Genuine brands deliver a distinctive promise that creates memorable value in their experience that reaches far beyond their customer base. We discuss gestalt in more detail in Chapter 5, The Brand Blueprint.

Customers evaluate brands based on their view of the cost to acquire a brand's offering, i.e., how much time is involved in the transaction, the monetary outlay, and how they will feel after all is said and done.

Finalizing the BrandPromise

Near the end of the *promise* brainstorming session, a brand team member should summarize all the salient points of the discussion in writing and prepare copies for each of the participants. Each participant should draft a "preliminary" three or four sentence *promise* before the session is concluded. In addition, each participant should create another draft of his or her *promise* within the next two days. Either through another meeting or by electronic distribution, a consensus draft of the *promise* should be created.

The *promise* should reflect a balance between the aspirations of the brand as well as the reality of what the brand can and is capable of delivering to its customers. It's important to note that a *promise* should be aspirational enough to signal everyone in an organization to "reach for the stars," with the understanding that successful organizations' *promises* reflect a constant migrational journey to fulfill their commitments.

The Reality Check

Once the consensus *promise* draft has been developed, it is time to review it with a sampling of stakeholders for a reality check. An example of a *promise* research questionnaire is included in Chapter 9. The brand team or a research company can help to finalize the questionnaire, and even complete the questionnaire through interviews with the target audience. The questionnaire should be reviewed in person with various stakeholders, and after the interviews have been completed, the *promise* should be modified to reflect reasonable expectations as well as the current brand situation.

One of the primary differences between the typical organization's vision or mission and the *promise* is this "reality check" aspect of stakeholder and customer input. A well-conceived *promise* can become a source of enormous power for a genuine brand's reputation and performance in the marketplace.

It should be understood that at this point, the organization has a recommended *promise*. However, the *promise* should not be finalized until the Brand Blueprint has been completed.

Tradition versus Innovation

Most of the time when new organizations are formed, the first thing to be decided is the company name. Next, the organization gets some form of graphic design assistance to create a logo, and then it is off to the printer to get business cards. Hopefully, it is obvious from our discussion thus far that the development of the *promise* should precede all other activities. Some may even ask, "How can we develop our *promise* when we don't have any customers yet?" The answer is to interview prospective customers. It has been our experience during this process that prospective customers are thrilled to be involved and welcome the opportunity to make a contribution toward the eventual outcome. Interestingly enough, our interviews with prospective clients of professional service brands have often resulted in an order or the beginning of a successful business relationship. The same thinking applies to established organizations. Clients and customers really appreciate being involved. After all, they consider themselves to be stakeholders! When a *promise* reflects the best interests of its customers, it provides a jump-start in the development of a genuine brand.

EXPERIENCING A BRANDPROMISE

The *promise* comes to life when it is understood by every employee or brand representative, and it energizes the brand when each employee "lives" the *promise* and delivers it consistently. Essentially, when the customer benefits from the delivery of an organization's *promise*, the brand is real.

Recently, while visiting Mexico to deliver a presentation, I had the pleasure of being a guest at the Westin Regina Resort in Los Cabos. The overall attitude of the employees seemed too good to be true. It seemed as if anything you needed, they were only too happy to accommodate. The opportunity came to ask the director general, Mr. Werni Eisen, a very successful hotel executive, why the service was so exceptional. His explanation was that when he meets with each group of new employees, he has but one request: that they be happy. If they are not happy in their jobs, he asks them to tell someone so the situation can be addressed or please not work at the resort. It sounds so simple. However, the rule in hospitality is: The way employees treat the guests is a direct result of how they themselves feel they are treated. So the *promise* at the Westin Regina Resort is very simple: Be happy!

The concept of the *promise* has deep roots, especially in the medical profession. The Hippocratic oath dates back to fifth century BC and Hippocrates, generally considered to be the "father of medicine." Hippocrates' writings have been widely interpreted and modified worldwide, as exemplified in Figure 4-11. A version of the Oath of Hippocrates was adopted by the General Assembly of

FIGURE 4–11

A DOCTOR'S PRAYER

JESUS CHRIST – DOCTOR OF MEN, PLEASE GIVE ME:
LIGHT – TO FOLLOW MY PROFESSIONAL KNOWLEDGE.
LOVE – IN MY EFFORTS TO CURE SICKNESS.
LIFE – FOR THE HEALTH THAT I BRING TO THE ILL.
HOPE – IN MY WORDS OF CONSOLANCE.
NEVER ALLOW ME TO SELL MYSELF FOR MONEY,
POLITICS, OR COMFORT.
JESUS CHRIST – GOOD DOCTOR, HEAR MY PRAYER, BLESS MY WORK,
AND GIVE DIGNITY TO MY PROFESSION.
AMEN

(Translated from Spanish and provided by Dr. Alberto Lomas, San Jose Del Cabo)

---

the World Medical Association in 1948 and more recently revised again.[1] The purpose of the Oath of Hippocrates is to provide a declaration of physicians' dedication to the humanitarian goals of medicine. In the United States there is not one universal oath that is taken by all physicians. In fact, various medical schools have their own versions of the Oath, and some medical schools give their students a choice. It is the subject of much discussion in the medical field today.

A consistently understood and applied medical oath for every person working in the medical profession in the United States could become a significant factor toward improving consumer confidence in physicians as well as enhancing positive perceptions of the entire medical industry. The power of a *promise* to communicate dedication, intent, and an assurance of excellence cannot be understated. Imagine the power of a singular oath embraced by all physicians and medical professionals.

Genuine brands make a promise and they deliver that promise consistently, eagerly, and at the customer's convenience. A genuine brand creates relationships with customers centered around its *promise*. The power of a *promise* is based on what customers say about a brand to their friends and their feelings toward the brand. Word of mouth can be one of the most important determinations of a brand's ultimate success.

The evolution of the Lexus automobile from Toyota Motor Corporation's empire is a classic example of the birth of a genuine brand. The following profile examines the Lexus brand and its promise to its customers.

BRAND PROFILE

LEXUS*
Living Their BrandPromise

Genuine brands dream big dreams. They match those dreams by setting their brand's vision for standards and expectations equally high. In 1987, if someone had suggested that a Japanese-manufactured luxury car would outsell the likes of BMW and Mercedes in the United States—and do it in five years or less—it would have been met by disbelief and criticism. But that is exactly what happened. Lexus, a new brand established by Toyota in 1987, began business in 1989 in the United States and took the luxury car industry by storm, surpassing Saab, Peugot, Sterling, Jaguar, Alfa Romeo, and Porsche in sales in its first year, and it came within 112 units of BMW. By January 1992, Lexus moved ahead of Infiniti, BMW, and Mercedes. The Lexus brand was the result of Eiji Toyoda's (Toyota Motor Corporation chairman) vision in 1983 that the timing was right for Toyota to produce high-end automobiles that appealed to buyers in the luxury segment. He understood that consumer expectations were already quite high for cars such as Mercedes, BMW, and Cadillac. Toyoda passionately believed that Toyota could design and build the finest luxury car in the world, and by accompanying it with unparalleled levels of customer service, would create a class of car-buying experience unheard of by buyers in the luxury segment.

FIGURE 4–12

---

*Information provided by Lexus and used with permission.

FIGURE 4–13

In less than 10 years, Lexus has become the gold standard for all luxury-class automobiles. Lexus has been able to accomplish these lofty levels of almost unparalleled success primarily because from day one, it has had a crystal-clear vision and understanding of its core customer. Lexus understood that to compete and be successful, just meeting customer expectations was never going to be good enough. It had to blow them away! Lexus has exceeded customer expectations and believes it shows in the numbers. Lexus has topped the J.D. Power and Associates Customer Satisfaction Index seven out of the last eight years. "Lexus and Infiniti have mastered the art of surprise and delight when it comes to customer care by going extra miles, but Lexus has had the better word-of-mouth marketing bounce from that," says Joe Ivers, director of customer service at J.D. Power and Associates.

While Lexus has earned its fair share of accolades, they are, according to Jim Press, Lexus CEO, "simply *representations* of customer satisfaction; they are not the real thing." Customer satisfaction at Lexus is best described by Press as a "way of life, treating people the way _they_ want to be treated. It's a kind of 'Say yes' culture. Lexus empowers its associates, field personnel, and dealers to always try to find a way to say *yes*."

FIGURE 4–14

To keep its promise to customers and exceed their expectations, Lexus has established three goals:

1. To produce the *best quality* products in the world.
2. To fix problems right the *first time – every time.*
3. To provide service and convenience to Lexus owners, *like nothing they have experienced before.*

Toyota has known from day one that the Lexus brand's success is due to the harmony it has created between a rich legacy and tradition of production efficiency and exceeding customer expectations in service, reliability, and value. The essence of the Lexus brand, "the relentless pursuit of perfection," serves both as tag line and the corporate rallying cry. Toyota knew that the Lexus brand had to stand for something more than a superior product.

Providing unheard-of levels of customer satisfaction was achieved in large part through a demanding selection process of dealers, selecting only 72 out of 1500 applications, and the establishment of a certification program for all Lexus associates. Lexus also implemented customer service support systems, such as the comprehensive Lexus warranty, the 24-hour roadside assistance program, the satellite network, the free loaner car program, and others.

"Lexus means providing a total experience that is reflective of a sincere, complete commitment to absolute excellence. It is ensuring that facilities, systems, and procedures cater to the customers' needs and wants. It is providing professional treatment borne of genuine concern by everyone who works at Lexus. It is efficiency, effectiveness, and professionalism," says Press.

Lexus is typical of other genuine brands that have created a new paradigm from which to differentiate themselves from the pack. Traditionally, luxury automobiles did not advertise price. Lexus did not adhere to tradition but listened to customers. Based on their research, Lexus believed consumers' attitudes about spending large amounts of money for a car had changed. To communicate their price advantage and positioning, Lexus broke with tradition and the longstanding belief and was the first luxury car brand to run "price" advertisements against Mercedes-Benz.

FIGURE 4–15

Lexus also differentiates itself from other brands by its philosophical approach to business plans. Jim Press says that the Lexus business plan

> is not built for sales targets. It is built for customer satisfaction targets. We had to avoid trading off long-term brand equity for short-term sales results.... We could have tried to pump more volume, but when you have customer satisfaction as the center of your business plan, as we do, you don't put heavy volume pressure on the organization. Volume is not what drives the division. Customer satisfaction is at the top. If we pump volume through, there is no way to maintain customer satisfaction and re-sale value. We think of our brand equity like it was a bank account. You are either making deposits or withdrawals.

By putting customers first, exceeding their expectations, and continuing their "relentless pursuit of perfection," Lexus will insure itself that the only future transactions into their brand equity account will be deposits.

Sources: Lexus corporate materials and "Creating the New Gold Standard" (pp. 27–30) and "Full Court Press" (pp. 22–26), *BrandWeek*, July 27, 1998.

ACTION GUIDE

THE BRANDPROMISE™

- A BrandPromise is written to define the key functional and emotional benefits from the customers' point of view after experiencing the product and service provided.
- A BrandPromise should address three fundamental questions:

  What business is our brand in?

  What differentiates our products and services from the competition?

  What is superior about the value we offer our customers?

- The BrandPromise is not designed to become the advertising message; however, advertisements and all internal and external communications should be consistent with the spirit of the BrandPromise.
- Today, every organization should view itself as in both the product _and_ service business.

- The formula for brand value is: Value = "What you get" ÷ "how much you paid." Customers pay in three ways: time, dollars, and feelings.
- Genuine brands understand that customers are moved by the *gestalt* of the brand, hence they are focused on delivering a distinctive promise that creates memorable value by tapping into the consumer's consciousness on an emotional and functional level.
- Genuine brands make a promise, and they deliver on that promise consistently, eagerly, and at the customer's convenience.
- The mistake new brands most often make is to believe that their initial differentiation is enough to last forever.

5

The Brand Blueprint

The Architecture of a Brand with a Brand Profile of Whirlpool Corporation

Nothing in life is more important than the ability to communicate effectively.
—Gerald R. Ford, 38th President of the United States

THE PHILOSOPHY BEHIND THE BRAND BLUEPRINT

It Starts with a Blueprint

You wouldn't think of constructing a building, be it a simple one-story dwelling or a very complex skyscraper, without the aid of a blueprint. One of the first top-of-the-mind associations we have of blueprints is that professional architects draft them. Architects are skilled practitioners in the profession of envisioning, designing, and planning all the necessary elements from which to build something—an office building, a home, a garden, whatever. In the language of building and construction, certain styles and types of structures are identified as "architecture." These styles often denote a time period in history, reflecting what was in vogue at the time. Brands are no different. Just as a distinctive architectural style sets the tone or establishes the nature of a building, so too are brands perceived in terms of their architecture.

A key component of the BrandMindset is the procedure for properly constructing and communicating a brand's identity. A deliberate methodology for developing a successful brand identity is crucial to maximizing brand equity. We call this a Brand Blueprint.* It is our methodology for building a successful brand identity in today's crowded marketplace. Brand Blueprint (*blueprint*) can be defined in this way: 1. The disciplined, detailed plan required to create, design, and communicate the intended brand perception. 2. That which determines the character or style of a brand. 3. A plan that reflects the BrandPromise and outlines the underlying *collective* architecture for the brand name, byline, tag line, graphic representations, and the brand story. Figure 5-1 shows how the *blueprint* fits into the overall BrandStrategy Doctrine Process.

FIGURE 5–1

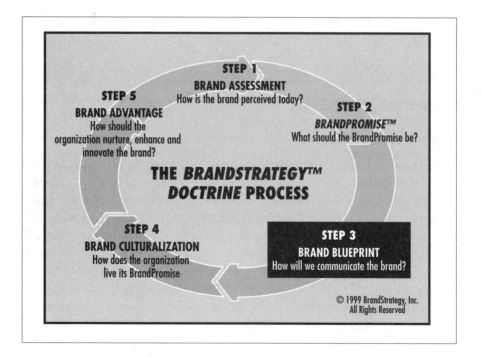

*For readability and ease of reference, Brand Blueprint is alternatively referred to as the *blueprint*.

We've already learned that the word *brand* means different things to different people. Brand is used almost generically today to refer to logos, trademarks, specific products, even company "names." While such usage is not incorrect, no single manifestation adequately captures the essence or the power that is a genuine brand. A genuine brand holds a very distinctive position in the consumer's mind's eye. As you will discover, the most successful brands are usually *genuine.*

A brand is forged from a multitude of components, which, if crafted properly, create an aura that is far greater in *perceived* size and value than the business alone. A highly complex entity, a brand is not just the actual product and services but also the complete set of perceived values, characteristics and attributes that differentiate it from other similar products and services. What is most important to grasp here is that brand identity *exists entirely in the mind of the consumer*. When it comes to brands, perception is everything. It has everything to do with what the consumer *believes* to be true about the brand. No matter what an organization's marketers have envisioned for a brand's position, it is the consumers who are the final arbiters. That is why we say a genuine brand is the internalized sum of *all* impressions received by customers and consumers resulting in a distinctive position in their mind's eye based on perceived emotional and functional benefits.

Let's lay the foundation for constructing a *blueprint* by first exploring the concept and history of branding.

The Psychology of a Brand

We introduced the term *gestalt* in Chapter 4, and it aptly describes the phenomenon of successful brands. Literally meaning *form,* or *configuration,* the theory of gestalt suggests that nothing is simply the sum of its individual parts. So the gestalt of anything has new and unique properties that are not derivable from the mere summation of its constituent parts.

Psychologists use the concept of gestalt to describe our process of perception, how we interpret and assign meaning to sensory input. They have shown that we interpret experiences holistically rather than responding to discrete elements. Thus, a drawn figure still has meaning to us, even if there are gaps in the drawing. We configure fragments of data into meaningful units in order to comprehend and learn.

Smart marketers understand that a branded product is not simply a set of objective features and attributes. Rather, consumers are influenced by the gestalt of the brand—all its tangible and intangible assets integrated into the consumer's consciousness.

Strong brands gain authority and stature in consumers' minds by offering credible, coherent, attractive, and consistent messages over time, from which consumers can form cohesive and meaningful patterns of association. Take Tiffany & Co., for example; everyone seems to recognize their signature Tiffany Blue™ color. What other brands can you think of that are known by a color alone, compared, say, to a symbol, name, or slogan? The Tiffany shopping bag and gift box stand out in a crowd; they are instantly recognized and evoke a full range of emotional responses and images, from envy to sheer delight. That is the power of a brand, the essence of a brand's gestalt. Figure 5-2 depicts the gestalt of a gift.

FIGURE 5–2

Photo by Craig Cutler; courtesy of Tiffany & Co.

Even brands that have lost their way can be successfully revived with the correct gestalt. In the 1960s the Volkswagen Beetle captured the imaginations of a young generation (the first wave of the Baby Boomers) and became a universally successful automobile. As the decades passed, the Beetle faded into obscurity, leaving a faded memory of its legacy and Volkswagen to a less-than-stellar position in the world marketplace. The Beetle may have disappeared, but the Volkswagen *brand* was not dead. Winner of *BrandWeek* magazine's Grand Marketer of the Year in 1998, Volkswagen has received much acclaim for its new Beetle. The successful return of the Volkswagen brand started by exploring the company's past to rediscover the core values and perceptions associated with the company. Volkswagen needed to decide which messages were relevant to communicate and who to target within a changing, diversified audience.

The Beetle's return is not necessarily the entirety of VW's comeback in the United States, but certainly it is the most visible aspect. Steve Wilhite, Volkswagen's senior marketing executive, says that "managing a brand for success has everything to do with understanding who you are, and not apologizing for it and not trying to be something you're not."[1] Wilhite further believes that at the heart of VW's comeback is the company's realization that it had to be comfortable with what VW is and where its products are designed and built. The Volkswagen ad theme that first appeared in 1995 typifies the spirit of the VW gestalt: "On the road of life there are passengers and there are drivers. Drivers wanted.®"

The Origins of Branding

Branding is not a new phenomenon. Craftsmen and manufacturers have long used marks of one sort or another to identify and distinguish their products from those of others, and examples of emblematic identification can be found throughout history. The earliest identity marks date back to prehistoric times, and even then the marks answered one or more of the same basic questions:

- Who made this?
- Who owns it?
- What is it?
- What makes it special?

Prehistoric hunters inscribed their weapons with marks to indicate ownership. Ancient Greek and Roman potters identified their work by pressing a thumbprint into the wet clay on the bottom of the pot. By the Middle Ages, the application of identifying marks onto livestock was commonplace. (To *brand,* indeed, comes from the old Norse word meaning to *burn.*)

Since ancient times, symbolic and ornamental figures have been used as tribal or national emblems to proclaim power and authority, by kings, emperors, and governments to proclaim ownership or control. The Japanese, for example, used the chrysanthemum; the Romans used the eagle; and the French employed first the lion and later the fleur-de-lis (Figure 5-3 provides examples of heraldic symbols).

Seals, too, were employed as forms of identity marks in the most ancient of civilizations. Their use, for example, in the Babylonian Empire was to authenticate the documents to which they were attached. For more than 30 centuries in China, Japan, Korea, and all over the far east, the use of beautifully hand-carved stone *chops* were used by Emperors and senior members of the imperial court to sign their rank and authority to authenticate official decrees and certificates. All persons—literate and illiterate alike—were well able to recognize the symbol of a ruler or other potentate.

FIGURE 5–3

HERALDIC SYMBOLS

FIGURE 5–4

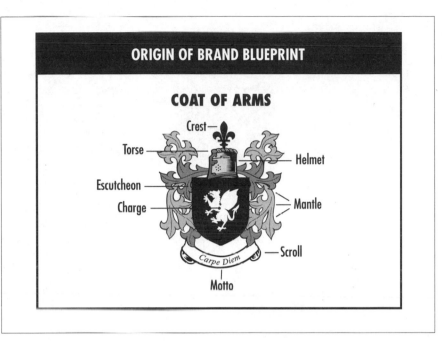

By the twelfth century in Europe a complex system of identifying signs was developed for use in heraldry. The practice of carrying personal symbols on shields and banners began during feudal times, when it was necessary for a knight, his face obscured by the visor of his helmet, to be recognizable at a distance. A coat of arms (see Figure 5-4) serves to distinguish families, corporations, and even states and nations. Its architecture was determined by a blueprint containing six elements: A crest, torse, helmet, mantle, escutcheon, and scroll with motto.[2]

Heraldry made explicit the connection between identity marks and value. Heraldic symbols drew upon a rich vocabulary and a strictly prescribed code to represent the identity of the bearer with accuracy and pride. Heraldic marks grew to denote not only identification but inherited social status and positions of privilege as well, with signs proclaiming aristocratic families, cadency marks distinguishing the birth order of sons, and symbols denoting adoption, alliance, property ownership, and profession.

FIGURE 5–5

Other kinds of emblematic identification have similarities with heraldry. An example is the totem system found among the indigenous peoples of America and Australia and illustrated in Figure 5-5. In these cultures an animal, plant, or other object serves as an emblem and heredity symbol of a family or clan.

The longevity and constancy of identity systems hints at the depth of the human need it fulfills. Marks on products have always indicated quality, craftsmanship, and pride. In addition, branding marks provide an effective means of condensing and communicating a complex reality into a single, simple statement that transcends literacy, language, and political boundaries.

Building a Brand

"If you build it, they will come" has always been a powerful concept. Our belief is that if you create the right blueprint for a brand, it's easier to achieve the desired brand perception, and that more customers will *come* to that genuine brand. Enduring brands can give businesses more leverage than any other asset, serving as an emotional shortcut between a company and its customers. A differentiated, "ownable" brand image can build an emotional and rational bridge from customers to a company, a product, or a service.

A brand's personality and reputation for performance can distinguish it from the competition, engendering customer loyalty and growth. Truly successful brands most often occupy unique positions in the consumer's mind's eye. A strong and motivating identity that customers know and trust can be elevated above price and feature competition. Owners of successful brands can be the beneficiaries of higher sales volumes, higher margins, and greater certainty of future demand. However, commanding brand identity does not happen by chance. To excel, a brand image must be well-planned, nurtured, supported, and vigilantly guarded.

Powerful brands (Figure 5-6)—such as Kodak, Coca-Cola, and Kellogg's—have all been *engineered*. They are the products of the deliberate actions of astute marketers who "live the brand," dili-

FIGURE 5–6

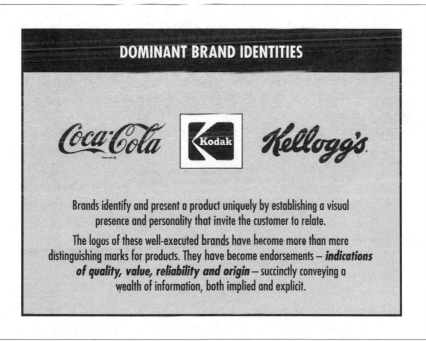

gently ensuring that all messages, representations, and innovations ring true to the governing *promise* and strategy. The brand is the focal point of the company's vision, the strategy against which all marketing and communication activities are gauged in order to maximize perceived value in customers' minds. Almost everyone recognizes the proprietary shape of a Coca-Cola bottle. In 1977 Coca-Cola was granted registration as a trademark for its uniquely contoured bottle by the U.S. Patent and Trademark Office, an honor awarded to very few other companies. In 1988 an independent worldwide survey confirmed Coca-Cola as the best-known, most-admired brand in the world, not bad for a brand that started inauspiciously in 1886 at the Jacobs Pharmacy soda fountain in Atlanta, Georgia, averaging nine servings a day. By 1998 Coca-Cola had grown sales of Coca-Cola and other beverages in excess of *one billion servings per day!*

THE BRAND BLUEPRINT METHODOLOGY

Developing a winning blueprint can be likened to designing a successful building. Just as the architect must embrace both aesthetic and functional requirements to achieve a structure that endures, so must a brand fulfill both practical and expressive mandates to construct a persuasive identity. For example, if a logo does not communicate what the company represents, it is simply not a good logo, no matter how creative or attractive it might be. Artistic and functional imperatives must both be satisfied.

Architects must see the big picture. They do not merely design four walls and a roof in a void. Rather, they create total environments to exist within the context of the physical and cultural landscapes. Similarly, the architecture of a brand should not be arbitrary. To flourish, it must be a reflection of corporate values and characteristics, securely rooted in the overall marketing strategy.

To be recognized by the customer as authentic, the brand should signal what the company delivers, both in its products and services, and in its attitude, culture, and the way it communicates with the customer. To meaningfully situate a product or company in the public mind as well as creatively and memorably convey the desired message, the brand architecture must address and consider the prevailing cultural and business landscapes. (Figure 5-7 provides an overview of the *blueprint* process.)

To position a brand for the future, it is necessary to first understand where it is today in the minds of the target audience. Building from a foundation of proper research is paramount. The Brand Assessment we described in Chapter 3, including a situational analysis and environmental review, is necessary to reveal consumer attitudes, industry and competitive trends, and other relevant forces in the marketplace. From this secure footing, the *promise* can be developed as outlined in Chapter 4, and the brand development cycle can advance to the *blueprint* process.

Branding today is an amalgam of all the concepts and strategies that have gone before. In fact, the vestiges of heraldic traditions and marks still permeate modern identity systems. However, the rich legacy of identity design and even our understanding of how and why brand attachments develop do not mitigate the high-

FIGURE 5-7

THE BRAND BLUEPRINT OVERVIEW

1. PURPOSE
- Create the architectural building blocks for the brand's communications.

2. PROCESS
- Develop:
  - The brand's name
  - Graphic representation
  - Byline
  - Tag line
  - Brand story and messages

3. RESULTS
- Ensures that all brand messages are consistent with *"what the brand stands for"* and the desired perceptions.

risk, high-stakes competitive environment of today's marketplace. That is why a prescribed technique for properly constructing and communicating a brand's identity is a fundamental component of the *doctrine* process.

The *promise* sets up the foundation for the *blueprint* as well as every brand message and every brand communication. The development of each component of the *blueprint* should reflect the primary tenets of the *promise.*

During the process of developing the *promise*, organizations may have included representatives of their advertising agencies or graphic design firms to participate in the process. In any case, it's time now to engage creative expertise to participate and contribute to the *blueprint* process and expected results.

Many organizations today have considerable creative expertise within their management teams and hence don't have to look to outside advertising, graphic design, or promotional assistance. Usually, the marketing department or division takes responsibility for the development of the *blueprint* and the associated visual communications and promotional executions. We recommend that a marketing executive assemble a team of internal and external expertise as appropriate to interpret the results of the *assessment* and the written *promise* to determine the *blueprint*.

The first step for this group is to agree on what the most important brand *signals* are—the essence of the *promise*—and how those signals should guide the creative process. As an example, let's say an Internet startup company has established that one of its *promise* signals should be a significant feeling of trust. The feeling and reflection of trust must then become a measured requirement for any proposed creative solution. The team's challenge is to identify a total of at least 10 signals (primary and secondary) to become guidelines for the brand's creative executions. Once the team has developed a consensus on the brand signals, then it should begin the creative journey to develop the proposed executions. It should be clear from our discussion thus far that creative execution should *not* be developed until after the brand signals have been agreed upon. After a review of all the *blueprint* components, we will revisit the process and the next steps.

The difference between our *blueprint's* philosophical approach and traditional marketing practice is that in many cases, organizations view each of the components comprising the architecture of a brand as separate and distinct units or variables. When a brand Website is designed, it should reflect and be "in sync" with the *blueprint,* and not necessarily take on an identity of its own. Utilizing the *blueprint* concept can optimize a brand's perception, thus advancing brand equity. Our Brand Blueprint consists of five basic components:

- A brand's name
- Graphic representations
- Byline
- Tag line
- Brand story

The five components are separate but whole, which is to say that no one component is more important than the others are. As a total unit, they should strike a harmony, a balance resulting in a synergistic connection with consumers. The blueprint's function is to direct and drive all brand communications and messages, including advertising, promotions, public relations, and the like. Let's explore the characteristics of each component and see how they work together to ultimately position a brand in the consumer's mind.

A Brand's Name

A name is the first and perhaps greatest expression of a brand. It sets the tone for all future expressions, from corporate identity to advertising to packaging. The genius of great naming is in the creation of a unique, ownable "sound symbol" that resonates in consumers' minds and hearts. An effective name empowers the value-building process, strengthening the worth of the brand.

An effective name is the first signal a brand can use to create a distinctive, positive positioning impression. The science and art of name creation, however, can be a highly complex and technical undertaking. The process can include, among other things, the consideration of linguistics (language structure), sound symbolism (inherent meanings), acquired meaning (associations accumulated over time), intrinsic meaning (root word derivations), phonetics (speech sounds), and ethological (behavioral) considerations. Most important however, is that a name for a new organization's products or services should be developed *after* the *promise*!

A brand's name affects an organization's identity at all levels, from the financial forecasts to the public's perception of products and services. According to the 17th annual Interbrand Corporate Name Change Survey, in 1997 a record 185 publicly held companies changed their corporate name, representing a 46 percent increase over 1996 and a 20 percent increase over the previous record set in 1987.[3] Interbrand Chairman Alvin Schechter, whose company is a branding consultancy, noted that corporations are "acutely aware of the power of branding. Brand [names] can convey a product's benefits, cement a corporation's positioning, and contribute enormous value to the bottom line."

Ideally, a brand's name should capture the essence of the brand and be ownable and usable across all markets. In order to best facilitate trademark protection, from the outset, it is wise to beware of names that may be difficult to distinguish from the generic product. The best, most creative names are derived directly from what Jack Trout and Al Ries call the "unique selling position," i.e., a brand's unique attributes.[4]

Naming experts also recommend that a brand name be pleasing to the ear. Brand names are often spoken out loud, but even when read, the mind translates words into sounds. Names should also be easy to remember and ideally, should integrate product positioning with the name, such as Die Hard batteries or Head & Shoulders shampoo. Good names are anchored to reality, conveying something meaningful about the product. If the name promises something, however, it should keep that promise.

Many factors must be considered in selecting a brand name for a product, including future marketing plans. Proper advance planning, from both a creative and a legal standpoint, is the key to maximizing marketing success. Criteria for developing an effective name include:

- *Availability*: Ensure that the name is available for use for a particular type of product by conducting a trademark search and an Internet domain name search. Internet domain names can be verified on sites such as www.internic.net.

- *Protectability*: Consideration should be given to registering the name as a trademark with the U.S. Patent and Trademark Office and in all other countries in which the brand will be marketed. Descriptive names are the least desirable from a trademark standpoint. Always use appropriate intellectual property symbols: ®, ™, or ℠. Basic copyright and trademark information is available on the Internet at http://lcweb.loc.gov/copyright/.

- *Acceptability*: Ensure that the name is acceptable in all cultures and languages in which the brand will be marketed. This screening should include pronunciation, name, obsolescence, connotation, slang, and related criteria.

- *Uniqueness*: To minimize preexisting associations, cut through complexity and ensure easy recall. Market research, including focus groups, surveys, and interviews are helpful to determine customer association of the brand name with a product.

- *Credibility*: The name should be appropriate, believable, and suggestive of a benefit or product association.

- *Reproducibility*: The name should be easy to pronounce, sound pleasing to the ear, look good to the eye, and be easy to spell.

- *Legibility*: It should be easily and effectively reproduced within all media and communications.

- *Durability*: It should have the flexibility to withstand cultural and business modulations for at least a decade.

- *Compatibility*: It should work easily with other information likely to be in close proximity.

A Unique Graphic Representation

From spear-marking and livestock-branding to the sophisticated corporate identity systems of today, graphic design technology has been revolutionized. However, the fundamentals of identity design have not changed significantly. Contemporary brand identities speak on behalf of products and companies, answering those same old questions and making qualitative value claims through a coordinated system of images:

- What is it?
- What makes it special?
- Who made this?
- Who owns it?

The most visible symbols of a brand's strategy, trademarks and logos, encapsulate the complex personality of products and organizations into a lucid and concise declaration. With the capacity to convey big messages in a small space, trademarks and logos form the most international language in the world, readily traversing borders and delivering unequivocal and uniform messages to consumers.

In 1998 The Conference Board, an international business membership and research organization, conducted a survey of senior marketing and communications executives from large companies in the United States and Europe. These executives identified three factors as key to the success of a strategy for a brand:

1. The strength of the brand logo/identity system.
2. The effective use of visuals and imagery.
3. The ability to capture the brand in a slogan.

Trademarks, the means by which manufacturers distinguish their products or services from those of others, fall into two main categories: *word marks* (such as the words *Shell Oil Company*) and *device marks* (such as the stylized scallop shell icon). Word marks are generally referred to simply as trademarks, while device marks are often called logotypes, or logos for short. Many of the world's most famous trademarks—like Ford, Xerox, and Coca-Cola—are a composite of a word mark shown in a distinctive graphic form.

The word *logo* comes from the Greek word *logos,* for *speech* and *logic*. The logo *speaks* to viewers, but its use must also *make sense*. (Some familiar trademarks and logos appear in Figure 5-8.)

As the name implies, trademarks were originally used by traders and merchants. With the advent of the volume manufacture of fine porcelain, furniture, and tapestries in France and Belgium during the seventeenth and eighteenth centuries, trade-

FIGURE 5–8

FAMILIAR TRADEMARKS & LOGOS

marks were used to indicate royal patronage, quality, and origin. The widespread use of trademarks, however, really only dates from the latter part of the nineteenth century, when the mechanization of printing and reproduction technology transformed mass communication and improvements in manufacturing enabled the mass-marketing of consumer products.

The appellation *graphic design* first appeared in print in 1922, and the buzzword *logo* became part of the marketing lexicon by 1937. Combining visual art with mass communication, graphic design became a mechanism to make ideas visible. A good brand identity could sell a product or confirm the legitimacy of a project. Logos became the graphic ambassadors of a brand's personality.

It has only been in the last 30 years, however, that we have seen a real explosion in the use of trademarks and logos. Television has had a lot to do with this, as has the rapid growth of secondary and service industries. Shipyards and coal mines had little interest in trademarks, while credit card companies, computer suppliers, and fast-food purveyors regard their trademarks and logos as the very heart of their business.

The diversity of choice that consumers face in a highly developed economy places significant pressure on organizations to create distinctive and differentiated brand personalities for products whose features, price, distribution, and availability may be quite similar. A strong brand is a potent weapon in the battle for market share.

Since the beginning of the nineteenth century, the laws of the United States, France, England, and other advanced countries have recognized that trademarks are valuable assets. It became possible to register ownership of a trademark or logo and to sell or license the value attached to a particular brand. Today, prominent brands are often sold for tremendous amounts of money. Consequently, the strategic legal and intellectual property considerations of trademarks and logos are vital.

In addition to the obvious advantages strong brand identities offer to manufacturers, brands are also useful to consumers in that they provide a roadmap through the maze of choices. Trademarks and logos have become the calling cards that enable us to recognize products, services, and organizations. They provide consumers with reassurance as to quality and origin, thereby permitting us to make ready decisions when faced with many choices.

Trademarks and logos are in essence "trustmarks,"[5] pledging the quality and authenticity upon which the consumer has grown to rely.

Widely known logos are recognized before they are even read. Their distinctive typefaces and other telling elements work together to facilitate recognition. This goes to suggest the manner in which identity design operates. It is faster than reading, preliterate, almost subconscious. It is a personal shorthand that enables companies to communicate as broadly as possible.

In addition to logos, a brand may come to be known by its overall image or impression (the product's "look" and "feel"), and the way in which the product is packaged and presented to consumers. These types of identifying features are commonly termed *trade dress*.

With thousands of images bombarding consumers every day, a product's distinct look can grab attention. Because trade dress often serves the same function as a trademark—the differentiation of goods and services in the marketplace—trade dress can confer legal protection under the trademark laws of the United States to the shapes of packages, containers, or products, and sometimes even décor, as indicated in Figure 5-9. Individually, such ordinary features as waiter uniforms, menu look, artwork,

FIGURE 5–9

plants, color, and architecture may not be very distinctive; however, in combination, they may represent a unique brand identity. Even sound is protectable as a brand, as evidenced by NBC's three well-known signature notes or the rhythmic four notes signifying that "Intel's inside." The unmistakable golden arches of McDonald's; Altoids' curiously unique tin; a Coke bottle's distinctive shape, color, and lettering; and Duracell's characteristic copper top are all examples of distinctive trade dress.

Excellence in identity design can suggest or signal a corresponding quality at the organizational or product level. However, design excellence is not measured in aesthetic terms only. Logos and trademarks must carefully balance artistic goals with the effective interpretation, differentiation, and communication of the real meaning of their brands. In other words, the question to consider is not how beautiful or creative a brand image might be, but whether it effectively and appropriately communicates the brand's promise.

In today's highly competitive marketplace, well-established brands are constantly under fire. As the intensity of competition grows and the costs of introducing new products and services escalate, competitors are tempted to emulate established marks and identities in order to derive the benefit of a successful brand's reputation and gain quick acceptance into the marketplace.

To avoid becoming "generic," a mark should identify the source or origin of the goods and not describe the goods themselves. Failure to take proper care can result in the loss of exclusive rights to a brand's name, marks, and image. For example, aspirin, cellophane, escalator, linoleum, shredded wheat, vacuum, and zipper were all once trademarks. When owners do not properly use and protect trademarks, valuable rights can be lost.

Take a look at a Frito-Lay® brand snack food package. Frito-Lay® correctly uses their valuable trademarks to identify the origin of the products and not to describe the products themselves. Their trademarks are properly used as adjectives to modify the generic product, as in Lay's® brand potato chips. Furthermore, the "ownership" of the trademark (i.e., the ® symbol) is consistently used and always readily apparent.

Good trademarks need not wear out or expire. Well-chosen marks can become more valuable as goodwill grows and are often

FIGURE 5–10

Used with permission.

the most important assets of established businesses. This is not to suggest, however, that a visual image may not benefit from a careful update from time-to-time in order to avoid becoming dated. Figure 5-11 provides an example of how Betty Crocker has undergone a "makeover" through the years. The challenge is to evolve an image in a way that keeps up with the times while maintaining all the visual meaning, heritage, and positive associations that have been previously garnered, as illustrated in Figure 5-12.

Trademarks, logos, and trade dress *identify* a product, service, or organization; *differentiate* it from others; *communicate* information as to origin; value, and quality; potentially *add value*; represent *valuable assets*; and serve as important *legal properties*. Criteria for developing an effective graphic representation include:

- *Protectability*: Consideration should be given to registering the mark as a trademark with the U.S. Patent and Trademark Office and in all other countries in which the brand will be marketed.
- *Acceptability*: Colors and shapes should be carefully considered to effectively cross cultural boundaries.
- *Uniqueness*: To minimize preexisting associations, cut through complexity, and ensure easy recall. Market research, including focus groups, surveys, and inter-

FIGURE 5–11

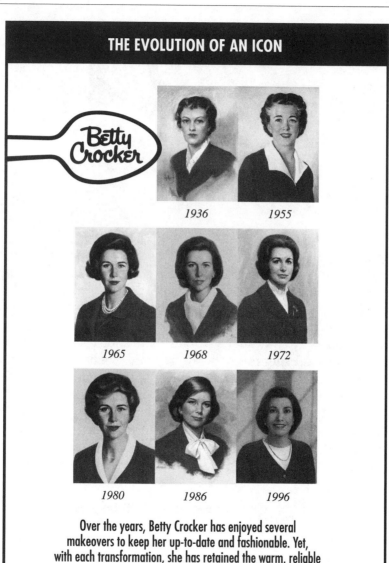

THE EVOLUTION OF AN ICON

1936   *1955*

1965   *1968*   *1972*

1980   *1986*   *1996*

Over the years, Betty Crocker has enjoyed several
makeovers to keep her up-to-date and fashionable. Yet,
with each transformation, she has retained the warm, reliable
image which consumers have come to know and trust.

Reprinted with permission from General Mills, Inc.

FIGURE 5–12

BRAND REVITALIZATION		
A&W RESTAURANTS	THE FRUIT OF THE LOOM SEEK NO FURTHER	fresh up with 7up it likes you
A&W RESTAURANTS 75 years	FRUIT OF THE LOOM	7UP
A&W ALL AMERICAN FOOD	FRUIT OF THE LOOM UNCONDITIONALLY GUARANTEED	7UP
A&W is a registered trademark of A&W Concentrate. Used with permission.	FRUIT OF THE LOOM® and the fruit designs are registered trademarks of Fruit of the Loom, Inc. Used with permission.	©7 UP is a registered trademark of Dr. Pepper/Seven Up, Inc. ©1999 Dr. Pepper/Seven Up, Inc. Used with permission.

views are helpful to determine customer association of the mark with a product.

- *Compatibility*: Graphic representations should work easily with other information likely to be in close proximity.
- *Flexibility*: They should be able to translate into various media, including paper, fax, and Internet.
- *Recognizability*: In every language.
- *Timelessness*: They should be timeless in style and not get caught in current trends.
- *Crispness*: Graphic representation should be crisp across multiple mediums, i.e., the Internet, packaging, print, television, etc.

It is important to understand that graphic representations do not function in isolation. They should be deployed as just one component in an overall coordinated strategic system, single prongs in an integrated *blueprint* approach that fulfills the *promise*.

A Byline

Among marketers, advertisers, and graphic designers, there is apparent confusion when the discussion turns toward distinguishing the relative differences between the use of a byline and a tag line. Bylines and tag lines are definitely distinct, playing very unique and important roles in the total *blueprint* execution.

At times, marketers expect consumers to work too hard. The byline should accompany the brand name, usually below the brand name to clearly describe the business that the brand is in. This clearly communicates to customers and potential customers where to place the brand's products and services in their mind's eye. A byline then, is the *descriptor* of the brand. The byline leaves no doubt where to place your brand. Whirlpool is profiled at the end of this chapter as an excellent example of a brand that utilizes all the architectural components of the *blueprint* to full advantage. The Whirlpool byline, "home appliances," is positioned right below their signature brand name in print advertising. In this way, consumers know instantly what Whirlpool is all about.

An organization with a very well-known brand might question why a byline is important to them. It's easy to forget that while most consumers may recognize a well-known brand in the United States, each year, millions of consumers either get married, move, get divorced, start a new job, or undergo some other major change in life. Consumers who may not have been interested in a brand's products or services previously, may now suddenly be in the market. Astute brands gain an advantage by using all of the *blueprint* tools to reassociate with those consumers who now find the brand's products and services quite relevant to their needs.

Some marketing experts may argue that if a brand's name is very descriptive, then it does not need a byline. It's true that the more descriptive a name is, the easier it is for consumers to position it in their mind's eye. The issue is to evaluate whether or not a descriptive brand name is enough by itself to communicate the brand's desired functional perception in a distinctive manner.

As we discussed previously, consumer research plays a key role in identifying all the critical attributes most important to consumers from an emotional and functional aspect as well as from an aspirational perspective. From this research, an organization can craft a byline that ultimately will last for many years. The byline reflects the core or essence of the business. Figure 5-13 provides examples of how some brands incorporate the use of a byline in their *blueprint*.

FIGURE 5–13

Brands that integrate bylines with their graphic representations.

A Tag Line

Tag lines have traditionally been referred to and defined as "jingles" or slogans. In creating a harmonious architecture for a brand, the tag line plays a unique and distinct role. In contrast to the byline, a tag line is the *expressive* line used to clarify or dramatize the brand's *emotional* and *functional* benefits to customers and potential customers. The tag line tells the consumer how they hopefully will *feel* about the brand.

Brands want to communicate positive feelings to their customers and potential customers. Strong brand identities are created when these emotional benefits are communicated. Consumers are concerned about how they will feel using the brand but they want to understand the practical or functional benefits as well. BMW's tag line is an example of how a brand conveys both messages in a short concise way. BMW is the "the ultimate driving machine." Consumers who would purchase a BMW hope to experience the excitement of driving a world-class car and also know that it is a well-engineered vehicle.

Nikon, the camera and optics manufacturer, was widely recognized as the "professional's camera." Nikon has a tradition of quality and product innovation among serious photographers and was once the preferred camera of professional photographers. However, competitors used innovation and marketing to make 35mm photography both affordable and easy with the introduction of the "point and shoot" cameras. So what are the emotional and functional benefits of purchasing a Nikon? Nikon's tag line tells consumers: "We take the world's greatest pictures."

The tag line can be used to help communicate your distinct point of difference from competitors. A tag line can help cut through the clutter to reach out and attract potential customers to the brand, and in some instances, a tag line is utilized to reposition a brand. The retail industry is highly competitive. However, successful brands have focused on a distinct point of differentiation that is communicated in their tag line. Target, the discount department store, provides an excellent example of a tag line communicating its brand's message. When consumers see or hear "Expect more, pay less," they connect with Target on *both* the expected functional benefit (price: "pay less") and emotional benefit (value: "expect more") of the brand. Further examples of brands utilizing tag lines to communicate emotional and functional messages to consumers are:

- Disney Institute: "You won't believe what you can do"
- Weber (barbecue): The Legend Lives On™
- Jeep: There's Only One™
- Philips: Let's Make Things Better

In contrast, Sears' use of a tag line attempts to reposition the image and identity of the brand with consumers. Sears has long been associated as a hardware and appliance retail and catalog brand. Throughout much of the 1990s Sears has used the tag line "Come see the softer side of Sears" in an attempt to attract potential customers to the brand and position Sears in consumers' minds as something other than just a hardware and appliance *brand*. However, a tag line is not enough by itself to reposition a brand. An organization must have a new *promise* and deliver its benefits if it expects to reposition a brand in the minds of its target audience.

A Brand Story

All genuine brands have a story, a legend about how they got started. Whether it's eBay.com, whose founder was investigating ways to sell and trade PEZ antique candy dispensers on the Internet, or FedEx, whose founder's idea for a special type of air cargo company did not impress his professor at Yale. In fact, Fred Smith, the founder of FedEx, received an unimpressive *C* on his undergraduate term paper, that outlined the concept of a specialized overnight delivery company. On the surface, these historical truths may not seem impressive. However, they really can be extremely powerful because they offer inspiration and optimism for everyone else. Preserving and enhancing a brand's heritage as it becomes more successful provides inspiration and motivation for customers, employees, and external relationships.

A brand's story puts a face on a brand, adds a personal touch, and can bring a brand to life. Genuine brands like Coca-Cola, Marriott, and Hallmark all have books that tell their brand stories. Summarized versions of a brand's story—on brochures, labels, guarantees, catalogs, etc.—can be very effective in communicating a brand's essence. Everyone appreciates authenticity, and that's what a genuine brand is all about.

THE BRAND BLUEPRINT BUILDING BLOCKS

Now that we have grasped the architectural components of the *blueprint*, let's focus on how the process should proceed to accomplish the desired result. As we discussed in the beginning of the chapter, the brand team should have agreed on the critical brand signals. Based on the creative foundation provided by these signals, it's time to engage the appropriate combination of internal and external expertise to develop three alternative recommendations for each of the *blueprint* components.

The secret is to draw upon the resources and talents from a variety of channels—creative, marketing, public relations, operations, customer service, and so forth. However, it's essential to test the communications and messages for each of the components of the *blueprint* with customers, employees, and other key stakeholders before reaching a final decision. Then a brand executive can view the "big picture" to ensure that the overall integrity and consistency of the Visual Vocabulary® (i.e., the visual translation of the brand into a flexible set of images, symbols, colors, typography, overall style, and ownable messages) produces the appropriate brand perceptions. Skilled executives understand how to incorporate these five components into a cohesive package that effectively communicates the right brand messages to consumers.

Once the recommendations have been tested, a brand's executive committee, in conjunction with the brand team, should decide the best choices for each component as well as the best combination, which will result in the desired overall brand perception. After the *blueprint* components are finalized, the next step is to focus on creating the actual messages (advertising, public relations, promotions, etc.) to be directed at the target audience. It's important to remember that messages and communications (internal and external) are developed after the *blueprint* is finalized and in conjunction with the culturalization plan discussed in Chapter 6.

Figure 5-14 shows how the various components form the "building blocks" of a *blueprint*.

Everything the organization does—everything—should be solely focused on enhancing a brand's equity. Guidelines and standards for proper use of a brand's representations (i.e., stationery, business cards, invoices, fax cover sheets, appearance on corporate vehicles, network screen savers, etc.), internal and external communications, and public relations and advertising should be articulated in the written *doctrine*. We will discuss this in more detail in the next chapter.

THE LIFE OF A BRAND

A fundamental measure of the success of a brand is its ability to be innovative, relevant, and preferred over time. Brands have the potential for a very long life, provided, of course, that they receive regular maintenance, i.e., guarding against lapses of quality, counterfeiting, product obsolescence, or an outdated image.

FIGURE 5–14

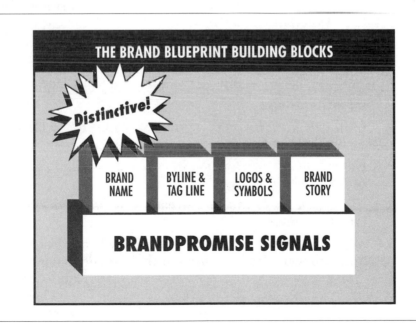

The best brands are potentially long-lived and robust. Though brand identity may require a minor remodeling from time-to-time, it should be done gently and carefully, just as Mercedes, Coca-Cola, and other owners of meaningful brands have done over the years. It takes a long time for consumers to develop brand associations, even with multimillion-dollar promotional budgets.

While some brands may wane because of shifting consumer needs or better competitors, others fall victim to derelict owners who neglect the necessary ongoing maintenance and investment. These brands fade from consumers' consciousness and suffer the consequences in their financial performance.

Genuine brands require a consistent commitment of time, attention, and creative effort to continue to engage and maintain their desired position in consumers' minds. In order to maintain the competitive edge and remain a leader, a brand must constantly protect its products, reputation, and market position. In addition, the development of new products and the improvement of existing products are requisites for a brand's continued growth.

Just as many homeowners have found that it is often cheaper and better to remodel or add onto a home than to buy a new one, so has the multimillion-dollar cost of launching a new brand stimulated corporate interest in *renovating* established brands. Dr. David Aaker of the University of California at Berkeley, one of the leading authorities on managing brand equity, describes the seven avenues for brand revitalization as:[6]

1. *Increase usage:* by increasing frequency of use and/or quantity used.

2. *Find new uses:* by researching and capitalizing on newly devised functional applications.

3. *Enter new markets:* which have the potential for new growth.

4. *Reposition the brand:* to refresh tired, dated, or obsolete strategies.

5. *Augment the product or service:* to newly differentiate and pull away from the rest of the competitive pack.

6. *Obsolete existing products:* by introducing new products or technologies to replace the existing installed base.

7. *Extend the brand:* by exploiting the established brand name from one product class to enter another product class.

Manufacturers have long been altering the characteristics of a brand's application or changing its packaging to revitalize brand image and boost sales. As illustrated in Figure 5-15, Arm

FIGURE 5–15

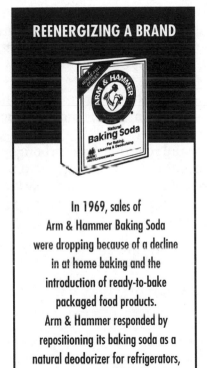

REENERGIZING A BRAND

In 1969, sales of
Arm & Hammer Baking Soda
were dropping because of a decline
in at home baking and the
introduction of ready-to-bake
packaged food products.
Arm & Hammer responded by
repositioning its baking soda as a
natural deodorizer for refrigerators,
freezers, and kitchen sink drains,
and sales skyrocketed.

Reprinted with permission from
Church & Dwight Co., Inc.

& Hammer is an excellent example of expanding a distinctive brand's application, i.e., a natural deodorizer. This has resulted in a whole new "life" for the product, while at the same time enhancing the brand's existing perception and equity. However, these kinds of changes are not without risk: Remember "New Coke"? Though updated formulations and packaging can be important, the best way to jump-start a brand is by understanding and capitalizing on its uniqueness and equity. Understanding the deeper meanings of brands to the people who buy them is the most significant way to differentiate one brand from another.

Almost every product and service category has become crowded, and organizations are under intense pressure to perform and stand out. Brands are everywhere and one would think that from all appearances there isn't room for another brand. This assumption is far from the truth. According to Tom Peters, business guru and author, branding is actually "the only way to stand out in a crowded marketplace." To that end, Mr. Peters also believes that branding is "nothing more (and nothing less) than creating a distinct personality—and then telling the entire world about it, any way you can, by hook or by crook."[7] Putting the pieces together to build a "genuine" brand requires a well-thought-out *blueprint*.

Whirlpool Corporation has a long history of understanding the value of a family of brands and the correct utilization of brand architectural components to communicate clearly and effectively with their target audience.

BRAND PROFILE

WHIRLPOOL CORPORATION*

Whirlpool Corporation is a leading manufacturer and marketer of major home appliances (see Figure 5-16). Headquartered in Benton Harbor, Michigan, Whirlpool manufactures appliances in 13 countries and markets them under 11 major brand names in more than 170 countries around the world. The world's leading manufacturer and marketer of major home appliances, the company makes washers, dryers, dishwashers, dehumidifiers, microwave ovens, ranges, refrigerators, freezers, and air conditioners.

---

*Information provided by Whirlpool Corporation and used with permission.

FIGURE 5–16

Whirlpool markets its successful family of branded products under such brand names as Whirlpool, KitchenAid, Roper, Estate, and Speed Queen (in Canada). Each brand has a distinct, distinguishable brand identity, image, and purpose. For example:

- KitchenAid brand appliances are marketed to upscale consumers who look for style and substance in the products they buy.
- Whirlpool is positioned as the brand that helps consumers manage their homes better.
- Roper brand appliances are value-priced and offer basic styling and features.
- The Estate brand line is limited to a few high-volume models distributed primarily through large retail chain stores.

Since 1929, when company founders Louis and Frederick Upton first decided to use the Whirlpool name, Whirlpool has grown from a family-owned machine shop located on Lake Michigan to being recognized as a leading global brand.

Whirlpool Corporation's strategy to shape and lead the emerging global home appliance industry is working because the company consistently improves the quality of its products and services, while refining its understanding of customers and what they want from Whirlpool appliances. Whirlpool's success is a result of a very disciplined, focused, and exhaustive strategic direction and planning process.

All successful brands have one thing in common: They have vision. Whirlpool is no exception. Whirlpool's vision is articulated as: "Every

Home...Everywhere with Pride, Passion, Performance." Vision becomes actionable through the BrandPromise. Whirlpool's *promise* is:

> *We create the world's best home appliances that make life a little easier and more enjoyable for all people. Our goal is a Whirlpool product in every home, everywhere. We will achieve this by creating:*
>
> *PRIDE—in our work and each other*
> *PASSION—for creating unmatched customer loyalty for our brands*
> *PERFORMANCE—results that excite and reward global investors with superior returns*
>
> *We bring this dream to life through the power of our unique global enterprise and our outstanding people... working together... everywhere.*

The Whirlpool culture is steeped in performance for the customer's benefit. Their culture reflects their story of success through dedication to creating value for customers. Whirlpool expresses their customer mindset this way: "Through the intense customer focus of all Whirlpool people, we will measure and deliver differentiated levels of customer satisfaction in all our markets, with all of our products and services, assuring that our brands are the preferred brands with our customers." To that end, Whirlpool was one of the first companies in the United States to establish a toll-free 800 number—referred to as "the Whirlpool Cool-Line"—for customer service in 1967. Renamed "the Consumer Assistance Center" in 1990, it gives customers direct, 24-hour access to Whirlpool. Whirlpool also prints their promise on mailing envelopes to consumers as shown in Figure 5-17.

FIGURE 5–17

FIGURE 5–18

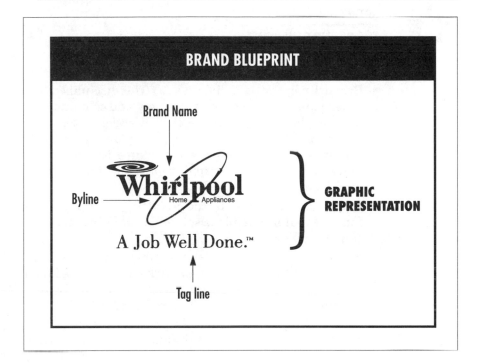

The Whirlpool brand serves as an excellent example of executing a Brand Blueprint. The Whirlpool brand name and distinctive logo never appear in print materials without a descriptive byline such as "home appliances." The company's tag line, "A Job Well Done™," is a reflection of their efforts to stay in touch with customers' needs and aspirations and is illustrated in Figure 5-18. The tag line will change as times and customers change. The tag line will express the emotional and functional benefits best capturing the moods and values of the day. Whirlpool's Brand Blueprint of 1998 can be seen in Figure 5-18.

THE BRAND BLUEPRINT

- Brand Blueprint is defined as (1) The disciplined, detailed plan required to create, design, and communicate intended brand perception. (2) That which determines the character or style of a brand. (3) A plan that outlines the underlying collective architecture for the brand name, byline, tag line, graphic representations, and the brand story.

- Consumers are moved by the *gestalt* of the brand, all its tangible and intangible assets integrated into the consumers' minds.

- Historically, brand has been the preferred way to identify and distinguish people, products, and services from others. Branding answers the questions: Who made this? Who owns it? What is it? What makes it special?

- Truly successful brands occupy unique positions in their customers' minds as well as the marketplace. The brand is *the* focal point of a company's vision, the strategy against which all marketing and communication activities are gauged in order to maximize perceived value in customers' minds.

- Building a successful brand is like being an architect: One must embrace both the aesthetic and functional requirements to achieve a structure that endures, and one must combine the practical and expressive aspects to construct a brand with a persuasive brand identity and strong image.

- Traditional marketing practices view and treat the components of a brand as separate and distinct entities. On the other hand, a Brand Blueprint ensures that the components are a *single cohesive unit* that can then optimize and advance brand equity.

- The Brand Blueprint's five key components are:

  1. *Brand name*—a unique, memorable, and distinctive name.

2. *Unique graphic representation*—an icon, symbol, or image that graphically depicts the brand's identity.

3. *Byline*—descriptive words or a phrase that tells consumers where to place the brand in their mind's eye.

4. *Tag line*—a message that expresses current functional and emotional benefits to consumers.

5. *Brand story*—preserves and communicates the brand's heritage.

- A well-conceived Brand Blueprint is all about design. Good design is the visual cue for everything the organization thinks, acts, and communicates relative to its brand. Remember, a brand can and should be perceived to have a larger "presence" than the "business."

CHAPTER 6

Brand Culturalization

Customer Service: "The Heart and Soul
of Genuine Brands"
with a Brand Profile of Hampton Inn

You can't build a reputation on what you are going to do.
—Henry Ford

BRAND CULTURALIZATION PHILOSOPHY

As we discussed in Chapter 2, the fundamental goal of the
BrandStrategy Doctrine Process is to provide a written roadmap
for everyone associated with a brand to follow. It also requires a
disciplined approach to brand decision-making, which is often
absent from organizations' day-to-day activities. (Figure 6-1 shows
that Brand Culturalization (*culturalization*)* is the fourth step
in the *doctrine* process.) *Brand Culturalization* can be defined as
the process by which all employees and associates (current and
future) are exposed or subjected to the sum total of beliefs, behaviors, and ways charactoristic to a particular brand, thus raising the level of awareness with a view toward improving the ability,
both individually and organizationally, to "live the *promise*."

---

*For readability and ease of reference, Brand Culturalization is sometimes referred to
  as *culturalization*.

133

FIGURE 6–1

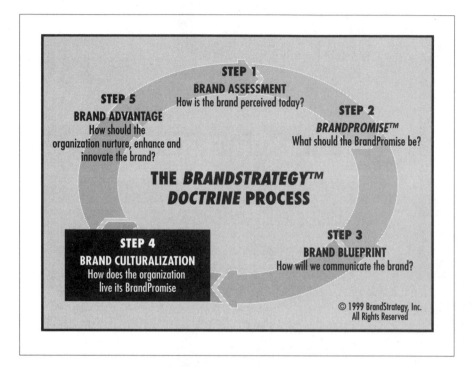

Therefore, the organization's goal during this step in the process is to establish the beliefs and behaviors, i.e., the *way,* necessary for its representatives to carry out its business. Then the organization must be sure that everyone is aware of the "brand way," and be sure that their behavior is trained and reinforced to produce the desired brand perception. The brand team's responsibility at this point is to capture all of the key elements of the doctrine process thus far and after the culturalization activities have been finalized, to develop the written *doctrine.* (See Chapter 9 for an example.)

One of the traits of genuine brands is their ability to create a consistent perception based on their transactions with customers. Consistent expectations are usually the result of a strong positive culture that exists within an organization. Therefore, the culturalization plan should define the correct culture and enhance its positive effect on each customer's experience. Cultures, like

FIGURE 6-2

BRAND CULTURALIZATION OVERVIEW

1. PURPOSE
- Everyone in the brand follows the same written roadmap in order to differentiate the brand(s) in the consumer's mind.

2. PROCESS
Develop a written BrandStrategy Doctrine.
- Create the brand principles.
- Establish brand equity goals.
- Outline a brand communication plan.
- Develop a brand culturalization plan.

3. RESULTS
- Determine how we will adopt and live the brand.
- Create the written BrandStrategy Doctrine which articulates the comprehensive action plan to reposition the brand over the next 12 months.

everything else, must "keep up with the times" in order to be relevant to consumers' changing needs and desires. All too often organizational cultures that once were "in sync" with consumers become passé or even wrong for a particular brand.

The *culturalization* process is outlined in Figure 6-2 and includes the following action steps:

- Creating the brand principles
- Establishing the brand equity goals
- Outlining a brand communication plan
- Completing a *culturalization* plan

The challenge of implementing any strategy is in getting everyone throughout the organization on the same page. Simply put, the goal of implementation is to obtain 100 percent total buy-in. If a *culturalization* plan is to be successfully implemented, then:

- Each and every employee and associate must understand and adopt the *promise.*
- The *promise* must become an integral part of the organization's culture and drive every decision.

Accomplishing this is no small task. *Culturalization* occurs as a result of consistent, persistent, and passionate teaching as well as role-modeling. It takes a comprehensive and multifaceted plan of attack to cause or influence employees at all levels of an organization to make the necessary changes in their thinking and actions. It's also essential that an organization's leadership create an atmosphere and work environment that encourages employees to open their minds and accept the new ideas.

The Brand Principles

Let's turn our attention now to the brand team's responsibilities for developing the brand principles. It's the team's job to gather all of the directives related to the organization's mission, vision, and strategic plans, both current and historical. This would include reviewing previous annual reports, magazine articles, employee manuals, advertisements, promotional brochures, and similar documents for clues about the source of the organization's cultural heritage. The purpose of this exercise is to uncover any valuable cultural signals that should be reflected in the culturalization plan. The *promise* signals that were discussed in relationship to the Brand Blueprint should be combined in a directional sense with any cultural signals that are uncovered. The brand team should next develop a list of words or brief phrases that will become the foundation of the brand principles. Examples of questions to review regarding a brand's principles and samples of brand principles are provided in Chapter 9 under Brand Principles (Sample Questions) and The Brand Doctrine Report, respectively.

Once the brand team has finalized up to 10 principles, they should be reviewed with representatives of all the organization's activities so that a consensus can be reached, and then the principles can be finalized. The brand principles serve as additional guidelines for the organization to operate its day-to-day activities.

It's essential that the principles support the basic tenets of the *promise* and set forth the fundamental beliefs that the organization intends to follow in order to manage its business, hire and train employees, measure its performance and progress, and build brand equity.

Establishing Brand Equity Goals

An organization's financial executives need to view the brand as an asset and not just as an expense. Historically, brand-related and marketing expenses have not been perceived by the finance and investment community as a strategic financial asset.

The primary reason corporate finance has not partnered with marketing and brand management in the past is because in many organizations, there is an adversarial relationship between the two functions. However, the situation is changing quickly, with more organizations realizing that it is essential to embrace a strategy for their brand that is integrated with all of their other functional disciplines. As Wina Woodbury, Vice President of Avon Products Inc., relates, "Five years ago, Wall Street's focus was on numbers and not too much on strategy. Now, the bulk of their scrutiny is on brands, especially where you're positioning your brand for the future."[1]

The brand equity goals are fundamental to the organization's ability to track its progress and performance. Unfortunately, in many cases the overwhelming focus is on stock price, and while that's extremely important, some would argue it's the result of other brand equity drivers that seem to be nonexistent or forgotten. Organizations that have changed their bonus plans to a payout based on a combination of customer loyalty, service excellence, and financial results have seen enormous improvement in earnings as well as overall brand equity. Just imagine for the moment that every monthly financial statement and budget report included the current and year-to-date customer satisfaction results as well. While there are a whole host of financial measures that can be a part of an organization's brand equity goals, there are many capable experts, such as Interbrand Corporation, The FutureBrand Company, or Mercer Management Consulting Inc., that specialize in measuring brand valuation. Market research companies have also entered this rapidly growing field. For example, Angus Reid Group, a global research company whose clients include *The Economist* and CNN International, has developed two products—Equity Reid™ and Reputation Reid™—that use a combination of consumer surveys and advanced statistical techniques to calculate the monetary value of both individual brands and corporate identity. This information can then be used to create strategies relating to brand extensions, product pricing, and advertising support. Our point of view is that the opportunity lies in an organization's ability to combine the traditional financial measures, R.O.E., R.O.I., EBITDA, discounted cash flow, etc., with consumer-related information, such as "intent to repeat," average purchase size, trust and esteem, shopper conversion, satisfaction, and perceived differentiation.

The brand team's responsibility is to work in partnership with the organization's finance department to develop realistic brand equity goals. However, as stated above, the brand equity goals should be representative of several factors that when combined, provide an accurate picture of the organization's progress in building its brand equity.

Let's assume as an example that Friendly supermarkets has set the following brand equity goals for the next 12 months:

- Customer satisfaction of 85 percent or better (85 percent or more of their customers rate their service excellent or good).
- A 10 percent increase in average receipts over the next year.
- A 3 percent increase in gross margin over the next year.

Given these goals, the organization must create incentives, measurement tools, and communication vehicles to be sure that everyone understands what the goals are, the progress being made, and what they can do to positively impact the results.

Outlining a Brand Communication Plan

In our previous discussions regarding the *blueprint*, we focused on selecting the correct architectural components to maximize brand equity. The culturalization plan should include the appropriate communication strategy to determine the optimal internal and external messages to bring the *blueprint* to life. Organizations use a widely varied nomenclature to describe their marketing or communication plans. If an organization has separate written plans for marketing, public relations, and internal communications, or other key activities that support the *doctrine*, then a "top line" summary of all of these plans should be incorporated in the brand communication plan. The actual documents themselves should be attached to the written *doctrine* as exhibits.

One of the significant values in this approach is that the *doctrine* provides the overall roadmap for the organization's commitment to developing a genuine brand. The *doctrine* should be easy to read and understand, as opposed to having to refer to several detailed department plans on a daily basis. Each of the organization's functional disciplines, such as human resources, operations, and marketing, should develop or utilize their own detailed plans to execute their day-to-day programs and projects that support their contributions to the brand's overall *doctrine*.

The brand team's challenge is to recommend an external and internal communication plan that will either position, maintain, or enhance the brand's desired perception based on all the information learned through the doctrine process.

The Culturalization Plan

As you can see, the entire purpose of culturalizing the brand *way* is to set the tone for the way everyone should feel about the brand; employees, customers, and all stakeholders.

We have devoted the majority of this chapter to the issue of customer service and its fundamental importance to the culturalization concept, because it is increasingly overlooked as a key in building a successful brand. Yet it can offer the most powerful payoff.

In summary, the culturalization plan is all about the activities an organization undertakes to create the appropriate brand attitude toward its customers.

Achieving increased loyalty from customers and potential customers goes hand in hand with a focus on customer service. In today's highly competitive marketplace, it isn't enough to just talk about delivering great customer service. Successful brands, as the old saying goes, let their actions do the talking. Linking customer service to the very essence of the brand requires the *culturalization* we've been discussing here. Delivering on a *promise* to provide outstanding and exceptional service to *all* customers, internal and external, is best accomplished when this concept becomes deeply rooted in the very culture of the brand itself. Providing exceptional customer service is aspirational. It begins with desire and is rewarded through the self-satisfaction of knowing you did the right thing by doing right for others. The benefits can be measured in small assurances or large returns. Smiling faces, exceptional morale, increased productivity, enhanced customer loyalty, and lower employee turnover rates are all tangible benefits of a customer service program grounded in *culturalization*.

The most frequently asked question in strategic planning exercises is, "What business are you in?" Usually, a discussion then takes place as to whether an enterprise is in the product or service business. For years, conventional wisdom has been that you are in one or the other, but not both.

It's time to dispel this myth and conclude that every enterprise is in both the product and service business. This has significant implications for the many organizations that spend the majority of their operational and management dialog focused on a "product/process mindset." An unbalanced preoccupation with product places the organization at a competitive disadvantage relative to potential differentiation. Certainly, product quality, selection, and engineering are important; however, a singular focus may disrupt the differentiation opportunity for a brand's strategic positioning. *Every* organization is in the product *and* service business.

A brand has to do with a customer's *perception* of the business and the level of service she or he expects. Companies can differentiate their brand by providing better quality, value, and most important, exceptional customer service. Successful brands in today's global marketplace understand what business they are in and that it always includes a service aspect. Exceeding customers' service expectations can be the defining factor in distinguishing a brand from competitors in the eyes and minds of consumers.

FIGURE 6–3

Dilbert © 1998 United Feature Syndicate, Inc. Reprinted with permission.

All purchase decisions are based on a perception of value. Nordstrom has achieved a mythical reputation and has successfully added value to its brand equity by offering outstanding customer service. A 1999 Seattle market research poll conducted by GMA Research and BrandStrategy, Inc., asked 400 adult consumers to name the best brands for customer service in several industries. Surprisingly, 35 percent of those surveyed could not name one health-care brand, nor could 39 percent name a computer manufacturing company that in their opinion had the best customer service. In addition, 44 percent could not name a superior customer service brand in cellular telephone service.

The opportunity is tremendous for brands to take a hard look at their customer service commitment, i.e., to make customer service an integral part of their perceived value and *promise*. Remember, when customers consider a brand to be a "friend," the feeling of trust and esteem can be a powerful contributor to brand loyalty.

The Essence of Genuine Brands

Why is it that customer loyalty continues to decline in the face of corporate downsizing, even during a period in American history with some of the lowest unemployment rates on record? And why is it that certain brands have become synonymous with the term *customer service*? In fact, an elite few, like Lexus and Disney, have become the very embodiment of customer service. Lexus customers are renowned for their devotion to the Lexus brand. Lexus obviously understands the difference between merely providing a service and nurturing loyal customers. This devoted loyalty and high degree of customer satisfaction has been the key factor in the Lexus story of success. Lexus has surpassed its rival Japanese brands, and trails only Mercedes among luxury cars in the United States. Toyota achieved this by focusing the Lexus brand on more than just the car or the product and extending a level of service unheard of in the automotive industry. Customers are treated to a uniquely different experience when they enter a Lexus showroom. Some customers have been treated to breakfast buffets, some to free lifetime car washes, and Lexus was one of the first automobile dealers to offer a replacement car while a customer's car was being serviced.

As a result of Lexus' brand standards for service and excellence, consumers' expectations of purchasing and driving automobiles have changed. Lexus has redefined brand value around delivering an exceptional customer service experience. For organizations like Lexus, customers consider the brand to be a friend. As a result, quality is not just an attribute of the product or process; rather, it is an extension of a service philosophy and a BrandMindset. At Lexus, customer service is all-encompassing. It is a way of life, personally and professionally.

Customer service can evolve into one of the most powerful ways to differentiate a brand, build long-term brand equity, and sustain competitive advantage. I routinely observe organizations discussing the following challenge: How can we get customers to purchase more often or make larger purchases in the future? The first goal of any organization should always be to create a perception of a brand as a customer's friend, then to focus on the task of creating purchase interest. In the first chapter, we concluded that customers generally fall into four categories of satisfaction: friend, loyal, disloyal, or suspect loyalty, as depicted in Figure 6-4.

It seems everyone has heard of Nordstrom's legacy for serving and exceeding customer expectations, even many who have never shopped a Nordstrom department store. Nordstrom, either by design or unconsciously, has discovered that customer service excellence is of paramount importance in building a genuine brand. From home-based businesses to the largest Fortune 500 organization, companies must realize that customer service is fundamentally the heart and soul of their brand. Customer service needs to be firmly entrenched in any organization's *culturalization* plan.

Customer service wears many hats and answers to different names: customer satisfaction, loyalty marketing, relationship marketing, one-to-one marketing, frequent-shopper, and so forth and so on. Customer service is probably one of the most documented

FIGURE 6–4

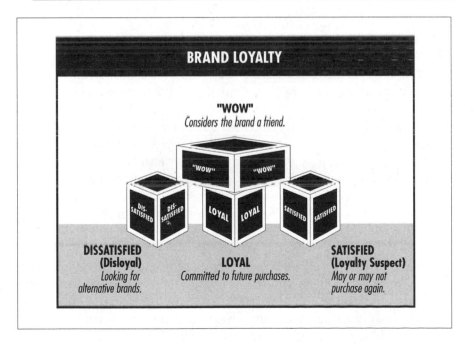

topics in all of business. Much rhetoric has been devoted to evangelizing customer-centered service and customer-focused initiatives. However, discourse alone is not enough to bring about change. Preaching loudly may get attention, and may accomplish the goal of getting all partners, associates, and employees within an organization to "sing from the same hymnal." But providing outstanding service to all customers as a part of a *promise* requires a uniquely different approach.

To customers, great service is an experience. It is the feeling that they take home with them after experiencing something positive, that "warm fuzzy" they're left with. Great customer service brings them back every time.

Exceptional Customer Service Pays Off

Customer service is one of the last great frontiers for a business to explore. The adventure is a journey fueled by purpose and desire. Great customer service is pure of heart and genuine. Its purpose is to serve the customer the best way possible, and its desire is to please customers in every way and earn the right to do business with them again and again. As D. Lee Carpenter, Chairman and CEO of *Design Forum,* says, "Although many retailers continue to focus on customer needs, we have evolved into a society of 'wanters.' Retailers should think and strategize from the perspective of what the customer wants, and that means choosing a target customer group and going after them. Give them relevant reasons for buying. Provide the ultimate in convenience and exceptional customer service and work toward building long-term relationships. Remember, a sale doesn't mean the end of a transaction; it signifies the beginning of a potentially beautiful relationship!"[2] It is a journey with no personal satisfaction until all customers are satisfied. The fundamental reason for every organization is to create a satisfied customer.

There have been many variables—interest rates, inflation, consumer confidence, economic climate—used to forecast trends in the stock market. While these various leading indicators have met with limited success in predicting the ups and downs of Wall Street, *Fortune* magazine has suggested that customer satisfaction may just be a better prognosticator of stock performance in the future.

A *Fortune* article suggested that the American Customer Satisfaction Index and the Dow are "locked in a remarkably tight tango."[3] A customer survey from the first quarter of 1995 through the third quarter of 1997 pointed toward an apparent relationship between the customer-satisfaction scores of individual companies and their stock performance. Campbell Soup, Heinz, and Procter & Gamble were all rated in the top quartile in customer satisfaction, and these companies' stocks were top performers. The American Customer Satisfaction Index (ACSI) is a comprehensive survey of how consumers rate a wide range of products and services. The ACSI can serve as a tool to help understand how customer satisfaction might be linked to the results that appear on the bottom line of the financial balance sheet or to stock price and performance. Figure 6-5 provides the 1998 satisfaction scores for the top 50 of the almost 200 companies tracked in the survey.[4]

This research indicated that overall, when customer satisfaction scores have moved up or down, stocks have followed three months later. Claes Fornell, a professor at the University of Michigan business school and who created the index, believes that "the correlation may not be as strong as the data suggests; however, he does believe that it will become a significant measure that says a lot about the future."[5]

The traditional business mindset is *transaction-process* driven. The new BrandMindset is driven with a focus on *relationships* and *customer service*. "To serve is to succeed" is the new mindset that everyone throughout the organization needs to adopt if the desire is to create a genuine brand. T. Scott Gross, author of "Unforgettable, Guilt-Free Selling," explains it like this: "Offering… comes from the context of *serving,* not selling. The result of serving is increased sales from customers who actually feel good about the transaction. The final step (in guilt-free selling) is to cement the relationship. If there is one word that customers hate, it is the word 'next!' Even when it is not said, if our actions imply 'next,' the customer may feel violated. Cement the relationship by saying or doing something that lets the customer know that the service is not over simply because the transaction is complete."[6] Mr. Gross has a slogan that he refers to as "POS (point-of-sale) Point." The slogan is, "Sell a customer, get paid. *Serve* a customer, get paid again and again."[7]

FIGURE 6–5

Rank	Company or Division	1997 Score	Change from 1996	Rank	Company or Division	1997 Score	Change from 1996
1	Mercedes-Benz	87	N.C.	26	Nordstrom	82	-1.2%
2	HJ Heinz, food processing	86	-4.4%	27	Oldsmobile	82	N.C.
3	Colgate-Palmolive, pet foods	85	N.A.	28	Philips Petroleum	82	3.8
4	HJ Heinz, pet foods	85	N.A.	29	Pillsbury	82	-5.7
5	Mars, food processing	85	-1.2	30	Ralston Purina, pet foods	82	N.A.
6	Maytag	85	2.4	31	Sanyo Fisher	82	1.2
7	Quaker Oats	85	3.7	32	Saturn	82	1.2
8	Cadillac	84	-4.5	33	Unilever	82	-1.2
9	Hershey Foods	84	-4.5	34	United Parcel Service	82	-5.7
10	Coca-Cola	84	-.4	35	Whirlpool	82	-3.5
11	Toyota	84	N.C.	36	Anheuser-Busch	81	2.5
12	Volvo	84	N.C.	37	Campbell Soup	81	-3.6
13	Zenith Electronics	84	N.C.	38	General Mills	81	-5.8
14	Buick	83	-1.2	39	Kellogg	81	-4.7
15	Cadbury Schweppes	83	-3.5	40	Levi Strauss	81	1.3
16	Colgate-Palmolive, personal care products	83	1.2	41	Lincoln Mercury	81	1.3
17	Nestle, food processing	83	1.2	42	Mars, pet foods	81	N.A.
18	Nestle, pet foods	83	N.A.	43	Miller Brewing	81	3.8
19	Panasonic	83	3.8	44	Mitsubishi Electric	81	-2.4
20	PepsiCo	83	-3.5	45	Sara Lee, food processing	81	8.0
21	Clorox	83	-1.2	46	Shell	81	5.2
22	Dial	83	-2.4	47	Sony	81	N.C.
23	FedEx	82	-4.7	48	Procter & Gamble	81	-4.7
24	Honda Motor	82	-1.2	49	VF	81	1.3
25	Kraft Foods	82	-3.5	50	Adolph Coors	80	1.3

Achieving a reputation for great customer service does not happen by talking about it. A brand's reputation is determined by what customers say about it and how they describe it in their everyday lives. The thing that matters most to customers is action. It would appear all too often that service training is left up to the customer to provide.

In *The Discipline of Market Leaders,* authors Michael Treacy and Fred Wiersema researched the characteristics of market leaders. They stated that to capture a larger share of customers' purchases, an organization needs to excel in one of three areas: operational excellence, product leadership, or customer intimacy. Studies have shown throughout the years that companies who dominate have excelled in at least one of these three areas.

In each case, the common denominator of market-leading companies is that they have figured out *how* to serve their customers. This is to say they have identified the customer's core need and dominated it.[8] We believe that any organization will find it difficult to hold a leadership position without a significant commitment to customer service excellence.

Keeping them satisfied is the first step to developing loyal, long-term friendships with your customers. A happy customer may be loyal; a *delighted* customer can be a friend for life. This is critical, especially when you consider the numbers: Countless surveys have shown that it costs about five times as much to get a new customer as it does to retain an existing one. Yet how much of a typical organization's marketing budget is invested in keeping current customers, as opposed to attracting new ones.

In order to discover how to culturalize a BrandMindset, it is important to understand where customer service concepts started.

The Customer Has Always Come First

Service is in the mind of the beholder. Customers really haven't changed all that much through the years. Even the earliest medieval bartering for goods and services was based on the goal of creating a satisfied customer. The difference between then and now is that in medieval times, a dissatisfied customer was just as likely to complain with his sword, whereas today's dissatisfied customer most often switches brands. In general, business has complicated the entire process and has lost sight of the essence of brand equity—*to make someone feel good.* When was the last time you read a return policy that sounded customer-friendly?

To explore the roots of customer service, one need look no further for a good example than the neighborhood grocery store. In the early days, when supermarkets, UPC codes, and scanning cash registers were concepts from Star Wars, the corner store was usually run by Ma and Pa and the rest of the family. They

FIGURE 6–6

WISE OLD PROVERB

It is well to remember these
reasons to treat customers as *guests*:

They are our friends.

They have present needs.

They will have future desires and...

any other reason!

Used with permission.

lived by one simple rule in those days: The customer is king! Ma
and Pa took pride in taking care of each and every customer that
came in. These hearty grocers were linked to their communities.
In rural areas, they felt the pinch right along with their farmer
customers when weather affected the crops and livestock. These
grocers were the pioneers in creating value. They experienced
and shared in the joys and hardships of each customer. They knew
each and every adult and child by name, not because some training manual told them to but because they believed it was just
"how people would want to be treated." Ma and Pa even knew
their best customers' favorite cut of meat or vegetable or cereal or
coffee, and they did all this without the aid of computers and
without invading the privacy of their customers.

Not much has changed. Even in this age of technological innovation, business is still about people. Today, just as then, the customer comes first (and is always right). Figure 6-7 is a great example of focusing on the customer. It's from our local Les Schwab Tire Store. Les Schwab Tires, with over 300 locations in the Northwest, is a regional legend for its exceptional service and customer praise.

FIGURE 6–7

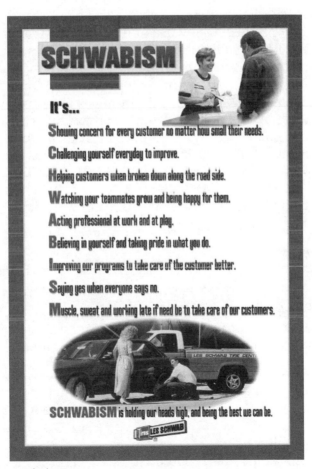

Used with permission.

Small-town merchants know their customers on a personal basis, they genuinely care about them as people, not just because it will improve margins or increase sales, but because it helps them do a better job. They believe in the golden rule of business: *Treat others as you would want to be treated. Then, because they are your customers, treat them just a little better yet.*

It's Still Service That Counts

In the late 1980s, the Ford Motor Company's advertising message was "Quality is job 1." While the emphasis may have been on such quality initiatives as total quality management at Ford and numerous other companies across the globe, total brand excellence cannot be achieved without a service component. If companies haven't figured it out yet, a brand's business heading into the new millennium is about service, not just having service, but *exceptional service*. It's difficult to get a lube, oil, and filter at a typical automobile dealership in 15 minutes any day of the week or weekend. However, Renton Honda is open seven days a week until 11 p.m. each evening, with overnight drop-off and pickup the next morning. The car is washed and the price is one of the most competitive in the area. Our informal survey of several Seattle-area domestic dealerships revealed that when it comes to servicing your car, it's not service when *you* want it:

- The average length of time for a lube/oil change was 50 minutes.
- The average business hours for the service departments, Monday through Friday, were 7:30 a.m. to 6:30 p.m.
- All were closed on Sundays.
- Thirty percent were closed on Saturdays.
- No one would guarantee that the car would be ready in 30 minutes or less.

Results such as these leave one wondering whether dealerships understand the difference between providing service and servicing.

Why should customers be inconvenienced? How can an organization defuse customers' bad attitudes when they have had to endure long waits and unfulfilled expectations? One of the best ways is by applying a little humor to difficult situations. Customer service can entail a sense of humor. Remember the old saying: *Service with a smile!* Southwest Airlines provides a real-life example that providing great service isn't a mundane, routine task. Southwest employees provide great service in a fun manner so that customers arrive at their destinations with a smile. (This is no small task, given the fact that Southwest offers no reserved seating, in-flight meals, or other traditional airline amenities.) An example of how Southwest's employees use humor to defuse tense situations and still live up to their customers' expectations of service appeared in an article in *USA Today*. It seems a Southwest Airline jet did not leave the gate at its regularly scheduled departure time. As it continued to sit at the gate, the passengers grew anxious and restless. According to passenger Jim Pelley, that is when the captain came on the intercom and "brought the house down." The captain drawled, "We're sorry for the delay; it seems that the machine that smashes your luggage is broken so we have to smash it by hand and that's taking a little longer."[9] The line worked. Passengers relaxed and settled in to wait patiently. The article pointed out that to the beleaguered business traveler, humor is a survival tool.

Customer service is not like stepping up to the plate in baseball.

A .300 batting average in customer service doesn't get you to the hall of fame;

it gets you to the *hall of shame* in your customers' minds.

Sadly, not all companies of the nineties "get it" when it comes to customer service. Joseph O'Leary, a partner and leader of Arthur Andersen's Customer Satisfaction practice, said, "With every release of the American Customer Satisfaction Index, customer satisfaction shows itself to be a powerful differentiator, yet too few companies are taking advantage of the opportunity to use satisfaction to gain a competitive advantage."[10] For example, personal computer brands ranked lowest among manufacturers of durable goods in the 1998 ACSI, falling into the bottom third of the nearly 200 companies tracked. As O'Leary observed, "The personal computer industry is a prime example. Its products are increasingly viewed as commodities, and as the industry has cut prices to attract first-time buyers, it has failed to upgrade its customer service processes to meet the needs of this novice group. There is a

FIGURE 6–8

Is There a "Smile" on the Other End of the Phone?

Customer call centers friend or foe? Depends on the experience. Customer call centers are described as "stressful and dysfunctional places to work" in a study by consultants Radclyffe Group, Fairfield, New Jersey. They found this to be true of 80 percent of the 130 centers studied.

Management oftentimes does not understand the dynamics involved in operating call centers. Call center employees require special care, nurturing, and constant communication to effectively serve customers on the receiving end. As the "human" contact with customers, the flow of critical information is necessary for call center staff to have a chance to create loyal customers.

Source: Albert E. Kerr, "Customer Call Centers Wind Up Another Summer of Discontent," Reprinted by permission of *The Wall Street Journal.* Copyright © 1998 Dow Jones & Company, Inc. All Rights Reserved Worldwide

clear lesson here that companies need to segment their customers and recognize that their needs may be vastly different."[11] An example of this lesson appears in Figure 6-8.

CUSTOMER SERVICE MYTHS

There are many myths about customer service. How many of these do you recognize?

Myth #1

> *Good customer service training costs a lot of money, and turnover is so high we can't afford to train people.*

Reality

> Although adopting a comprehensive customer service learning program is ideal, beginning with just a simple service aptitude test can increase the level of customer service significantly.

Myth #2

> *We train every employee to provide good customer service.*

Reality

True, many companies train employees. However, when you review the training programs, you will find that 90 percent of the program is focused on functional and transactional skills, leaving only 10 percent or less for guidance on how to create a great customer service experience or how to build brand loyalty.

Myth #3

We don't need a customer service program because we receive very few complaints on our customer comment cards.

Reality

The world's foremost research organizations have proven repeatedly that less than 5 percent of unhappy customers actually take time to complain. Unfortunately, approximately one-third of unhappy customers quietly switch brands or complain to others, which further depreciates a brand's overall value. Comment cards or voluntary feedback can be an effective part of a customer loyalty measurement program, but they cannot be the only determination.

Myth #4

If we have the lowest price or the best technology, we don't have to worry about customer service.

Reality

The business environment is littered with unsuccessful low-priced brands, and great new products that have failed to provide appropriate customer service. However, it would seem that many companies focus most of their resources and strategy on products as opposed to service. Even the software giant Microsoft announced in February of 1999 plans for a major reorganization to focus on customer service and the Internet. Microsoft's president, Steve Ballmer, has been reviewing operations, and according to Rob Enderle, an analyst with Giga Information Group who is familiar with the plans, "When Ballmer did his review, he realized the organization was disconnected from customers—organized around technologies and not customers."[12] Technology companies can find it difficult to embrace the value of exceptional customer service and customer satisfaction.

Myth #5

Large organizations cannot provide the same level of "intimate" service as smaller organizations.

Reality

If you believe you can't, then you can't and won't. However, large companies such as Safeway are proof that an organization of *any size* that makes a commitment toward customer service can change their culture and reap the benefits of improved customer satisfaction and brand loyalty on their bottom line. Steve Burd, Safeway's CEO, believes that service and efficiency are the most important things to his organization.[13] Gregory TenEyck, a Safeway spokesman, explained it this way, "If you're in the retail business, you deal with people every day. If you don't want to be friendly, you shouldn't be in the retail business. But it's a way for Safeway to set ourselves apart from our competition, to provide the best shopping experience for our customers."[14]

Myth #6

I'm a small company and I can't compete with the service reputations of someone like Nordstrom.

Reality

You only have to be legendary with your own customers, not everyone else's. Many genuine brands began as small entrepreneurial enterprises. Take care of your customers and they will spread the word about you. Customer service is about focus. You don't achieve an outstanding service reputation among customers and consumers because you *tell* them you have great service. Advertising won't get you a great service reputation. You have to earn it. If you stand behind your *promise* and deliver, customers will give you due recognition.

Myth #7

Customers are for life.

Reality

While most CEOs would like to believe that customers stay for life, the reality is that this is a difficult if not an unattainable goal.

According to John R. Graham of Graham Communications, no customer is for life. They exist for measurable periods of time. As in life, where it is nearly impossible to attain 100 percent of anything, the same is true of customer loyalty. As Mr. Graham points out, "Gucci shoes are worn by Wal-Mart customers as well as Nieman-Marcus shoppers."[15] Low price does not breed customer loyalty. Customers become loyal to the price, not the brand. Price is used to lure customers away.

When you consider the customer service myths, you can begin to understand that the reasons for poor customer service are predictable:

- Organizations rarely have standards established to independently measure their customers' *perceptions* of exceptional customer service.
- Organizations have viewed customer service training as a cost, or overhead, not a profit or brand investment.
- Job applicants are not properly screened—or screened at all—for the behavioral attributes that predict customer service aptitude.
- Employees are trained to do the technical or routine tasks of a job, such as operating a cash register, but are rarely taught how to delight a customer.

Regardless of the reasons, organizations are losing billions of dollars a year in lost brand loyalty because they are investing in job training and not in customer service *learning*. Customer service learning is not about cost; it's about long-term brand equity. Poor customer service may be predictable, but it is also preventable. The processes and technology exist that can reverse the trend of poor customer service. The message is clear: *To optimize profit, learn to optimize excellence.*

BRAND CULTURALIZATION METHODOLOGY

Who would think such a little word like *yes* could carry so much weight. *Yes* transforms and empowers. *Yes* breaks down any walls attempted to be built. *Yes* is the most powerful tool employees and associates can carry with them throughout the workday. *Yes* makes the small opportunities seem great in the eyes of customers. *Yes* allows you to be *service-ready*. *Yes* frames the essence of a can-do brand attitude, as opposed to a can't-do attitude. *Yes* lowers the levels of anxiety. The power of *yes* is waiting to be unlocked.

Probably one of the best examples of adopting a service-ready attitude is the Internal Revenue Service. Talk about the power of *yes* breaking through old stereotypes. Once thought of as the immovable force, even the Internal Revenue Service has come to realize that the key to improving their age-old image as the bad guys is through customer service improvements. From tax collection, the IRS has shifted its emphasis to "provide first-quality customer service and make life easier for the taxpayer," says IRS commissioner Charles Rossotti. Talk about stepping outside the box!

Mr. Rossotti has focused the IRS's direction on emphasizing customer service and technological change. He says that by 1999, taxpayers can expect:

- Phone representatives 24 hours a day, seven days a week, expanded from 16 hours, six days a week in 1998.
- 250 IRS offices open Saturdays from the second week of January through mid-April for taxpayers to walk in for help and problem-solving. In 1998, only a few offices were open on Saturdays late in the filing season.
- Simpler communication. Seventeen IRS notices have been rewritten to make them shorter and more understandable. Most are for taxpayers who may have made minor mistakes in filing, such as mathematical errors, or sent other inaccurate information.

Mr. Rossotti realizes that for taxpayers to experience better service, the IRS has a "massive job to fulfill." Figure 6-9 compares the old Internal Revenue Service mission statement with its newly revised statement, reflecting an entirely new promise for taxpayers.

As another example, Nordstrom tries to hire people who will fit their system and culture. Nordstrom would rather hire nice people and teach them to sell than hire salespeople and teach them to be nice. It is said of Nordstrom that they "hire the smile and train the skill."[16] Nordstrom doesn't have all the answers;

FIGURE 6–9

A Whole New Attitude

A Comparison of the Internal Revenue Service's Old and New Mission Statements

Old: The purpose of the Internal Revenue Service is to collect the proper amount of tax revenue at the least cost; serve the public by continually improving the quality of our products and services; and perform in a manner warranting the highest degree of public confidence in our integrity, efficiency, and fairness.

New: The IRS mission is to "provide America's taxpayers top-quality service by helping them understand and meet their tax responsibilities and by applying the tax law with integrity and fairness to all."

Source: Kerry Hannon, "IRS Unveils Plan to Focus on Customer Service," *USA Today,* September 24, 1998, p. 38. Copyright 1998, USA TODAY. Reprinted with permission.

however, they do understand that their salespeople are the most valuable people in their company. It's essential for them to be able to transfer their tradition of great service to a new generation of employees and customers. This requires that service aptitude and attitude be firmly entrenched and linked to their brand's culture. Nordstrom, like Disney and Lexus, is a living example of the saying: Attitude determines altitude. Patrick McCarthy is Nordstrom's longtime leading salesperson and has achieved almost celebrity status as a result of living the Nordstrom Way. He typifies the spirit and attitude that exists among the vast majority of Nordstrom employees. Mr. McCarthy explains his attitude toward work this way: "This job is more than selling clothes; it's important for me to give back to the bucket of life."[17]

It doesn't take long to figure out if customer service is imprinted in the culture of the local supermarket, department store, bakery, telecommunications company, catalog retailer, automobile dealership, or the insurance agency we all deal with. Examine your feelings after the next interaction with an organization's brand representatives, and in just a few minutes, you will have the answers. It takes only that long to determine if they *genuinely* look forward to serving you, or if you are a task, a necessary evil of the workday. Customers who are treated exceptionally well will become brand "fans." A fan is one who rewards brands with loyalty and devotion. When customers want or need something,

FIGURE 6–10

CULTURALIZATION *NOT* TRAINING

*Of course, the key to a unique customer service program is **the learning** that all employees, associates and representatives experience...* **THE POWER OF YES** is *centered on three unique philosophies:*

– *When you start by hiring the best, training becomes culturalized.*

– *A customer is a commodity, a guest is a valued resource.*

– *The practice of continually benchmarking (internal and external) best-demonstrated practices for customer service will transform culturalization into guest loyalty.*

---

genuine brands are the first to come to mind. A satisfied, loyal customer speaks highly of your brand, not your competitors.

Every Customer Is a Guest

A *guest* is a person who stays at someone's home when they come to visit. Guests should be able to expect to receive the hospitality of the home, business, or Website they are visiting. A guest patronizes a particular place or purchases a specific product or service because it promises to satisfy a need, want, or desire. The "guest" mentality can be utilized. To differentiate an organization's brand usually requires a different mindset and attitude toward customers and consumers. Target stores now refer to customers as *guests*, and their motto (printed on every receipt) is: *At Target Guest Service Is Job One.*

A customer is someone who makes a purchase or patronizes a business or organization. A *guest*, on the other hand, is someone a brand's representative looks forward to serving with anticipation and can't wait to welcome. Guests are entertained, and they are thought of differently than customers. Guests are friends. This is why we believe that genuine customer service learning revolves around the acronym G.U.E.S.T. (Figure 6-11 lists the primary reasons why customers should be treated like guests.)

Break the Rules: Discover New Paradigms for Service

What was the last great innovation in customer service? Some would say possibly UPC codes and electronic scanning. Would customers agree? They may not view scanning technology as in their best interests. It took perseverance to attain a consumer mindset that scanning really is faster and better in the long run. However, the electronic scanning process has given many a company a black eye, as time and again, the integrity of pricing accu-

FIGURE 6–11

G.U.E.S.T. stands for:

Greeting	The initial guest greeting is always designed to communicate, "We're glad you're here."
Understanding	Listen, learn, and understand as much about your guests, their needs, and their feelings as possible: "We always listen for the way our guests feel."
Efficiency	Efficiently handle requests and concerns. Fast and easy is always the answer: "We respect your time; we know it is valuable."
Special Treatment	There is always something you can do to make your guests feel special! Remember: "We have the power to provide a pleasant surprise for our guests."
Thankfulness	Thank each and every guest for his or her patronage:
	"We don't take your business for granted, we want you to be a friend, and we understand the lifetime value of your patronage."

racy has been questioned. And while electronic scanning has provided the means to collect all sorts of customer purchasing behavior data, consumers are beginning to voice privacy concerns and question the benefits to them of collecting so much data.

Technology can certainly be utilized as an extension of a brand's total customer service strategy. For example, consumers today want customized apparel. Levi Strauss recognized this emerging trend and opened retail outlets devoted to those customers wanting to custom-order jeans according to their personal measurements. Companies such as GAP, Lands' End, and Eddie Bauer have also integrated customized personal shopping features into their Internet Websites.

Companies can take advantage of mass customization and the use of information to provide personal attention via technology (consumer personal databanks). Computer systems and programs now provide three-dimensional body imaging and high levels of interactivity. Self-checkout is not just a dream but a reality. Supermarkets have been testing this concept, and Winn-Dixie, a leading chain in Florida, is implementing self-checkout.

L.L. Bean has been a benchmarking role model for companies from a wide assortment of industries. As a catalog retailer, 80 percent of their orders arrive by phone, to the tune of over 50,000 calls a day, on average. They studied best practices from other companies all over the world in an attempt to exceed customer expectations. By integrating a FedEx station into the design of their new Order Fulfillment Center, L.L. Bean has come close to approaching its goal of turning around 100 percent of its orders within 24 hours. Five years ago, customers could expect to receive their order within two weeks. Today, there is a span of about two hours between the time the order is received over the phone and the time it's ready for FedEx to deliver.[18] Figure 6-12 summarizes a new service approach for movie theatres.

FIGURE 6–12

A Little Extra Popcorn Adds Up to a Lot of *"Peanuts"*

On their way from box office to theater seat, moviegoers pass through a critical selling window for exhibitors—the lobby. That's where popcorn, candy, and soft drink purchases add between $1.50 and $2.00 to each ticket sale, and at considerably higher margins. For a national movie chain with 500 locations, adding only 10 cents to each of these impulse purchases can mean an extra $10 million dollars a year in revenue. How to do it?

KURT SALMON ASSOCIATES

KSA

Kurt Salmon Associates (consultants) are currently employing three approaches to maximizing the potential of this selling window for a movie chain client: improving service, expanding the product line, and sales promotion.

Improving service involves training mostly teenage part-timers to work more efficiently as well as improving engineering methods (prepacked popcorn boxes) and rationalizing candy counter layouts. For theater managers, it means more analysis and measurement, regardless of what's showing this week. Staggered starting times would widen selling windows, for example, but could complicate projection and cleanup schedules.

In the product line area, the goals are to get current buyers to trade up and induce potential new customers to sample more-appealing, nontraditional choices. Sales promotion efforts include packaging tickets and popcorn at a single price, spreading the aroma of popcorn in the lobby, and more aggressive signage and video screens to presell customers as they wait to buy their tickets.

Similar narrow selling windows exist at sports arenas during halftime, in newsstands at hotels and airports, at fast-food counters in shopping malls and terminals—anywhere time-constrained, captive audiences can be sold something in a hurry.

Source: Kurt Salmon Associates, "The Popcorn Window," *KSA New Connections*, Winter 1996, pp. 2–3.

Bill Gates's vision to have a computer in every home is coming closer and closer to reality. One day in the not-so-distant future, PCs will achieve the lofty status that the television has reached. As personal computing power continues to enter each and every home, more and more consumers will embrace technological innovations and applications. The question becomes one of how technological advances can enhance a brand's perception and support improved customer service, as opposed to how customer service can support the technology. It's amazing how many organizations implement substantial customer-related technologies without ever involving or testing customers' reactions.

Self-checkout, in-store computerized kiosks, and computer

stations providing customers access to catalog Websites are examples of some organizations' attempts at applying technology to better serve their customers. What do consumers think of using in-store kiosks, computers, and self-checkout? Figure 6-13 provides a table with consumers' overall responses to three key questions: (1) Would you use this technology? (2) Would it make shopping easier? (3) Would you shop at the store more often as a result of using this technology?

How can brands discover new paradigms for customer service? Where do organizations look for ideas that will be relevant to their brand's customers and potential customers? The first place to look is at your competitors. In his book, *Techno Trends: How to Use Technology to Go Beyond Your Competition,* Daniel Burrus provides 30 basic rules with which to apply technology breakthroughs. The book and the 30 rules are built around the analogy of playing a high-risk card game. Rule 21 is: *Find out what the other guy is doing and do something else.*[19] Assess your competitors' customer service attitudes, aptitudes, personnel, programs, and services. Are there any areas where you can differentiate yourself so that from your customers' and potential customers' perspective, you appear to offer something new and wonderful?

The Internet has become the latest technological marvel to capture our imagination. The same principles of customer service apply to conducting electronic commerce on the Internet. Via the Internet, a brand becomes accessible to an entirely new customer base. Because of this enormous exposure, a brand's Website should be an extension of the organization's culture and reflect a real-life customer service attitude. The Internet provides brands

FIGURE 6–13*

	In-store computer	In-store kiosk	Self checkout	Automatic price check
Would you use this technology?	62%	57%	69%	78%
Would it make shopping easier?	43%	27%	56%	69%
Would it cause you to shop at the store more?	23%	14%	28%	30%

*Based on Kurt Salmon Associates Apparel Solutions Survey, 1998.

with another tool to serve customers and potential customers in entirely new ways. It's another answer for organizations that really desire to become genuine brands by becoming faster, easier, and more efficient than ever before.

How About an Unconditional Guarantee?

The *promise* must be an integral part of the customer service guarantee. From your customers' perspective, the *promise* is your word, your commitment to them to stand behind your products, services, *and* their experience with you. The more extraordinary the promise—and deliverable—the more effective it is in differentiating the brand. Most businesses have guarantees in some form. Some require customers to read the "fine print." Others require a legal expert to interpret their meaning. And many drive customers away! The design and implementation of a guarantee *worthy of a privileged position* tightly links the brand with its customers and builds long-term loyalty. As the saying goes, "the proof is in the pudding." In the case of extraordinary guarantees, actions speak louder than words.

The Spire Group's founder, Christopher Hart, has pioneered the concept of taking the seemingly routine guarantee and elevating it to the status of "extraordinary." An extraordinary guarantee strategy ensures the organization a measurable way to boost satisfaction and loyalty among consumers and customers. According to the Spire Group, product and service guarantees are in abundance, but most of them are limited in scope and power. Later in this chapter, we profile Hampton Inn, an excellent example of the "best practice" for a genuine brand.

In the catalog industry, two pioneer companies built their brands, and *earned* their service reputations, largely as a result of their extraordinary guarantees. L.L. Bean and Eddie Bauer are well-regarded retailers of quality outdoor and casual wear. The two brands are competitors, yet they share a similar commitment to a 100 percent guarantee of satisfaction. L.L. Bean believes that they should "sell good merchandise at a reasonable profit, [and that if you] treat your customers like human beings, they will always come back for more." The founder of L.L. Bean personally tested his products in the field and backed them with

FIGURE 6–14

L.L.Bean®   Eddie Bauer®

Our Values of 100% Satisfaction	**Our Guarantee**
"Our products are guaranteed to give 100% satisfaction in every way. Return anything purchased from us at any time if it proves otherwise. We will replace it, refund your purchase price or credit your credit card, as you wish. We do not want you to have anything from L.L. Bean that is not completely satisfactory.	*Every item we sell will give you complete satisfaction or you may return it for a full refund.™* **Our Creed** *To give you such outstanding quality, value, service and guarantee that we may be worthy of your high esteem.™* *– Eddie Bauer, 1920*

Used with permission.

his unique guarantee. Figure 6-14 provides the "words" of their guarantees. However, only shopping the brands will indicate how well they have culturalized their *promises*.

History shows time and again that customers take promises very seriously. We all remember the pains AOL suffered in their efforts to recover from near-disaster and numerous lawsuits. The lesson here is that customers may very well hold you to your promise—or the lack of one—all the way to the courthouse. Another lesson learned from these examples is that a good idea, a new product, and even a stated commitment to customer service do not guarantee customer satisfaction. Employees and associates are the key to delivering the promise, and determining how customers will feel.

Measuring Service Effectiveness

Let's assume you've worked on integrating the BrandMindset into the very core of your company's culture. You believe passionately that customer service is mission-critical to long-term success and have begun the systematic implementation of your new service strategy. How will you measure its effectiveness? How will you ensure that you are actually creating satisfied, delighted customers?

This is where internal and external benchmarking are vitally important and independent consumer research is necessary to identify the critical service elements of the transaction and interaction environment as well as competitors' relative performance. In addition, ongoing periodic research is required to measure customer satisfaction with and loyalty to specific brands and specific industries.

Assessing associates is an integral aspect of internal measurements. For the *promise* to be successfully and thoroughly culturalized, all employees' and associates' customer service aptitude should be assessed, including that of *all* senior executives and management. New hires should be assessed prior to entry and periodically thereafter, along with their fellow associates. Customer service scores should be integrated into the employee's informal and formal performance appraisal review.

The goal most brands aspire to is 100 percent customer satisfaction. But how do you know, from your customer's perspective, if you are truly "delivering the goods?" GMA Research Corporation, Bellevue, Washington, outlines seven steps to plan, implement, and achieve a successful customer satisfaction measurement program. GMA's seven steps[20] are:

> *Step 1: Ascertainment.* First recognize the need and value of measuring customer satisfaction for your organization. Review examples of what others are doing and how well it helps them. Review the organization's mission statement, business plan, or *promise* to see how customer satisfaction measurement will provide support in accomplishing the strategic objectives.
>
> *Step 2: Focus groups.* Conduct several focus groups with a small number of customers and employees. Discuss their attitudes and opinions regarding customer satisfaction: What drives it? What is most important in achieving 100 percent quality? What improvements need to be made? What are some examples of highly satisfied customers? And so forth.

Step 3: Establishing measurement attributes. Based on the ascertainment analysis and focus group discussions, develop a list of key attributes that are important to achieving a high degree of customer satisfaction. *Each attribute must be measurable.* Examples include fast service, product quality, reliability, friendly service, customer recognition, product selections, good value, and convenient location.

Step 4: Selecting the appropriate methodology. There are a number of techniques available for conducting customer satisfaction surveys. These range from customer comment cards, more extensive customer questionnaires completed at the business location or taken by customers and returned via the mail, telephone surveys, and executive interviews. The important issue is picking the technique that works best in each specific environment, and usually a combination of techniques produces the most projectable results. Consideration must be given to making the interview process satisfying to the customer, such as a reasonable interview length and professionalism on the part of the interviewer. Various techniques have a range of incurred costs.

Step 5: Pretesting. Once the key attributes and interview techniques have been decided, the customer questionnaire is drafted and pretested on a number of actual customers to determine how well the questions work. The quality of this measurement tool must be defined. Modifications are made prior to implementation. A group of employees should also test the questionnaire as part of this phase and provide input and suggestions.

Step 6: Implementation. After modifications are made, the organization is ready to implement a customer satisfaction measurement system. Hours of operation, customer flow and distribution, seasonal fluctuations, as well as external factors are all considerations in deciding when and where to implement the system. For some organizations, once a year is sufficient, whereas others require continuous measurement. Always consider how actionable the results will be in deciding the timing and frequency for the survey.

Step 7: Feedback. The true worth of the customer satisfaction measurement system is in how well the results are understood and applied. This measurement is not to be kept secret but rather communicated to all areas. The feedback system should report results to all company levels (and be included on the financial statement), which facilitates use and understanding. Graphical presentations work well in giving employees a quick view of how satisfied customers are and reasons driving the ratings. Periodically, results are summarized and reports issued at staff meetings and published in the employee newsletter.

The key to *culturalization* is getting everyone to understand that it is important to strive to be better today than yesterday, and even better tomorrow than you are today. Customer satisfaction is measurable and based on how people feel. Selected attributes may change over time in their importance for achieving high customer ratings. A watchful eye on these trends will maintain the effectiveness of the customer satisfaction measurement system and accomplish the long-term *culturalization* goals.

All too often, people suggest that only upscale or luxury brands can afford to unconditionally guarantee their customer's satisfaction. Fortunately for consumers, this is not the case, and Hampton Inn, which is profiled next, is a perfect example of an organization that has embraced the *culturalization* mindset to become a genuine brand.

BRAND PROFILE

HAMPTON INN'S EXTRAORDINARY GUARANTEE*

Many companies say they guarantee satisfaction. Few really stand behind their guarantees. Fewer still offer a level of guaranteed satisfaction that can be described as *extraordinary*. In October 1989, Hampton Inn, a subsidiary of Holiday Corporation, began offering a unique proposition to guests staying with them—an *unconditional* guarantee of their satisfaction. Guests could define on *their* terms whether or not they

---

*Used with permission from Promus Hotel Corporation as well as permission from Chris Hart, Ph.D., author of *Extraordinary Guarantees: Achieving Breakthrough Gains in Quality & Customer Service.*

were satisfied. Hampton Inn guaranteed their satisfaction without ne-
gotiation! These two elements made the guarantee extraordinary. This
type of unconditional guarantee was unheard of in the hotel industry at
the time and provided Hampton Inn with a competitive advantage in its
lodging segment and within the hotel business in general.

It wasn't easy being in the "shadow of the Great Sign," Ray Schultz
(the founder of Hampton Inn) says. He is referring to being the startup
sister brand to Holiday Inns. To those inside the Holiday Corporation,
the original Holiday Inn sign was known as "the Great Sign." Upon
reflection, Schultz added, "I thought the 'birthing' of the brand was difficult enough, but changing the culture of franchised hotel owners was
equally as difficult."

While a few competitors imitated the Hampton Inn 100 percent satisfaction guarantee, mere imitation did not produce the results achieved
by Promus.** Competitors did not have Promus Hotel Corporation's
unique culture, absolutely empowered employees, and the *attitude* that
makes the guarantee more than a slogan.

Initially, the Hampton Inn guarantee was viewed as a proactive approach to what Schultz, (who became chairman of the Promus Hotel
Corporation) referred to as "the heartbreak of franchising." Schultz

FIGURE 6–15

**The Promus name change came as a result of the sale of Holiday Inn Hotels to Bass
    PLC in the late 1980s.

was determined that Hampton Inn would not fall prey to the all-too-familiar deterioration of a lodging chain that traditionally plagued the hotel industry. He recognized how easily quality and service standards could slip as properties aged and franchised hotels increased. And he knew how often investments in properties—either hard dollars put into capital improvements or so-called "soft dollars" put into employee training—for example, were compromised to support short-term earnings.

Schultz asserted, "Deteriorating quality inevitably will result in declining guest satisfaction, lower guest loyalty, and negative word-of-mouth. It is easy to lower service standards, but once lowered, it is very difficult to raise them. We *must* maintain the brand consistency that fuels the fires of excellence and pride throughout the chain. This is the basis for the strong financial performance that results from satisfying our guests."

As a business-building program, the 100 percent satisfaction guarantee (depicted in Figure 6-16) has been an overwhelming success. It has attracted new guests into the system, while also serving as a powerful guest-retention program. At least as important, it proved to be an indispensable tool for identifying previously unrecognized opportunities for quality improvement and creating the impetus to make those improvements. In this regard, the 100 percent satisfaction guarantee "turned up the pressure in the hose," showing where leaks existed, and provided the incentive to plug them.

As Schultz says,

The 100 percent satisfaction guarantee is the cornerstone for establishing trust with our customers that we will satisfy them. The 100 percent satisfaction guarantee aligns all our people and processes toward one goal: guest satisfaction. We are not interested in maximizing today's earnings at the expense of the long-term health of our lodging system. The hotel industry is littered with the corpses of once-great chains that either did not understand this view—or lost sight of it.

Hampton Inn's success with the 100 percent satisfaction guarantee prompted a change in the parent company's name from Holiday Corporation to Promus, which in Greek means "to serve." The fit between the Promus name and what the 100 percent satisfaction guarantee promises was not accidental. Michael Rose, the former chairman of Holiday Corporation, relates, "After the sale of Holiday Inns, we searched hard for a name that would truly reflect our core values. After months of discovery, [we learned] 'promise' had already been taken. However 'Promus' was available and became our first choice."

FIGURE 6–16

HAMPTON INN GUARANTEE

Hampton Inn

100%
SATISFACTION
GUARANTEE

We guarantee high
quality accommodations,
friendly and efficient
service, and clean,
comfortable surroundings.

If you're not completely
satisfied, we don't expect
you to pay.

Benefits of

the 100%

Satisfaction

Guarantee:

– Unifies organizational commitment to
guest satisfaction.

– Focuses organization on guests' perceptions of
product and service.

– Empowers employees and motivates them to
deliver excellent product and service.

– Reduces employee turnover.

– Attracts new guests.

– Increases positive word-of-mouth.

– Acts as an insurance policy that increases
guest retention.

– Uncovers opportunities for service improvement.

– Assures consistent high-quality service delivery.

– Improves financial performance.

– Attracts high-caliber franchisees to the
Promus system.

Reprinted with permission from Promus® Companies.

The following example illustrates the power the 100 percent satisfaction guarantee delivers to both employees and customers:

> An alert hostess noticed that two guests from an Australian tour group were passing up her hotel's popular complimentary breakfast. On the second morning, she asked if anything was wrong.
>
> "To be honest, the food is just not what we're used to at home," they replied, describing a typical Australian breakfast.
>
> When they came down the next morning, the hostess greeted them cheerfully. "I think we might be able to give you some breakfast this morning," she smiled, laying out items they had mentioned the previous day. She had made a quick trip to a nearby supermarket and added items from her own kitchen at home.
>
> The guests were thrilled. "So this is what 100 percent satisfaction means?" they asked. "We get to define satisfaction?" They were so impressed that they arranged to have the other members of their tour group, who were staying at another hotel, moved to the Hampton Inn. The two weeks worth of unexpected revenue from the tour group certainly was a more than adequate return on the extra time and money spent by the hostess to satisfy her guests!

When Schultz and Rose originally embraced the guarantee in late 1988, they knew it had to be an absolute commitment to their guests' satisfaction. With competition among hotels in the moderately priced range intensifying, they recognized that only a concept as bold as an unconditional guarantee would differentiate them from competitors and provide a competitive advantage.

What would guests expect from an unconditional guarantee? Research revealed that guests were most interested in the quality and cleanliness of their accommodations, friendly and efficient service, and a moderate price. They also wanted a guarantee that was simple and easy to invoke if warranted. Quite simply, the 100 percent satisfaction guarantee gave Hampton Inn's guests what they wanted. Hampton Inn created delighted customers. As a result, Promus earned long-term customer loyalty *and* a healthier bottom line from higher occupancies and better margins than competing brands.

BRAND CULTURALIZATION

At the end of the day, remember these key points to help create a genuine brand:

- Brand Culturalization is accomplished when every associate understands the beliefs and behaviors of the brand and lives the BrandPromise every day.

- Every organization is in the product *and* service business (and should spend as much time and money on service as products).

- Exceptional service is an experience, the *feeling* a customer takes home.

- Adopt a *service-ready attitude*, have a *guest aptitude*, and remember the power of *yes*!

- Customer service is the heart and soul of successful brands. Every customer should be treated like a *G.U.E.S.T.!*

  Greeting

  Understanding

  Efficiency

  Special treatment

  Thankfulness

- Hire only those employees who really have a *desire* to serve, as opposed to *having* to serve as a condition of employment. Train for customer service learning first, then for functional learning.

- Technology is the key to discovering new customer service paradigms. Internet Websites should be an extension of your organization's service attitude.

- Offer an unconditional, 100 percent guarantee. Live your BrandPromise. Reputations are earned, not purchased.

- Guests define satisfaction on *their* terms. Offer and deliver a unique BrandPromise to differentiate your brand, sustain competitive advantage, and build customer loyalty.

- Measure customer service every month and put the results on the front page of the financial statement.

CHAPTER 7

Creating Brand Advantage

Leveraging and Maximizing Brand Equity

with Brand Profiles of
Federated Department Stores and
Starbucks Coffee Company

Whenever you see a successful business, someone once made a courageous decision.

—Peter Drucker, American business philosopher and author

BRAND ADVANTAGE PHILOSOPHY

There are many strategies available to organizations to leverage their brand equity and achieve ultimate success. We have chosen four concepts, which we believe to be relevant to most brands and which we hope will be the most helpful. They include private brands, FutureBrands^{SM}, and brand alliances (*alliance*).

As Figure 7-1 illustrates, creating Brand Advantage is the last step in the BrandStrategy Doctrine Process. The three strategies outlined in this chapter are examples of how to sustain, innovate, and nurture a genuine brand.

FIGURE 7–1

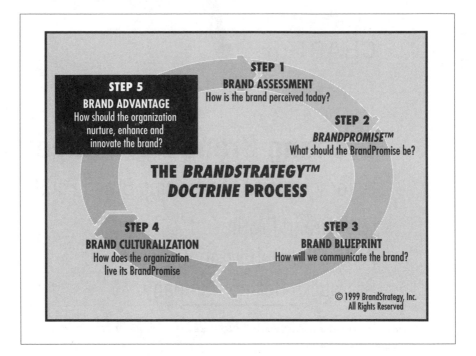

PRIVATE BRANDS

Private label isn't a brand. The customer can be brand loyal, but not label loyal. What retailers did was take brands and turn them into labels.

—Larry Light, president of Arcature Corporation

The Private Label Philosophy

Over the years, a diverse vocabulary has been created by retailers and suppliers to categorize different brand types. In the traditional retail trade, such as supermarkets or apparel, a *national* brand is a widely known brand within a product category—for example Del Monte in canned vegetables or Ralph Lauren in sweaters. *Private label*, or a "store brand," is generally used to refer to types of products provided by suppliers to the retail industry that bear the "name" of the respective retailers, such as the Gap, Nordstrom, and especially supermarkets, such as Safeway, Albertsons, Shaw's, Publix, etc. Other types of private labels include those created and owned by suppliers who allow certain retailers to sell the products in their stores, such as President's Choice. Retailers have long desired to sell other types of brands such as private labels for a variety of reasons that we will examine in more detail later.

In many cases *private label* and *private brand* are used interchangeably to refer to the same thing. However, as we will explain in detail, they should be very different. Other designators include *generic* brands, which are generally used to describe products that are sold in a package without a brand name, such as a generic drug. They are typically regarded by consumers as "no frills" products, in which case the product's contents become the brand, as with generic peanut butter, for example.

In the recent past, to improve the bottom line, many national brand manufacturers have decreased their research and devel-

FIGURE 7–2

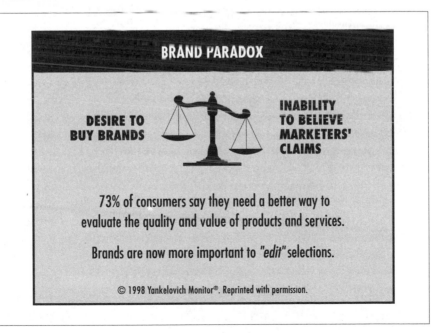

BRAND PARADOX

DESIRE TO BUY BRANDS

INABILITY TO BELIEVE MARKETERS' CLAIMS

73% of consumers say they need a better way to evaluate the quality and value of products and services.

Brands are now more important to *"edit"* selections.

© 1998 Yankelovich Monitor®. Reprinted with permission.

opment efforts as well as promotion and marketing expenditures. As a result, some of these brands have lost their competitive edge. Many retailers have realized that private label products can compete successfully with national brands, with the benefit of a higher profit margin. Correctly executed, a private label strategy can also build store loyalty. In an effort to recapture lost market share, some national brands have had to reduce their premium pricing. Articles have appeared with titles like "Brands Are Dead" or "Generic Brands Are the Future," suggesting national brands are a thing of the past. The notion that somehow brands are passé couldn't be farther from the truth. In fact, the 1998 Yankelovich Monitor,® a proprietary report on consumer behavior in the United States published every year since 1971, concludes that nearly 60 percent of consumers say that a known, trusted brand influences their purchase decisions. This represents a significant increase over the past several years. Barbara Caplan of Yankelovich notes that brand influence dipped from a high of 65 percent in 1996 to 58 percent in 1998. "In no way, however, does that decrease represent a weakening of the importance of brand," she adds. "In fact, it suggests a more urgent need for organizations to build their brand equity." In consumers' hectic lives today, the shortage of time requires that brands help "edit" the overwhelming array of choices in a crowded marketplace.

The primary reason brands lose favor with consumers is because their perceived value proposition has eroded or they have failed to live up to their BrandPromise. Any product or service, regardless of whether it is a national brand or a private label, is vulnerable if it either does not have an appropriate *promise* or doesn't deliver on it. If a private brand consistently delivers a superior *promise* to its customers, then it may well be able to outperform a national brand. It doesn't matter what position the brand seeks; what matters is how it lives up to its *promise*. Many category-leading national brands have fallen off their premium pedestal because they failed to innovate their product or service offering or allowed their perceived value to erode in the consumer's mind.

Retailers' Desire for Private Labels

The primary reason retailers are interested in growing their percentage of private label products is to increase their gross profit margin and create loyalty. Generally speaking, a private label product can be acquired by the retailer at a much lower cost than a national brand of the same product. Therefore, a retailer can generate a larger profit margin on a private label product, even if it sells at a retail price lower than the national brand. In grocery stores, "strong (gross) margins of 35 to 40 percent make store brands attractive for retailers who may be getting only 27 percent on national brands."[1]

While private label products can help retailers increase their margin, and possibly sales, retailers need to develop a *merchandising mix* strategy for all the brands they want to offer. As retailers become more strategic in their approach to their merchandise mix, they will be searching for the optimum combination of various types of brands to maximize their customers' loyalty as well as the store's profitability and success. As Susan Zimmerman recently wrote in Progressive Grocer, "Store brands are on the threshold of an unprecedented growth throughout all major retailing outlets."[2] Shaw's Supermarkets, Inc., of Massachusetts racked up 40 percent of its $2.8 billion annual sales from its store brand products in 1997.

In the early development of private labels and store brands, there was generally less emphasis on differentiation and more focus on lower price. However, that has begun to change, with more emphasis now on innovation and the development of unique products instead of "me too" commodity products.

The caveat in the rush toward the development of store brands is that if an organization is to have any kind of brand, it should have a well-conceived strategy for its brand and be willing to invest in it. Brands of all types require constant assessment, innovation, and nurturing if they are to be successful.

The Private Brand Methodology

As many retail organizations evolve their existing private label programs or create one for the first time, they can improve their chances of success by learning to think like a brand. This means they should address the following issues:

- Define each type of brand from the consumer's perspective (i.e., desired and perceived benefits).

- Determine the optimum mix of the appropriate types of brands and pricing for their target audience.
- Develop a *promise* for each type of brand.
- Adopt a written *doctrine* for each controlled brand, which sets forth the investment, outlines the goals, and measures customers' satisfaction and the desired brand equity.

Retailers are creating private brands for their exclusive use, which provides the opportunity to create an independent brand image while offering their consumers distinctive product and service benefits. A retailer who understands the importance of private brands will be able to leverage both its private brand products and its store brand. For example, if a retailer is well regarded for its perishable departments (gourmet meats or deli foods, for example), it can create a "dinner to go" product that will be perceived by its customers as credible and lead to acceptance. The retailer's expertise or brand can help "jump-start" the good feelings and trust toward certain categories of products. At the same time, a good quality product will reflect back toward the store's brand and should increase its value. However, just because a retailer places its store brand or "name" on certain merchandise, it doesn't necessarily follow that it will have a successful private label or brand. The definition of brand still applies. The key to any type of brand's success is its commitment to being *distinctive* and offering real value and benefits to its customers over the long term.

Regardless of what type of brand it is—whether a product is identified by a store brand, private label, or private brand—it still is only as good as its perception in the minds of its target audience. Building or managing a successful private brand program is a complex undertaking that requires the application of the brand thought process, understanding how the consumer perceives all the competing brands within a segment, and then successfully executing the appropriate strategy.

Federated Department Stores has implemented the appropriate private brand strategy, and the following profile outlines their Charter Club brand's success.

BRAND PROFILE

FEDERATED DEPARTMENT STORES
Charter Club®: A Private Brand Success Story*

As retailers are challenged to differentiate their offerings, private brands can play a pivotal role in helping department stores redefine and shape their overall store image. For Cincinnati, Ohio-based Federated Department Stores, Inc., the exclusivity of successful, genuine private brands offers them a strategically differentiated and distinct advantage over their competitors. The creation, management, nurturing, and ultimate success of their private brands is the responsibility of the Federated Merchandising Group (FMG), a division of Federated Department Stores. FMG is also responsible for managing branded vendor relationships (e.g., Liz Claiborne, Tommy Hilfiger, and Ralph Lauren) and for the process of conceptualizing, designing, sourcing, and marketing Federated's private brands exclusive to Macy's, Burdine's, Rich's, Lazarus, Goldsmith's, and The Bon Marche.

FMG markets and manages seven exclusive private brands: Charter Club, I*N*C International Concepts, Style & Co., Badge, Alfani, Tools of the Trade, and the licensed Arnold Palmer brand. Private branded merchandise represents about 15 percent of Federated's total sales annually, or more than $2 billion at retail. Federated believes that private brands provide an excellent opportunity to increase sales, protect margins, and offer exceptional value to their customers. The private brands are comparable in style and quality with national brands and designer

FIGURE 7–3

Used with permission of Federated Department Stores, Inc.

goods, but they have their own differentiated attributes as well. Each private brand at FMG is developed through significant research into the needs, expectations, and perceptions of target customers. As a result, Federated's private brands are not just copies or "knockoffs" of national brands.

FMG provides a strong support program for each brand in the form of targeted advertising, visual presentation at retail, and in-store promotion. FMG understands that to build and maintain brand integrity, they have to remain focused on each private brand and remain true to each brand's distinctive image, identity, and attributes. Of the seven private brands, the most successful to date is Charter Club.

Charter Club is Federated's oldest and largest private brand, established in 1982 in Women's Sportswear. Since then, Charter Club has expanded to offer products and collections in the Women's Ready-to-Wear, Accessories, Men's, Home, and Children's categories, offering about 40 collections each year. Three to four collections hit the sales floor every month for a total of more than 700 items annually.

Charter Club private brand development is a total team effort at FMG. Designers, product managers, and overseas associates work closely to create innovative apparel, accessories, and home goods. Inspiration for products comes from many sources, such as lifestyle trends, European influences, and customers. Each product team integrates inspiration with all the other various aspects of research and perceptions to decide what the customer for each private brand will relate to and then crafts the collections eight to ten months before they are seen at retail.

Charter Club has been a private brand success story for Federated's department stores due to its ability to use compelling words and strong images to communicate its "sense of self," or personality. National brand competition keeps private brands fresh, alive, and current with today's customers. Charter Club compares with national classic clothing brands such as Liz Claiborne, Tommy Hilfiger, Ralph Lauren, L.L. Bean, and Lands' End.

Federated has executed its Charter Club brand strategy very well. A leading consumer magazine recently compared the men's Club Room by Charter Club blazer to a leading national brand's blazer. The magazine pointed out that the Club Room blazer (retail $235.00) has reinforced stitching in the armhole lining as well as armshields that prolong the life of the jacket and extra details that the competitor's blazer (retail $275.00) didn't have.

Charter Club is viewed by Federated as the "family" or "lifestyle" brand, meeting their consumers' needs for classic yet casual clothes and furnishings. It must be a good fit, since sales of Charter Club home products have grown so exceptionally.

FIGURE 7–4

Few people have the luxury of changing clothes for the many roles they play in the course of their day, which is one reason the casual lifestyle has become so dominant, both in the workplace and around town. Charter Club helps its customers make the transition from office to home, weekday to weekend...stylishly, comfortably, and effortlessly. The private brand delivers consistent styling, value, and quality, which Federated believes translates into customer loyalty, a key to brand growth. The word often used to describe Charter Club and Club Room by Charter Club is *classic*. Classic is often associated with luxury. One implies the other. Regardless of price, you know that a classic is "right."

Club Room is designed to take the men's business of Charter Club a little further in reflecting sophistication, substance, and value. These clothes take inspiration from timeless men's fashions, reinterpreting classic fabrics and patterns with modern appeal and affordable pricing.

The challenge for the FMG Charter Club team is to stay in step with customers' changing lifestyle expectations. The question always at the forefront of any product consideration is: Is this brandable under the Charter Club name? The creation, placement, and marketing of Charter Club best exemplifies how to build a brand's equity. With Charter Club's disciplined focus on its *BrandPromise*, that is, its relevance, newness, fashion, quality, and value, Federated is assured of continued private brand leadership and success with its customers and consumers in the years ahead.

CREATING FUTUREBRANDS^{SM}*

> *The art of prophecy is very difficult, especially with respect to the future.*
>
> —Mark Twain, American author

FutureBrand Philosophy

The last two decades have seen major structural changes in most industries around the world. The confluence of new technologies, globalization, and changing regulatory environments has forced many large companies to significantly change their business strategies and practices.

Because of the structural—rather than cyclical—nature of the change, these changes have, in many cases, meant more than just the redirection of business strategy. They have created the need for a wholesale metamorphosis of many corporate reputations. Banks, telephone companies, airlines, utilities (gas, water, electric), pharmaceutical companies, and others have had to convince their various stakeholders of their ability not only to change course but to change their entire personalities as well!

---

*Information provided by The FutureBrand Company (formerly Diefenbach Elkins) and used with permission.

In this type of environment, it has been only natural for corporations to turn to cost-cutting, downsizing, and a frenzy of consolidations and mergers to demonstrate that they can behave and survive in a more competitive world. After all, they are fighting two battles at once: defending existing markets from new and untraditional entrants while also trying to grow in unfamiliar territories. Often, heroic efforts at improving service or introducing new products have gone unnoticed or had little effect at changing the perception of the corporation's reputation or stock price. More is often necessary.

There are no levers to pull once a company has gone through the often-painful "rightsizing" exercise. It is difficult to "save" your way to the future; therefore, a growth strategy and a way to communicate that the metamorphosis is underway is required. A change in a corporation's identity is a powerful tool. It can be used to express a new and aspirational positioning that signals a desired FutureBrand reputation aligned with a growth strategy. In some circumstances, a change in name is required as well.

A Case in Point

Most companies change their corporate brand because of a merger or acquisition, spin-off, major change in business strategy, or occasionally because the company's operations have changed so significantly that the brand reputation has lost relevance for the business.

In 1997, the Woolworth Corporation closed the last of its "five & dime" stores in North America and with a sense of dignity retired the Woolworth name and launched its FutureBrand, Venator Group.

The retirement of a venerable brand like Woolworth was not done lightly. As background, Frank Woolworth opened his first store in 1879 and over time became the premier general merchandiser, with 2600 stores worldwide. The Woolworth Corporation added specialty stores over time including Kinney, The Footlocker (Kids and Ladies), Champs, Colorado, and others, so that in 1994, when new management was brought in, there were over 40 formats. Many of these formats were soon eliminated as underperforming assets and new inventory processes and forecasting systems were put in place in a major information technology transformation.

The shutdown of Woolworth stores in the United States was dramatic but not unexpected. It was consistent with the new business strategy and underlined how much the company had changed, leaving the Woolworth brand irrelevant at best and at worst misleading. The brand had become an anchor with many negative attributes and hence became an inhibitor in communicating the company's achievements and aspirations.

All Woolworth's audiences, employees, analysts, investors, and landlords were waiting for a signal that would confirm the company's strategy and signal its aspirations for the future. The FutureBrand Company was engaged by the new Woolworth management to partner with the executive team to manage a process to create a true FutureBrand.

The FutureBrand Methodology

Step 1: Positioning.

The development of a positioning statement involved a thorough understanding of the best practices of several global retailers, near-in competitors, and in-depth interviews with industry analysts, employees, and other key stakeholders. A "future landscape" of the industry revealed a unique position that fit the personality of the company and the ambitions of the executive team. Given the reputation of the old organization, the positioning was carefully screened to be credible, sustainable, differentiated, and relevant.

Step 2: Brand Creation

Both name generation and design exploration was conducted around a limited number of "spike," or most important, attributes that were the key underpinnings of the positioning statement. The new identity had to be cleared in 20 countries around the world. The creative exercise started with a galaxy of names driven off of the spike attribute platforms, carefully narrowed by legal as well as aesthetic considerations. Prior to the official launch, the company released the following statement:

Venator is inspired by a classical word for sportsman, whose energy and skill bring home the prize. In that spirit we have chosen Venator Group as the name for our worldwide team, keeping pace with our customers in the active pursuit of life. The challenge of the marketplace invigorates us; we are driven to set new standards of excellence as we strive to win the global retail game.

Figure 7-5 illustrates the new brand identity.

Step 3: Brand Management

The launch. From breakfast at Wall Street to mall meetings in shopping centers around the world, 75,000 employees, analysts, and others were communicated with directly. New signage on the Woolworth building; newly designed stock certificates; corporate advertising in North America, Europe, and Asia; and other vehicles announced the new FutureBrand, Venator Group, in various tailored messages that in one way or another explained the genesis of the brand:

The Venator Group wordmark, with its solid, classical proportions, exhibits stature, harmony, and balance. Letters of gold and silver, the colors of achievement, reflect its high performance standards in the retail marketplace. The interlocking letters denote the connections—corporate to division, division to division, and among different countries—that create one successful team from the company's many parts.

This is just the birth. The ongoing management of the brand through all aspects of communication is now essential to its future success.

FIGURE 7–5

Step 4: Brand Measurement

Managing the brand as a financial asset is paramount to the creation and sustainability of a FutureBrand. This entails two separate but linked measurement activities. The first is the benchmarking at the outset of the financial value of the brand. The FutureBrand Company uses a proprietary method of discounted cash flow analysis to assess the value of the brand to the existing business, less other tangible assets and goodwill not related to the brand. Combined with a market position multiple, this gives a starting point of value. In addition to a financial value, the progress of the FutureBrand attributes is measured at three levels among the stakeholder audiences: tablestake, valued, and spike.

These measurements provide important accountability for investments in the brand on an ongoing basis.

A brand is both perception and reality. Organizations must deliver on both. Creating a FutureBrand requires that as much importance be placed on the reality as on the promise. Otherwise, what starts out as well-intentioned aspirations turn into exercises in redecoration.

BRAND ALLIANCES

> *I think we are entering a new age of collaboration in business where the paradigm shift is to think in terms of "we," not "me."*
>
> —Sandy Jap, assistant professor of marketing at MIT's Sloan School of Management

Brand Alliance Philosophy

In an age of intense competitive pressure, branding is still the best way to differentiate an organization in the minds of consumers. Successful brands have discovered the advantage of brand partnerships to compete, survive, and thrive. The concept and spirit of collaboration is fundamental to the creation of strategic alliances. Collaboration is all about working and cooperating with others, even competitors.

Alliances occur when two or more brands agree to merge their best interests, forming a mutually beneficial relationship that results in competitive advantage for both brands. We define an *alliance* as a philosophical partnership with other *appropriate* brands to enhance, leverage, and maximize an organization's total brand equity.

There may be some confusion as to what constitutes an alliance. Alliances are different from many cobranding, sponsorship, product endorsement, cooperative advertising, and licensing agreements. Alliances are inherently strategic in nature, long-term oriented, outside a business's four walls, and focused on creating a paradigm shift in the marketplace, not just an advertising strategy. Offering Pepsi products in a restaurant as the only soda fountain beverage would be an example of cobranding. Alliances create the perception in the minds of consumers of exclusivity or preferred status, a "step up" from the traditional cobranding deal.

Alliances are necessary because today's customers demand them. Customers give their hard-earned dollars to brands that deliver solutions. Consumers' lifestyles today require brands to provide solutions that will save them time, make life's choices easier, and be hassle-free. Brands have to translate this to a new way of thinking, and executives need to look beyond the "four walls" of their own organizations, reaching beyond the physical and mental limitations of the status quo, to envision future possibilities. This new way of thinking extends to how competitors are perceived as well.

Brands can no longer always view other competing brands as "the enemy." Organizations cannot only think in terms of squashing or wiping out competitors. Creating win win situations used to apply to relationships between an organization and its suppliers or vendors. Organizations that hope to create genuine brands in the twenty-first century will be required to embrace the concept of creating win-win situations involving many parties, including consumers and sometimes even competitors. The losers will be those brands that don't think in terms of creating strategic alliances.

There is risk involved in forging new relationships. The long-term success of any relationship is ultimately dependent upon choosing the right partner. When new relationships are developed and properly nurtured with the *appropriate* brand partner, the outcome proves beneficial to both organizations. Successful alliances create new levels of equity for the brands involved, generally greater than any one brand could achieve on its own. Two or more brands working together with a well-defined strategy and partnership can reach potential customers that they may not be able to individually.

Howard Schultz, chairman and CEO of Starbucks, calls this "investing ahead of the curve." Starbucks serves as a model for developing, cultivating, and nurturing alliances. Starbucks, which is profiled at the end of this chapter, believes that it is critical for a successful brand not only to do things right but to do *the right things*. We like to think of "doing things right" as running a business correctly and successfully (i.e., producing near-term results), and "doing the right things" as, for instance, strategically managing a brand to achieve long-term equity.

Leveraging Brand Equity

Fifteen years ago, finding a true alliance would have been difficult. They were few and far between and generally limited to production or industrial applications. The business environment of 15 years ago was not as complex as today's marketplace, and the rate of innovation has increased pace consistently.

The advantages of an alliance can be significant: immediate credibility enhancement, reducing the risks of innovating new products and services, and enhanced speed of exposure, market access, or distribution. Successfully combining resources and jointly assuming risks can yield benefits beyond the capabilities of individual brands. Michael Shrage, author and futurist, describes the spirit of collaboration as "the process of shared creation: two or more individuals with complementary skills interacting to create a shared understanding that no one had previously possessed or could have come to on their own."[3]

One of the greatest benefits resulting from an alliance is the opportunity to create new ways to differentiate the brands. As Carla Cooper, vice president of customer marketing for Coca-Cola USA Operations, says, "Consolidation levels the playing field. But it also creates strong players looking to differentiate themselves—and the need for differentiation forces you to seek another ally."[4]

An organization can leverage its brand's equity through an alliance with the right partner, thereby strengthening its management skills, enhancing its competitive position, and gaining improved overall operating and distribution efficiencies, not to mention a faster response.

An alliance can be the means for a brand to enter a new category, enhance their identity or image, and build overall awareness. Barnes & Noble was not necessarily the expert in the coffee or food service business. Starbucks is the expert in the coffee business and has a powerful brand identity among consumers for what Howard Schultz refers to as "the third place," a stimulating place where people can relax and indulge themselves. The alliance between Barnes & Noble and Starbucks created something bigger in the minds of consumers than either brand could have accomplished alone. The result is a customer-friendly, intellectually stimulating shopping environment that is the realization of each executive's vision. The alliance between Barnes & Noble and Starbucks further enhanced the exposure and equity for both brands.

It takes vision, leadership, and focus to leverage your brand's equity. Daniel Burrus, author of *TechnoTrends* and leading technology forecaster, states that from a historical perspective, real success comes when individuals and companies focus on leadership in the marketplace and teamwork internally. He used the term *competers* to better capture the opposition between innovation and competition.[5] Some of Mr. Burrus's key observations regarding the differences between competers and innovators can be seen in the characteristics listed in Figure 7-6.

It would appear from Mr. Burrus's characteristics of competers that they would be less likely to seek and develop an alliance. On the other hand, innovators would welcome and embrace the concept. Innovators would be inclined to seek out and forge relationships with the right partners because they are always looking for new opportunities and ways to grow and sustain their position of leadership with customers and potential customers.

Brand Alliance Methodology

Organizations are seeking to form partnerships and alliances in record numbers; however, it's the quality of the relationship that counts. As the saying goes, its quality, not quantity, that matters most. Succeeding in an alliance means that customers perceive the end result to be something special, preferred, and exclusive.

FIGURE 7–6

Competers	Innovators
Tend to copy what others are doing	Constantly looking for better ways of thinking and acting
Are locked into set patterns	Constantly cultivate a creative mindset
Believe the future will take care of itself if they take care of the present	Focus on their future goals and building a path to get there
See scientific and technological developments as threats to their status quo	Focus on how they can apply new technologies to open up new opportunities
Collect and swim around massive amounts of data	Look for ways to translate raw data into useful information
Tend to react to trends	Learn how to predict and even create trends and profit from them
Dread change and resist it as long as they can	Seek to remain adaptive and to master change
Often avoid anything that would cast them as being significantly different from their competitors	Seek to maximize their differential advantage
Often think about how they can use high technology to cut workforces and save money	Seek to integrate strategy, technology, and people
Are annoyed by problems and see them as enemies of progress	Go looking for problems they can turn into opportunities

Exclusivity can elevate even the smallest companies to a new position of privilege in the eyes of customers and potential customers. Take the case of Saxony Ice, located in Mamaroneck, New York.

Saxony Ice's owner, Richard Hendler, recently shared some of his insights. In 1978, Saxony Ice was faced with a puzzling problem: Their products suffered from a lackluster image—frozen water. Not a very glamorous product to go to market with, but one that generally satisfied consumer needs. Hendler calculated that perhaps a strategy for his brand might be the right thing for his company. Unlike a brand such as Perrier, Saxony didn't have the marketing resources to launch an all-out brand identity campaign singlehandedly. What Richard was able to do was develop an alliance with another ice company, A.T. Reynolds & Sons, in Kiamesha Lake. Together they formed Leisure Time Ice Inc. The logo evoked the image of a snowcapped mountain against a blue sky surrounded by lush forests. The name conveyed convenience in packaged ice. Their total strategy differentiated Leisure Time Ice from traditional ice companies and their packaging. Hendler and Reynolds had the brand image printed on bags, trucks and stationery for a total cost of about $5000.

Leisure Time licensed other ice manufacturers to use their brand image, which resulted in a wider distribution area. Over the course of the next several years, Leisure Time Ice grew to as many as 25 licensees, selling 40 million bags of ice annually.

At the outset, Richard Hendler had to create the right foundation for his company and the other licensees who joined the alliance. It would have been difficult for Saxony Ice to become a significant brand in the minds of its consumers. Leisure Time Ice, on the other hand, evoked an *exclusive* image, provided geographical leverage, and became a special brand. The alliance was successful in attracting customers outside its core and in building brand equity.

Successful Brand Alliances Follow a Strategy

A strategic alliance is a serious business relationship built upon mutual trust, ideology, and business opportunity. Only a few business relationships can actually be classified as genuine alliances. Alliances can occur without a merger, acquisition, or other business asset combinations. They can be based simply on an agreement to leverage brand equity. The conditions must be right for the alliance to succeed. There are five criteria that should be evaluated prior to developing an alliance:

1.   *The business cultures and ideologies of the organizations should be similar and in sync.* There should be a similar dedication to quality and integrity, and their brands should have compatible images and reputation. It is because of this cultural and philosophical match that the brands select each other. It takes a lot of work

to develop and maintain an alliance. Hence, if the business cultures match and key executives "think alike," they will have a much better chance for success.

2. *Senior management of the companies must buy into the concept of the alliance and agree to meet regularly.* With buy in, an alliance can be supported at all levels within the participating organizations. As in any relationship, it cannot be forced upon an organization or brought about simply by contractual arrangement.

3. *An alliance should never be viewed as a "short-term fix" to anything.* A brand alliance usually involves multiple initiatives. These initiatives should create a competitive advantage for each brand. The advantages should be measurable, understood by the parties involved, and monitored regularly so that each partner feels equally treated.

4. *Since the brands usually become preferred partners to each other, they should continue to seek out additional ways to work together.*

5. *An alliance must be approached as a relationship in the purest sense—like a marriage.* As defined by *Random House Webster's Unabridged Dictionary*, *relation* is "an aspect or quality that connects two or more things or parts as being or belonging or working together or as being of the same kind... the state of being mutually or reciprocally interested." The goal is enhanced competitive advantage for each brand in its respective industry.

The most successful alliances result when an internal foundation is built to integrate the alliance goals into each brand's long-term vision and strategies. Building alliances requires that a strategy be tailored to both brands' culture, style, and processes.

If you want to perform a self-assessment to see if the time and conditions are right for you to consider developing a strategic alliance, use the following questions as a guide:

- Which brands address a problem or compete in a category for which our company's brand is a superior solution?
- Which brands need our solutions?

- Which channels do we need to leverage our brand? (Distribution? Financial? Marketing?)
- Are we the real or perceived leader in our category or industry?
- Which brands will our new product or service take market share from?
- Which brands are the market leaders (perceived or otherwise) in the category we aspire to enter?
- Can we get to where we want to go (achieve our goals and objectives) alone?
- Do we all have the resources, technical expertise, logistics, etc., to carry our brand beyond where we are today?
- Can our brand enter another category or "place" with the help of others?
- Are we open to working with other brands, or will egos get in the way?
- Is there another brand that shares our beliefs, values, and goals, or that complements our culture and management style?
- What are the risks involved in working with another brand? How can they be overcome or diffused?
- What core competency does our brand bring to the party?
- What are our strengths and weaknesses? Are we aware of a brand with which we can align to improve and enhance our brand equity?

The Walt Disney Company is envied and much copied. When competitors have nipped at their heels, the ever-resourceful (and imaginative) company has made quantum leaps to position Disney on an entirely new playing field. They serve as a model of excellence on many strategic marketing fronts. What is remarkable is that with so many entities as a part of their corporate structure, 70 percent of their profits come from Disney-branded products.[6] In his book, *Work in Progress*, Michael Eisner, Disney's CEO, talks about Disney focusing its efforts on rethinking and reinventing the company to stay ahead and maintain its leadership positioning. Toward that end, in June 1998, Disney "created" an alliance with the Internet's fourth largest gateway, Infoseek, when they purchased a 43-percent share of the company. Michael Eisner views the Disney-Infoseek alliance as a "unique and unprecedented collection of brands, advanced technology, and marketing experience."[7] This alliance offers consumers the combination of Infoseek's search engine capabilities and the best of Disney's content. In July 1999, Disney announced they would acquire the balance (57 percent) of Infoseek and create a new Internet company called go.com.

Obviously, this substantial investment makes the relationship more than just a alliance. However, interestingly enough, just because two brands have a significant financial interest in each other, it does not decrease the importance of following the alliance strategy. In fact, based on the recent problems with high-profile brand mergers, a financial investment between two brands may actually make the alliance more difficult.

The Future for Brand Alliances

Brands of any size and level of success are turning to the Internet to build awareness and reach potential new customers on a global basis that was unheard of just a few short years ago. The rapid pace of technological advance gives brands an entirely new medium in which to conduct business. Virtual brands, or "E-brands," have emerged to capture the imagination (not to mention dollars) of a new generation of cybershoppers. Traditional brands can use the technological advances and applications of the Internet to form alliances or create an electronic hookup with another brand known as a *hyperlink*. In his recent book, *Webonomics*, author Evan Schwartz does an excellent job of addressing the issues related to brands on the Internet. "Major brand names are up for reevaluation in the Web economy. Those that build Web ventures that live up to and exceed their reputations will become even more valuable. Those that do not stand are in danger of losing their eminence."[8]

An example of brands coming together on the Internet is GreatFood.com. Founded by Ben and Donna Nourse in 1996, GreatFood.com was one of the early e-commerce retailers on the Internet with a focus exclusively on the specialty food industry.

GreatFood.com links many new suppliers of specialty foods, by invitation only, to create the ultimate virtual specialty food store. The site has been featured in *Time* magazine's *1998 Technology Buyer's Guide*, has been acclaimed by such publications as *The Wall Street Journal* and *PC World,* and was declared one of the top 25 shopping sites on the Web for overall customer satisfaction by the *Biz Rate Guide*. Noted for quality, selection, service, and its secure ordering process, GreatFood.com features over 1400 global products from more than 60 different leading specialty food companies.

Once an organization has decided to contemplate a specific alliance, it is essential to have shared values and goals. Starbucks has set the standard for many brand-related strategies, and their use of brand alliances has been a fundamental reason for their success.

BRAND PROFILE

STARBUCKS COFFEE COMPANY*
Brand-Building Beyond the Four Walls

The Starbucks brand has literally outgrown the walls of its existing stores, offices, and roasting and production plants. Increasingly, people everywhere come into contact with, experience, or at least have heard of the Starbucks brand. It has easily become the brand success story of the 1990s. As a result of this broadening exposure, Starbucks has been forced to rethink its brand positioning.

Starbucks Coffee Company was founded in 1971, opening its first store location in Seattle's Pike Place Market. Today, Starbucks is North America's leading brand retailer and roaster of specialty coffee. Starbucks has become one of the premier icons of success in the 1990s; more than 8 million people visit Starbucks locations each week. Their brand is easily one of the most recognized brands in the world today. "Our mission as a company is to establish Starbucks as the premier purveyor of the finest coffees in the world, while maintaining our uncompromising principles as we grow," states Howard Schultz, Starbucks chairman and CEO. When Schultz first arrived on the Starbucks scene in the early

---

*© 1998 Starbucks Coffee Company, excerpts reprinted with permission of Starbucks Coffee Company.

FIGURE 7–7

1980s as director of retail operations, Starbucks was a local, highly re-spected roaster and retailer of whole bean and ground coffees. What transpired, as a result of Schultz's vision and passion, is all part of the well-documented Starbucks success story.

Starbucks doesn't franchise, at least not in the traditional sense. They retain total control over their growth and look for logical, appropriate partners with whom to attract new customers. As Schultz stated in his book, *Pour Your Heart Into It*:

> Franchising is almost a forbidden word at Starbucks. To me, fran-chisees are middlemen who would stand between us and our cus-tomers. We prefer to train all our own people and operate all our own stores, so that each cup of coffee you buy from Starbucks is the real thing. At first, we were immovable in our position: Our customers could buy Starbucks coffee only in a Starbucks store. I was just as opposed to wholesaling as I was to franchising, and I wouldn't let our coffee be sold at any other type of store.

So how does a company whose business is selling "the best cup of coffee" and whose brand's business is "the third place" continue to grow and prosper?

Starbucks realized that in order to sustain long-term profitability and growth, the existing brand model had to be revisited. Schultz is a believer in doing things right and doing them extremely well. Over a nine-year period, Starbucks has grown 50 percent or more on an annual basis, and more important to Schultz, the global equity of the brand has grown even more dramatically. The essence of any successful brand is not judged by the size of the company. The true size of Starbucks brand equity is more subjective than quantifiable. Consider that Starbucks has built their brand not through advertising, promotion, or the lowest price, but as Schultz refers to it, "one customer at a time." The Starbucks brand has grown in direct proportion to the number of customers they intimately serve and satisfy every day.

Schultz says that in the past 10 years Starbucks has spent more money on training than on advertising. He staunchly believes that it's their partners (Starbucks terminology for their employees) that will take Starbucks into the next century and meet its goal of 2000 stores in the year 2000. Starbucks' investment in people as a growth factor is distinctively unique in any industry. Because of this core belief, one can see why external relationships have become a natural fit in Starbucks brand expansion plans.

As Starbucks burst into the mainstream consciousness and became a symbol for the modern culture, more and more companies wanted to climb on the bandwagon and be associated with the Starbucks name. From the outset, Starbucks recognized that it had to judge its partners judiciously. Successful partners with Starbucks were going to be those organizations who clearly understood the essence and mission of the Starbucks brand, and who were also in harmony with Starbucks core principles and values.

To Starbucks, it was all about reinventing themselves. They did not want to limit themselves by location, traditional methods, or conventional wisdom. Starbucks did not want to limit coffee to coffee drinkers alone. Thus, Frappuccino® was born, a result of responding to consum-

FIGURE 7–8

ers' desires. In an alliance with the Pepsi-Cola Company, Starbucks was able to create a *bottled cold* coffee beverage that appealed to an entirely new audience. This expansion "beyond the bean" allowed customers new access to Starbucks and furthered the overall awareness and perception of the Starbucks brand mystique.

Brand alliances allowed Starbucks to make their visions become reality. These strategically developed and nurtured relationships allowed Starbucks to transform ideas into blockbuster brand extensions. However, the alliances were being formed when Starbucks was not the largest specialty coffee retailer. Consider Figure 7–9. It depicts the number of retail stores Starbucks had at the time brand alliances were formed

FIGURE 7–9

Number of Starbucks Retail Locations by the End of 1998: Over 1700 in North America

Year	No. of Starbucks Store Locations	Strategic Brand Ally	Brand Alliance Activity
1991	116	Host Marriott	First licensed state ferries and airport location
1992	165	Nordstrom	National coffee account
1993	272	Barnes & Noble Bookstores	Locate and operate Starbucks stores in conjunction with B&N bookstores
1994	425	ITT/Sheraton Hotels	National coffee account
1994–1995		Pepsi-Cola	Frappuccino development and distribution
		Horizon Airlines	Begins serving Starbucks in-flight
1995	676	United Airlines	Serve Starbucks brewed coffee in flight
1995		Chapters, Inc. (Canada)	Operate coffee bars inside superstores
		Canadian Airlines	
1995–1996		Dreyer's Ice Cream	Develop and distribute line of coffee ice creams
1996	1006	Aramark Corporation	Open first licensed Starbucks on campus at University of New Mexico
1997	1381	"Oprah's Book Club"	Contribute to literacy fund within The Starbucks Foundation

with each of its strategic partners. For example, Starbucks was a relatively small company of only 116 retail stores (compared to the more than 1800 retail stores it has today) when it formed one of its first alliances with Host Marriott in 1991. That year marked the beginning of a long-term partnership in which Host Marriott agreed to sell Starbucks coffee exclusively on Washington state ferries and also began the joint venture operation of licensed airport-terminal coffee bars at Sea-Tac International Airport.

For example, careful crafting and flawless implementation with partner Dreyer's Grand Ice Cream carried Starbucks coffee ice cream to the privileged-first place position in the category. Starbucks admits that they were not the first to think of coffee ice cream. As they put it, "We were the first to take the coffee part seriously." They now offer approximately 10 flavors—in a variety of packages and types—in retail food stores across the United States.

Starbucks is a big brand. But in the context of the total coffee business, Starbucks is not the major player. In fact, two-thirds of all coffee is sold in supermarkets. Over two years, 1996 and 1997, Starbucks tested and introduced six newly created blends, in whole bean and ground versions, in Portland, Oregon, and selected areas of Chicago. These market areas were the test of Starbucks' ability to leverage its brand recognition to attract new customers in this new channel of distribution. Based on the positive test market results, Starbucks announced in September 1998 that they were forming a long term partnership with Kraft Foods to accelerate the growth of the Starbucks brand into supermarkets across the United States.

What is to be learned from Starbucks' strategic brand alliances? When you are in a relentless pursuit to *exceed* customers' expectations, all possibilities should intrigue you. Brand alliances are consistent with the Starbucks corporate culture. Starbucks has a culture that passionately cares about each and every one of its partners (employees). Starbucks believes that their success is a result of nurturing the unique skills, talents, and characteristics of these partners. Starbucks could not be the company it is today were it not for their partners. They believe that future success can only come about as a result of nurturing its relationships with both internal and external partners.

Starbucks turned 25 in 1996. In its 1996 annual report, Starbucks gave a progress report on the coffee revolution and the business phenomenon. Among the vast number of things that could be said and attributed to Starbucks' meteoric rise, the report featured 25. For that year, Starbucks recognized six different brand alliances among its 25 proud accomplishments.

FIGURE 7–10

Memo

To: People Who Work in Offices Everywhere

Fr: Starbucks Specialty Sales and Marketing

Re: Coffee Breaks

Your coffee break will never be the same! Thanks to our alliance with U.S. Office Products, 1.5 million offices will soon have the chance to reward their workers with great coffee—and elevate the quality of the office coffee break. Additionally, our strategic alliances with Barnes & Noble Booksellers, United Airlines, Nordstrom, Costco, Westin Hotels and Resorts, and ITT/Sheraton, and our licensing agreement with Host International, Inc., allow us to reach customers in the many places they work and play.

Starbucks 1997 Annual Report.

Starbucks seeks the kinds of strategic partners that will enhance their brand, not dilute it. They only seek out those brands that are the proper fit and are consistent with the Starbucks reputation for quality, leadership, and expertise. Having a vision and developing the right type of alliance with the *right* partner propels the Starbucks brand into new product categories, sustains competitive advantage, and ensures growth for years to come. There isn't a structure big enough to house the Starbucks brand. It truly is bigger than any store and cannot be contained with four walls.

ACTION GUIDE

BRAND ADVANTAGE

- A strategy for private label or controlled brands should accomplish the following:

  Create definitions for each type of controlled brand from the consumer's perspective.

  Determine the optimum mix of the appropriate types of brands for an organization's target audience.

Develop a BrandPromise for each type of controlled brand.

Adopt a written BrandStrategy Doctrine for each controlled brand that sets forth the investment and measures the customer's perception and desired brand equity on a regular basis.

- The key to a private brand's success is its commitment to being distinctive and offering real value.
- Building or managing a successful private brand program is a complex undertaking that requires the application of the brand thought process, understanding how the consumer perceives all the competing brands within a segment, and then successfully executing the appropriate strategy.
- It is important for organizations contemplating a strategic brand alliance to share similar values and goals. At the outset, the most fundamental issue is to determine the right fit, bringing together the cultures and systems of different brands to work together and trust each other enough to accomplish mutual goals and objectives.
- A brand alliance must be approached as a relationship in the purest sense—like a marriage. As defined by *Random House Webster's Unabridged Dictionary*, *relation* is "an aspect or quality that connects two or more things or parts as being or belonging or working together or as being of the same kind... the state of being mutually or reciprocally interested." The goal is enhanced competitive advantage for each brand in its respective industry.
- A change in a corporation's identity is a powerful tool. It can be used to express a new and aspirational positioning that signals a desired FutureBrand reputation aligned with a growth strategy.
- A brand is both perception and reality. Organizations must deliver on both. Creating a FutureBrand requires that as much importance be placed on the reality as on the promise. Otherwise, what starts out as well-intentioned aspirations turns into an exercise in redecoration.

CHAPTER 8

brandstrategy.com

The man with a new idea is a crank until the idea succeeds.
—Mark Twain

AN INTERNET PHILOSOPHY FOR A GENUINE BRAND

The Internet represents an unparalleled opportunity—and challenge—for organizations aspiring to be genuine brands. Some experts predict World Wide Web users will increase from more than 100 million today to over 320 million by the year 2002, with electronic-commerce sales growing to as much as $900 billion in that same period. It took radio 30 years to reach 60 million people and television 15 years, the Internet accomplished this in just 3 years. The University of Texas has concluded that the NET economy is doubling every nine months. Even the most conservative forecasts affirm the significant opportunity that the Internet presents for building and maintaining brands. However, more than simply a new medium through which to extend a brand's image, the so-called information superhighway is having a profound impact on how economic value is created and extracted in what has been described as the transformation from market*place* to market*space*.

In this new electronic marketspace, transaction costs are reduced as a result of decreased paperwork, advertising, inventory, ordering, shipment, and design costs. Transactions are more convenient, with 24-hour service, easy access, and wide selection, all available at the customer's location. They are also ubiquitous, providing virtually all customers access simultaneously.

On the Internet, the traditional marketplace exchange between physical seller and physical buyer is eliminated. The location of inventory and the actual transaction site are irrelevant. As a result, cyberspace customers learn about products differently, they make purchases differently, and they have products delivered differently. Accordingly, how consumers grant their brand loyalty can also be very different.

In this information-defined transaction space—with no physical product to touch or feel, no familiar bricks-and-mortar emporium to loyally patronize, and hundreds of similar-sounding sites from which to choose—the conventional formula for brand differentiation doesn't always work. In the virtual world, the traditional marketing mix no longer applies, for in this new arena *product* becomes *place* becomes *promotion*.

Research shows us that Internet users are online for practical reasons, and to be successful, brand efforts must reflect that consumer goal. It is important to recognize that on the Internet, brand attitudes are driven by *experiences*, not necessarily by traditional advertising-induced perceptions, and that consumers are not using the Internet because they love technology per se. It's because, as we pointed out in Figure 7-2, most consumers desire a better way to evaluate the quality and value of products and services. The common theme among successful online brands such as Dell Computer Corp., Yahoo!, AOL, and Amazon.com is that they help the consumer *do* something, offering a practical benefit online.

A well-known brand name may draw loyal customers to a Website, but unless it delivers something of value, consumers won't stay long or return. Reebok, for example, understands that its customers won't visit their site to simply read about sneakers. Rather, individuals interested in sports fitness can find numerous features to enhance their physical fitness, including a personalized fitness schedule based on activities they like. Similarly, American Express doesn't simply relate the benefits of card ownership on their site, but more appropriately creates a real sense of brand identity by offering useful travel-related services, events, articles, shopping services, and tips that enhance a brand's reputation as the leader in travel services.

The egalitarian Web offers the opportunity for any brand to become a genuine brand. In the virtual world, size may not matter, since anyone with the resources to rent space on a server and to generate some fanfare for their brand can become a competitor. Established brands that don't understand or comprehend the Internet brand philosophy will not only miss out on opportunities but also leave themselves open to attack and brand erosion as well.

THE METHODOLOGY FOR CREATING GENUINE BRANDS ON THE INTERNET

There are multitudes of technical resources available to consult when developing or evaluating a Website: books, consultants, even other Websites dedicated to the process. The intent here is not to replace these resources, but rather to provide an overview of just some of the important considerations in the context of building genuine brands.

Creating a genuine brand on the Internet requires the application of the same basic principles outlined in preceding chapters. As we stated earlier, the genuine brand consists of three key concepts:

- Distinctiveness (possesses unique characteristics)
- Perception (is perceived as a distinctive brand by the target audience)
- Benefits (offers functional and emotional benefits)

The 24/7/365 (24-hours-a-day/7-days-a-week/365-days-a-year) nature of the Internet offers a brand the unique opportunity to embrace a true "at the customer's convenience" mentality, making all of a brand's activities, products, and service offerings available to the target audience whenever and wherever desired. Remember that genuine brands make a promise, and they deliver on that promise consistently, eagerly, and at the customer's convenience. If crafted correctly, the Internet forum seems tailor-made to amplify a genuine brand's position.

When creating or evaluating a Website for a genuine brand, it is helpful to consider the following tips:

- A compelling opening is important to capture a visitor to a Website. After about 10 seconds, however, human beings begin to lose focus, so the first page must be experienced within that time. (For an average reader, that amounts to about 40 words.) If the welcome page contains a large, multicolored graphic that takes too long to download, frustrated visitors will stop the download and move on.

- Content must be of interest or value to the target audience. Relevant and interesting content is *the* most important component of a good Website. If a site offers little more than a company's brochure, it will attract few visitors and even fewer *return* visitors. The more times a person returns to a site, the more likely they are to become a customer. Regular and frequent updates of content give visitors a reason to return. Including a "What's New" area and reminders to visitors to "bookmark" the site for an easy return visit is beneficial.

- Every Web page should be error-free: graphics should load properly (across multiple browsers and hardware platforms); links should be valid and working; and all copy should be free of spelling and grammatical errors. Excellence in execution is testimony to the excellence of a brand.

- It is important to design the site, not individual pages. Thanks to search engines, a visitor may enter a site at any point. Therefore, a consistent look and methodology across all pages will allow users to know immediately where they are when they enter a particular site (and will help them remember it as well). This does not mean that every page must look exactly the same, but rather that the structure and metaphors used in the site should be consistent throughout. Consistency can also help reduce viewer frustration and download time. If graphics are repeated (for example, a logo or navigation bar), once it downloads, it should stay in cache memory so the browser does not have to download it again.

- The site design should be absolutely consistent with the established strategy for the brand. Everything about the Website should live a BrandPromise and be consistent with the look and feel of a brand's image and architecture. A consistent brand representation should be included on every page. Every opportunity to enhance existing customers' loyalty and engage new consumers as friends of a brand should be addressed. Every feature of the Website should be viewed as an opportunity to build brand equity and enhance a brand's perception.

- A Website should be as *platform-independent* as possible. Unlike print media, when a page is created on the Web, what we see may not necessarily be what others get. The World Wide Web is a multiplatform, nonbrowser-specific medium. This means that there is a wide variation of technological capabilities in the marketplace. Therefore, a site should be designed for multiple browsers to provide easy access to the widest possible audience. (In other words, make the *message* the issue, not the medium.)

- While graphics and multimedia effects are important to capture and retain viewer attention, they should not be overdone. Users frequently do not wait for long downloads associated with complex graphics files. Half of the users of the Web do not view it graphically, either because they do not have a graphics-capable browser or because they have their graphic viewer turned off to save time. To ensure a graphically dependent page can also be readable and navigable by textual browsers, alternative text information should be included for each image on a page.

- Web pages should be viewable on any monitor, regardless of window width. The average user on the Internet has a 640x480 screen, a 14.4 or 28.8 speed modem, and often has as little as 256-color video. If a site is not easy for all users to view, it has failed to achieve its visual goals as a brand, no matter how wonderful the design is.

- A site should be easy to navigate. Design the site to serve—rather than impress—the customer. Easy navigation and fast download times become a part of the *promise* on the Web. Users will appreciate a site that loads quickly and gets them where they want to go in as few "clicks" as possible. In general, a visitor should be able to get anywhere in a site in a maximum of *three* clicks.

- Clever design can reduce the download size and time of pages. Smaller graphics, thumbnail graphics, and repeated graphical images are all ways to speed up pages with graphical effects. Textual labels embedded in graphics not only allow text-only browsers to interpret them but also allow all viewers to read the labels and make choices without waiting for the image download to finish creating an overall positive brand impression.

- Links on every page to a search mechanism and site map are good ways to help customers easily find what they are looking for. For those who want to browse, a navigation bar on every page that highlights product categories is of great benefit, and every page should contain a link to HOME and a link to an e-mail address or some sort of contact information.

- Too many hyperlinks can make a page confusing or difficult to read. Furthermore, after working so hard to get customers to a site, why invite them to leave before they experience all that the Website has to offer? Each page should contain no more than 10 links, ideally clustered at the bottom. Better yet, links should be organized on a separate page. Be judicious about the links used, and be sensitive to the impressions they create for the host brand. Include only links to sites that add value to the content of the site and enhance the perceived benefits to the host brand.

- It's always important to promote a brand's Internet presence in offline communications by including e-mail and Website addresses (URL) on business cards, fax cover sheets, letterhead, brochures, and advertising. The goal should always be to help potential customers communicate with a brand. Choose the categories and words that best represent the site, and submit the site address to search engines and subject directories. Include all the *keywords* and tags for a site that are appropriate. It's important to carefully select other brands for links and to exchange links (banner ads) with other sites. If links are included in the Website, request reciprocal links from their Webmasters. Place paid advertisements on sites that attract potential customers.

- As we have discussed previously, a brand's Website should not be an exception for great customer service. One of the great expectations of the Internet is speedy communication, and fast responses to e-mail indicate that a brand is serious about relationships with customers. Consumer trust is built with timely and accurate information, quick responses to inquiries, and by being there over the long haul.

- Many experts suggest it is wise to avoid the use of "frames." Some sites have adopted frames to ensure that visitors have access to a menu bar at all times. However, frames can cause problems in some cases. Frames make bookmarking difficult, so users will find it harder to return to the same page another time. Some browsers may not support frames, so they could potentially exclude some customers. Frames also consume a large part of the screen and they slice the screen into parts, thereby restricting design and the brand's presence and valuable content visitors came to see.

- Security is at the forefront of everyone's mind on the Internet, so don't scrimp on security. The words *Secure Server* can have a remarkably calming effect on customers and provide the right kind of brand assurance. Creating the most secure environment possible in which to process transactions and collect confidential data reinforces a customer's peace of mind. Provide a link to a Security Practices page, and explain the policies and publish all business practices in a straightforward manner.

- If a brand's Website is using "cookies," (the string of numbers that is put on a visitor's hard drive to identify the visitor to the Website), explain what they will be used for. Recent horror stories have generated real animosity toward cookies. If a Website uses them, communicate the appropriate assurances about the privacy of the information. It's all about building trust and customer loyalty.

- Remember, a brand's Website is a guest in the viewer's environment. Here is a list of Internet *don'ts*:

Don't waste their time!

Don't insult them by telling them they need a new browser, larger monitor, etc., in order to view the site.

Don't consume valuable bandwidth unnecessarily.

Don't intrude on their environment with sound or other effects without notice.

Don't "spam" (send unsolicited e-mail) a brand's existing customers.

Offer visitors the option of receiving notifications of sales or new products, but make sure to obtain their permission before sending anything.

Figure 8-1 outlines the Internet brand review criteria, and in Chapter 9, as a part of the Brand Tools, we present an evaluation and rating guide to use when examining a brand's or its competitors' Web presence. In evaluating and scoring a brand's Web presence, the key criteria are quality of content, visual appeal, ease of use, and brand equity enhancement. The goal is to achieve an Internet Website that best capitalizes on the potential of this dynamic medium and creates positive perceptions for a brand.

FIGURE 8–1

Internet Brand Evaluation Criteria

Content	Criteria
Opening	Is there an interesting or compelling opening and an appropriate brand representative? Is it viewable within a reasonable time (10-second rule)?
Purpose	Is there a clear purpose to the site?
Target	Is the content of value or interest to the brand's target audience?
Copy	Is the copy well-written and error-free? Does it "sell?"
Links	Do the hyperlinks add value to the site and enhance the brand image? Is the information of value to the target audience?
Updates	Is the site content updated regularly? Is there a reason to return? Does the brand appear innovative?
Customer service	Is there an FAQ or Q&A forum? Is there an e-mail link to customer service? Is there a prompt response to e-mail inquiries? What is the site's response commitment?
Entertaining	Is the site fun and entertaining? Does the brand come alive?
Atmosphere	Does the site have an inviting atmosphere? If a retail site, is it compelling?
Consistency	Is there a consistent brand image or trade dress and methodology across all pages? Across related sites? Is there synergy with the corporate brand identity?
Online shopping	Is it possible to purchase products online? How easy is it? Is there an appropriate depth of products?

Visual Appeal	Criteria
Engaging	Are graphics and other multimedia elements attractive, fun, and appealing? Do they enhance the brand's image?
Useful	Do the special effects have a purpose? Do they add value? Do they distract from content? Do they interfere with readability? Are they readable by both graphic and text-only browsers?

Navigation	Criteria
Speed	Are the pages useful to the viewer in a reasonable amount of time (10-second rule)?
Site map	Is there a site map or table of contents that is easy to understand? Is navigation clear and logical?
3-click rule	Can any spot in the site be reached in a maximum of three clicks?
Descriptive links	Can users tell if the information they are linking to will be of use to them?
Links to home	Is there a link to the homepage on every page in the site?
Platform independence	Is the site accessible to less-feature-rich and text-only browsers? Are textual tags available in the graphics to speed navigation?

Overall	Criteria
Finding the site	How easy is it to find the site? Are URL and keyword queries to search engines logical?
Expectations	Does the site meet or exceed expectations, based on the desired brand perception?

ACTION GUIDE

brandstrategy.com

- Internet users are online for practical reasons, and to be successful, Web brands must address that consumer goal. On the Internet, brand attitudes are driven by *experiences*, not necessarily by traditional advertising-induced perceptions. Successful online brands help the consumer *do* something and offer a practical benefit.
- Creating a genuine brand on the Internet requires the application of the same basic principles outlined in preceding chapters. A genuine brand consists of three key components:

Distinctiveness (possesses unique characteristics)

Perception (is perceived as a distinctive brand by the target audience)

Benefits (offers functional and emotional benefits)

- When creating or evaluating a brand's Internet presence remember in cyberspace customers learn about products differently, they make purchases differently, and they have products delivered differently. Consequently, how consumers grant their brand loyalty can also be very different.

- The Internet offers a brand the unique opportunity to embrace a true "at the customer's convenience" mentality.

- The content and format of Websites should serve the customers' interest, not a brand's.

- The technical considerations and limitations of implementing a Website should be transparent to the customer.

- Everything about a Website should deliver on a BrandPromise. Every opportunity should be taken to enhance existing customers' loyalty and engage new consumers as friends of a brand.

- Successful sites have an emphasis on customer service. Quality online information, prompt responses to e-mails, toll-free helplines, and can-do attitudes demonstrate a serious commitment to customer service and an Internet presence.

- Implementation of Secure Servers and Encryption Technology is critical to consumers' "peace of mind" and trust.

9

CHAPTER

Brand Tools

Organizing Your BrandStrategy
Doctrine Process

INTRODUCTION TO THE BRAND TOOLS

In the previous chapters we have provided a step-by-step guide for building a genuine brand, regardless of its situation, life cycle, or size. This chapter provides a variety of appraisals, sample reports, and evaluation guides to make the process of developing a doctrine for a brand much easier. The only caveat is that the commitment to be a genuine brand is neverending. Brands constantly evolve (whether they want to or not) with changing times and with customers' changing needs, wants, and desires. The secret, then, is how an organization can continually stimulate the process to renew and reinvent its brand. If there is one destination on this roadmap, it is this: The brand must always stay *connected* with its customers and in touch with its stakeholders.

The first set of tools includes self-administered appraisals that an organization can utilize as models to design specific questions that can be used for personal assessments or to promote discussion at brand-related meetings or retreats. These include three sets of questions:

- Test Your BrandMindset
- Customer Service Altitude Check
- Brand Advantage Evaluation

FIGURE 9–1

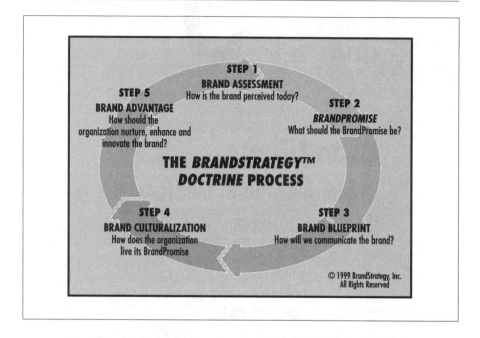

The second set of tools has been developed as guides through the *doctrine* process. If you can see what something is supposed to look like when it's finished, the process is much easier and more rewarding. The sample tools shown are:

BrandStrategy Doctrine Workplan Overview

BrandStrategy Doctrine Workplan Detail

Brand Assessment Executive Summary (Sample Report)

BrandPromise (Research Questionnaire)

Brand Principles (Sample Questions)

Living Our Brand's Promise (Culturalization Guide)

Internet Brand Evaluation Matrix

BrandStrategy Doctrine Report (Sample Document)

These brand tools are intended only as guidelines and are not intended to be all-inclusive or comprehensive. They are provided only as directional suggestions for ideas and approaches. Each and every brand situation is different and hence requires and deserves its own specific strategic methodology to address its special circumstances. The examples represented by these brand tools are deliberately general in nature. Let's review each one and see how they can be used.

The Brand Doctrine Workplan Overview is designed to provide an easy-to-follow outline and description of the steps to be completed. The second tool, the Detail, follows the Overview format except with much more detail. These forms provide organizations, and brand teams in particular, with the answers to such questions as "Where do we start?" "What comes next?" and as my daughter used to say, "Are we there yet?"

The Brand Assessment Executive Summary is a generic version of a completed assessment report. This is intended to demonstrate in a general sense what a report should look like when an organization has completed its Brand Assessment.

The BrandPromise Questionnaire is a guideline for testing a draft of a brand's promise with various customers and, of course, all stakeholders. We recommend the use of a professional research firm, if at all possible, to ensure projectable results.

The Brand Principles Sample Questions have been created to assist in the process of finalizing the principles during the culturalization phase. Many times, it is hard to ask all the right questions in order to establish the appropriate foundations for the brand principles. This makes it easier.

Hopefully, it's obvious at this point how important the right service attitude is to the ultimate ability of an organization to build a genuine brand. We have provided a culturalization guide entitled "Living Our BrandPromise" to be used to design a brand's customized culturalization program. A version of this guide has been used successfully with thousands of employees to help them embrace a brand's promise, as opposed to being "trained."

Because of the importance of the Internet today and its influence on all brands' futures, we have provided an evaluation matrix for brands on the Web. This evaluation follows directly from Chapter 8, brandstrategy.com, and provides a concise reality check before an organization puts its brand on the Web, or it can serve as a guideline for evaluating an existing Website.

Last, but certainly not least, is the Brand Doctrine Report, which is a summarized sample of what the written document could look like when an organization has finalized the process.

TEST YOUR BRANDMINDSET

To aid your self-discovery and determine if you are "thinking like a brand," please complete the following quiz. Answer YES or NO to the following:

The BrandMindset	Yes	No
1. Does your organization have a BrandPromise, mission, or vision statement?		
2. In general, can most employees recite the BrandPromise, mission, or vision statement or their key messages?		
3. Are senior executives' discussions focused on innovating products and services?		
4. Is the majority of your marketing budget for public relations?		
5. Do you have written guidelines for your brand's graphic representation and usage?		
6. Does your brand have a byline description that usually appears with the brand name to let consumers know what business you are in?		
7. Does your brand have a tag line that usually appears in advertising to communicate to consumers the emotional and functional benefits of your brand?		
8. Does your brand conduct regularly scheduled consumer research in the form of interviews and/or consumer focus groups?		
9. Do you know how your customers view your brand compared to your closest competitor?		
10. Are your strategic and business-planning processes all directed and focused on building, developing, and growing brand equity?		
11. Does your organization's leadership own the responsibility for your brand's equity, as opposed to the marketing department or an advertising agency?		
12. Does your brand occupy the leadership position in its respective market, category, or industry?		
13. Does your organization measure and analyze every activity—products, services, and customer interaction—to determine whether it is fulfilling the BrandPromise?		
14. Does your organization have a consistent methodology to measure and monitor brand equity based on cumulative results?		
15. When important decisions need to be made regarding the brand, does someone represent the customer's viewpoint?		
16. Do you have a regular process in place to capture important consumer and customer input?		
17. Do you have any unique proprietary assets such as patents, trademarks, and attributes that consumers can recognize and which will help them sift through the cluttered marketplace?		
18. Do you place a priority on being perceived by consumers, first and foremost, as a "friend"?		
19. Does everyone throughout the organization have a personal understanding of what your brand stands for and how they deliver the brand's essence?		
20. Do you know, from your customer's perspective, what the most distinctive attributes are that differentiate your brand from competitors?		

Scoring:

Give yourself 5 points for every YES answer.

80+ Excellent Brand Mindset: You are thinking like a brand.

60+ Good: You have the foundation to develop a BrandMindset.

<60 Brand opportunity: You may have a significant opportunity to benefit from changing the current brand mentality.

CUSTOMER SERVICE "ALTITUDE" CHECK

The following questions are designed as a self-appraisal to help you determine the "altitude" to which your brand has climbed. Remember, customer service starts with attitude, and *the brand attitude determines the brand altitude in your customers' minds.*

Score the accuracy of each statement as:
0 – Not accurate
3 – Somewhat accurate
5 – Accurate

Rate the accuracy of each statement:	Score
1. We measure customer satisfaction several times throughout the year.	
2. 75% of our marketing budget is targeted toward maintaining or growing current customer loyalty versus getting new customers.	
3. 100% of the time, our new programs, services, and products and changes in price are reviewed or tested with our customers before reaching a final decision.	
4. Our company officers work in a customer service position at least one day a year.	
5. We make it extremely easy for anyone—customers, vendors, suppliers—to contact us (our phone number is on every product, package and external document).	
6. Our customers always talk to a "real" person—7 days a week, 24 hours a day, 365 days a year.	
7. We convert at least 60% of consumers who attempt to do business with us, i.e., complete a sale versus "just browsing."	
8. When our customers call in, they always have an option to bypass the recorded message and talk to a real-live person.	
9. Our phones are almost always answered within one to three rings.	
10. Every employee and sales associate *always* greets customers by first name whenever speaking to them.	
11. A minimum of 50% of new employee training is devoted to customer service as opposed to job-specific functional training.	
12. We screen all applicants with a test to determine "service aptitude" and their desire to serve customers.	
13. Each and every customer is thanked, acknowledged, and invited back to visit and/or shop our brand.	
14. We offer an unconditional 100% guarantee of satisfaction for everything we sell or service.	
15. We make it easy for customers to return products, without hassle and without exception.	
16. We believe that our employees and associates are the best ambassadors of our brand.	
17. Every one of our employees and associates is motivated to exceed customer expectations and thoroughly understand what it means to deliver our brand's promise.	

18. We welcome and handle all customer complaints personally, quickly, and responsibly, with results reviewed by senior executives on a weekly basis.	
19. We trust the judgment of our employees and empower them to resolve customer complaints on the spot.	
20. We don't view customer service training as an expense factor; rather, we view it as an investment in the future of our brand to benefit our employees, associates, customers, shareholders, etc.	

Evaluating Your Score:

80+ High altitude: Keep it up with a watchful eye.

50 – 79 Medium: On the border, caution is advised; lots of opportunity for improvement.

< 50 Flying too low: The brand may be at risk.

BRAND ADVANTAGE EVALUATION

To aid your self-discovery about your mindset regarding brand alliances, please complete the following quiz.

Score the accuracy of each statement as:
0 – Not accurate
5 – Somewhat accurate
10 – Accurate

Rate the accuracy of each statement:	Score
1. Within the past 12 months, we have innovated a specific aspect of our brand with significant positive impact on brand equity and growth.	
2. We have a history of excellent, positive relationships with other organizations in our industry.	
3. We are focused on and committed to applying unique technologies as the pathway toward gaining, leveraging, and exploiting opportunities.	
4. We have a disciplined process to explore problems that can be turned into opportunities.	
5. A well-defined and -executed private brand can be perceived by customers as offering superior value to a national brand.	
6. Our private brand(s) are genuine brands in that they have a distinct strategy, promise, and blueprint.	
7. At best, our brand has seen insignificant new growth and market share increases.	
8. We have seen other organizations benefit from brand alliances and can see how our brand could also benefit.	
9. Senior executives in our organization believe in and encourage brand alliances.	
10. Our organization has solutions that could benefit other companies.	

Evaluating Your Score:

75+ Excellent You possess a well-developed, positive Brand Advantage mindset.

60+ Good You're definitely on the right track. There is plenty of room to grow, develop, and nurture your Brand Advantage mindset.

<60 Poor There is a lot of work ahead to develop a positive Brand Advantage mindset.

BRAND DOCTRINE WORKPLAN—OVERVIEW

Actions	Steps to Be Taken
Step 1: The Brand's Assessment (How is our brand perceived today?) Understand the importance of building a brand and learn to think like a customer; conduct customer research and gain consensus on where the brand is currently positioned.	– Review existing research – Complete consumer/market research (research firm) – Written report completed – Presentation to executive committee – Consensus on current brand position
Step 2: The Brand's Promise (What does our brand stand for?) Develop a promise for the brand that signals "an expressed assurance of benefits and future excellence."	– What business is our brand in? – What differentiates our products and services from the competition? – What is superior about the value we offer our customers?
Step 3: Brand Blueprint (What is our brand, how do we want our brand to be perceived in the future, and how will we communicate it?) After understanding our brand's core benefits to customers, communicate that understanding to everyone, using the right messages and graphic signals.	– Brand architecture building blocks completed: brand name, byline, tag line, graphic representations, and brand story – Create visual communications and messages (agency/design firm)
Step 4: Brand Culturalization (How will we adopt and live the brand?) Create the doctrine that articulates the comprehensive action plan to reposition our brand over the next 12 months.	– Brand principles – Brand equity goals, brand alliances, brand communication plan, and brand culturalization plan – Written doctrine
Step 5: Brand Advantage (How to leverage our brand) Leveraging our brand to create sustainable competitive advantage.	– Private brand development, if applicable – Position the brand for the future – Create brand alliances where appropriate

BRAND DOCTRINE WORKPLAN—DETAIL

Actions	Responsibility	Target Date	Completion Date
Step 1: Brand Assessment			
Conduct formal brand team meetings to introduce a brand mentality and outline a workplan.			
Conduct interviews with the key stakeholders.			
Analyze brand's current position by conducting a team review of the current marketing strategy, research findings, retail, technological and transaction trends, and consumer behavior.			
Conduct customer and market research and review results (research firm).			
Draft a written assessment of the current brand's position.			
Review assessment with the brand team.			
Finalize written assessment document.			
Present assessment to executive committee and gain consensus on the brand's position.			
Suggest a directional *promise* for the brand that simply states what the function and emotional benefits are from a customer's point af view, now and in the future.			
Step 2: The Brand's Promise			
Develop the brand's promise. (The objective is to create a long-term value proposition that describes the brand's core benefits for customers.)			
Step 3: Brand Blueprint			
Based on be brand's promise, develop the architectural building blocks, i.e., the written guidelines for graphic representations, brand name, byline, tag line, and creating the brand story.			
Develop the brand messages and actual communications (advertising, Internet, and graphic design expertise, etc.)			

Step 4: Brand Culturalization

Formulate the guiding principles, based on the brand's promise, which outline the brand's commitment to offering superior value to customers.

Develop brand equity goals to ensure that every department creates perceived value in the customer's mind.

Outline a brand communications execution plan: employees, community, public relations, advertising, promotions, Internet, catalog, publications, etc.

Develop a culturalization schedule and activity outline so that everyone can learn to live the brand's promise.

Develop measurements that will determine if the organization is living the brand's promise.

Step 5: Brand Advantage

Constantly assess and position the brand for the future.

Investigate whether a strategy for a private brand would be appropriate.

Identify brand alliances with other brands to maximize our brand equity.

BRAND ASSESSMENT EXECUTIVE SUMMARY
(Sample Outline Report)

I.   **Contents**

Background

- A brief outline of project goals, team, and workplan.
- Overview of the brand doctrine workplan.

The Brand Mentality

- A summary of key ideas relating to, "Thinking like a brand."

Consumer Research and Related Trends Affecting the Brand

- 10 key impacts

Conclusions Regarding the Current Brand Position

- 15–20 key points with reference to supporting information or research.

Recommendations

- Directions for the brand in the future.

Appendix

- Listing of all resources, articles, research, and sources of information. (A permanent assessment file should contain actual copies of everything listed above.)

II.   **Background**

A brand team was organized to complete an assessment as the first phase of a comprehensive workplan to develop a strategy plan for the brand. The team included internal executives as well as external experts. (List participants.)

The goal of completing the brand assessment was to address the following:

- Characterize the perception of the brand based on internal management interviews; external interviews with advertising, media, and research partners; and customers, consumers, and other key stakeholder research.
- Conduct a "transaction analysis" for the most frequent customer experiences with the brand and observe key competitors' transactions also.
- Review the current and future business environment, technological trends, and competitive landscape.
- Enhance the brand team's expertise related to "branding" and introduce a paradigm shift (*a change in the model*) in the approach to developing the future positioning for the brand.
- Determine the existence of a current promise for the brand and recommend a direction for the future.

III. Brand Mentality *(Examples)*

The key to building a genuine brand and enhancing brand equity is to understand how to think like a brand. A few paradigm shifts to consider:

Commonly Held Beliefs	New Brand Paradigms
Compelling advertising builds great brands.	A superior value proposition builds great brands.
Awareness is first.	Differentiation is first.
Business plan drives the organization.	Brand drives the organization.
Marketing owns the brand.	The executive team and everyone in the organization own the brand.
Marketing and brand management are one and the same.	Each requires a different focus, but they must be integrated.

Brand influence over purchase decisions is more important than ever because everyone has less time and therefore depends on brand perceptions to "edit" the choices and save time.

Thinking Like a Brand

Organizations that have created great brands, like Starbucks and FAO Schwartz, claim their brands with pride and are very focused on what they represent to the customer. A brand should position itself specifically as a friend to customers. To create long-term customer loyalty, the total brand experience has to be perceived as distinctive.

IV.   Consumer Research *(Examples)*

The top five attributes most important to customers are as follows: (*examples*)

- Awareness
- Trust
- Convenience/Access
- Feeling good
- Relevance

Consumer research—500 telephone interviews with the brand's customers and noncustomers—is summarized as follows:

- Consistent brand perception across various customer segments.
- Customers want fast service and more attentiveness.
- Disparity between customers' self-perception and the brand's priorities.
- The customer's experience with the brand is not consistent across different departments and divisions.
- Customers want to feel special about their experience with the brand.
- Good customers like the brand but are declining because of new competition and slow customer service.
- Inconsistency and low cross-selling across departments.
- The brand does not exceed the customer's expectations.
- Lapsed customers still feel positive about the brand.
- New, nontraditional competition is the biggest threat.

An internal comparison of the customer transactions at the brand and two competitors indicated the brand's experience was not a competitive advantage and needs attention. It is the opinion of the brand team that there is not presently a current promise for the brand. The mission statement is over 15 years old and no one remembers it. The future promise for the brand should be to establish the brand as the "preferred and trusted relationship for our segment." New category competitors are entering the market and the brand's market share continues to erode. The brand must change dramatically to own the relationship with its target customers, and we should not continue with a "business as usual" mentality.

V.   Preliminary Conclusions *(How is the brand perceived today?)* *(Examples)*

The brand has established significant awareness because of its aggressive promotional strategy and execution. While this has been very positive, it has not developed a sustainable competitive advantage through the creation of a distinctive brand perception. The brand faces the possibility of decreasing sales growth, and mall traffic has been regularly declining. Chart 1 indicates our customer's future intent to purchase our brand as compared to our competition. The market for the brand's products is highly competitive; however, product segments A & B favor the brand based on current preferences and behavior.

CHART 1

Future Demand *(Example)*

Product Segment A		Product Segment B	
The brand	15%	The brand	15%
Competitor X	13%	Competitor X	12%
Competitor Y	4%	Competitor Y	7%

Based on the five attributes most important to customers comparing the brand and two of its key competitors (Chart 2), none of these brands occupies a "position of privilege."

CHART 2

Brand Attribute Comparison

Factor *(Examples)*	The Brand	Comparison X	Comparison Y
Awareness			
Trust			
Convenience			
Feel good			
Relevance			
Quality products			
The best service satisfaction			
Value			

- While competitor Y gets the highest scores, in general, they do not own the total brand advantage, and in fact, if their current brand messages continue, they are inviting another brand to take their advantage away. The opportunity for the brand is to improve their perception of trust and quality.
- A review and internal rating of the brand's employees revealed a fairly consistent opinion of the brand's current status. On a scale of 1 to 10, the overall average of employee satisfaction was 7. The highest rating was 8 for new employees, and the lowest was 5 for the customer service employees.

VI. General Brand Observations *(Examples)*

- Value is defined as customers' perceptions of what is spent compared to what they receive in return.
- The one-to-one relationship with the customer is the key to loyalty.
- It's important to be a successful business from an accounting point of view; however, from the consumer's point of view, the brand should be genuine.

- Every business activity should be focused on improving the brand's relationship with customers. Building a strategy for the future begins and ends with making the commitment to better serve our customers our first priority.
- A brand that values the customer relationship will challenge internal policies and procedures that are inconsistent with building and maintaining the position of trust.
- Today's customers are not satisfied with the traditional propositions anymore. Having large selections, the latest products, unique advertising and attractive promotions may meet only the minimum requirements. While these elements comprise the foundations of the category, they won't guarantee success because every competitor can provide the same attributes.
- Because the brand's customers are exposed to more sophisticated marketing campaigns and increased retail choices, they yearn to find differentiating elements that can add value to their lives. Once shoppers find this differentiation, they will seek to develop a relationship with the brand that can simplify their lives.
- A customer should not be thinking, "I am going to visit the brand," but "the brand will take care of my needs."
- The customer pays the organization's salaries and should be treated accordingly.

VII. Recommendations *(Examples)*

- Migrate the brand from a process mindset "business as usual" to a brand mentality to become the customer's "preferred choice."
- Utilize the strengths of the brand's awareness to differentiate the brand in ways that will build brand equity with the customer in an "emotional" sense.
- The executive team of the brand needs to "own the brand" and become actively involved in developing the new value proposition that will gain the "position of privilege."

- It is essential that once the future brand's promise has been developed, every single employee will take pride in and want to live the brand's promise.
- Determine which of the positive attributes are the most important to the brand's target audience and which ones the brand can really deliver on; then own that position in the consumer's mind.
- The brand's products and services must become fundamentally different in order to be perceived as differentiated from the competition.
- The brand needs to become the preferred choice with its target consumers and deliver on the promise of "anytime, anywhere, at the customer's convenience."
- The brand should develop alliances that will have a positive influence on the customer's perception with three other appropriate brands.
- Take advantage of competitor X's confusion created by their reorganization. Change the brand's perception and direction to catch them by surprise.

VIII. Appendix

Include a list of all the information, sources, and research used to reach the assessment conclusions. (A permanent assessment file should contain actual copies of everything listed above.)

Date: The Brand: Location: Interviewer:

PROMISE RESEARCH—QUESTIONNAIRE

"Hello, my name is _____. We are conduct-
ing a survey asking people their opinions about _____.
We are giving a free gift *(explain what the gift is)* to those who
agree to assist us. May I take a couple minutes of your time?"

Observe quotas—Gender: _____% female, _____% male.

Age: _____% 18 to 35 years old
_____% 36 to 59 years old
_____% 60 or older.

1.   Gender (record, *do not ask!*)   a. female   b. male
2.   During these past 12 months, how often have you
       been a customer or guest at **The Brand**? *(circle one
       below)*

       at least once a month   4
       every 2 or 3 months   3
       twice a year   2
       once a year   1
       never   0

3.   What words or ideas first come to mind when you
       think of **The Brand**? *(allow time to think)*

       _____

       _____

4.   Briefly, how would you describe **The Brand** to some-
       one who has never heard of it before?

       _____

       _____

Date: The Brand: Location: Interviewer:

PROMISE RESEARCH—page 2

5.   Now, think about your experience at _____.
     On a scale of 1 to 10—1 meaning it is **completely
     unimportant** and 10 meaning it's **extremely impor-
     tant** to you—please rank the following attributes
     (read list, circle applicable number):

		unimportant				**important**					**don't know**
a.		1	2	3	4	5	6	7	8	9	10 DK
b.		1	2	3	4	5	6	7	8	9	10 DK
c.		1	2	3	4	5	6	7	8	9	10 DK
d.	*(Insert attributes)*	1	2	3	4	5	6	7	8	9	10 DK
e.		1	2	3	4	5	6	7	8	9	10 DK
f.		1	2	3	4	5	6	7	8	9	10 DK
g.		1	2	3	4	5	6	7	8	9	10 DK
h.		1	2	3	4	5	6	7	8	9	10 DK

6.   On a scale of 1 to 10—1 meaning **completely inaccu-
     rately** and 10 meaning **positively accurately**—how
     does the following statement describe what **The
     Brand** is all about? (read statement below)

(Insert proposed promise for **The Brand** here.)

inaccurately						**accurately**			**don't know**
1	2	3	4	5	6	7	8	9	10 DK

Date: The Brand: Location: Interviewer:

PROMISE RESEARCH—page 3

7. Are there any words or ideas in this statement that you find inconsistent with what you know or how you feel about **The Brand**? *(allow time to think)*

_____

_____

8. Which ones?

_____

_____

9. In your opinion, what words or ideas would make this statement reflect more accurately what **The Brand** stands for?

_____

_____

10. When was your last transaction with **The Brand**? Approximate number of days _____ months _____ never _____
    (If not recent, continue; if recent, skip to question 12.)

Date: The Brand: Location: Interviewer:

PROMISE RESEARCH—page 4

11. Why have you not been a customer lately of **The Brand**? *(do not read list; circle as many as necessary)*

a.

b.

c.

d.

e.   *(Insert various options for answers)*

f.

g.

h.

i.   don't know/not sure

(continued from Q10; from Q11, skip to Q14)

12. On a scale of 1 to 10—1 meaning **completely disagree** and 10 meaning **absolutely agree**—how would you rate your last customer experience at **The Brand**? *(read list, randomize)*

		disagree					agree				don't know
a.		1	2	3	4	5	6	7	8	9	10 DK
b.		1	2	3	4	5	6	7	8	9	10 DK
c.		1	2	3	4	5	6	7	8	9	10 DK
d.	*(Insert attributes)*	1	2	3	4	5	6	7	8	9	10 DK
e.		1	2	3	4	5	6	7	8	9	10 DK
f.		1	2	3	4	5	6	7	8	9	10 DK
g.		1	2	3	4	5	6	7	8	9	10 DK
h.		1	2	3	4	5	6	7	8	9	10 DK

i.   I was extremely pleased with my last experience at **The Brand**.

Date: The Brand: Location: Interviewer:

PROMISE RESEARCH—page 5

13. If you had not chosen **The Brand** today, or the last time you were a customer, where would you have gone instead?

_____

_____

14. Is there anything **The Brand** could do to make your experience better? Yes _____ No _____. If yes, what?

_____

_____

15. Finally, please tell me the zip code(s) where you live.

_____

_____

16. Any other comments or suggestions?

_____

_____

_____

_____

Thank you for your time and assistance!
(Present the gift!)

BRAND PRINCIPLES—SAMPLE QUESTIONS

1. What business is your brand in?
2. What differentiates your service and product from the competition?
3. How do you offer superior value to your customers?
4. What are your core values and beliefs?
5. What are your brand's strengths and weaknesses?
6. What are the most important factors, from the consumer's perspective, when choosing your brand?
7. What are the least important, from the consumer's perspective?
8. What reasons does or would the consumer give for using or choosing your brand?
9. If your brand were an automobile, what kind of automobile would it be? Why? (Asked internally and externally of all stakeholders)
10. If your brand were an animal, what kind of animal would it be? Why? (Asked internally and externally of all stakeholders)
11. What do you want your brand to stand for; what principles would be the brand's primary core drivers?
12. From an internal perspective, what do you believe are the most important factors?
13. Who are your brand's primary competitors?
14. How do their customers perceive your brand? (strengths and weaknesses)
15. What words would consumers use to describe your brand?
16. Does your brand position allow you to be *first* in any aspect of the market, category, or industry?
17. Is there another brand, organization, or company that is very similar to yours?
18. What are the best demonstrated practices in your brand's business?
19. What are the customer's expectations regarding a guarantee of satisfaction?

20. What is your brand's story? (history, unique points, founders, etc.)

21. What are the messages your brand will communicate?

22. Are there any relevant associations for your brand that consumers will be drawn to?

23. What features of the brand's products and services are most important to consumers?

24. What other brands do your customers use or purchase? Why?

LIVING OUR BRAND'S PROMISE

Leader's Culturalization Guide

Introduction

- Discuss reasons for being here

  Our goal is to *delight our customers.*
  Demonstrate specific behavioral skills essential for
  success.
  *(engage every customer; absolute guarantee of satisfac-
  tion)*
  Improve from good to better to best.

- Our promise and five key values

  Understand promise and values

- Why a promise is important

  Understand relationship between your satisfaction,
  personal happiness, and delighted customers.
  Caring is the key to your happiness and success here.
  Components of service *(putting the human touch first).*

- Additional topics for discussion *(list from participants)*
- Open discussion or Q&A
- Closing

  Thank you for your patience and participation.
  I would appreciate your rating on this session at its
  conclusion *(hand out forms).*
  I wish you delightful, successful, caring relationships.

Presentation needs:
- Name card on desk for participants
- Promise and values handout for each participant
- Rating sheets for each participant to complete
- Speaker phone
- Flip chart, greaseboard, pens

Our Promise

> Only Friendly's combines the freshest foods available
> and special values every day in stores that are as
> clean as Disneyland.
> We are dedicated to our customers' enjoyment of fine food.
> Our customers appreciate our engaging,
> knowledgeable associates, who are fast and friendly.

Our Values

(**Freshest**)   Freshest food in town

(**Fastest**)   5 minutes or less

(**Cleanest**)   A delight to all the senses

(**Quality**)   Nothing but the best

(**Value**)   Our customers decide what is on sale

What Is a "Customer?"

- Ask the question: What is the definition of a *customer*?
  (List participants' answers on flip chart and discuss)
- Answer: A customer is: "Everyone you come in contact with."

Cus'tom-er **1.** One who regularly, customarily, or repeatedly makes purchases of, or has business dealings with, a tradesman or business establishment; a buyer or purchaser, a patron; **2.** A person with whom one has dealings or doings of any kind.

Source: Webster's *New International Dictionary*, 2d ed.

- Changing Service Perspective

Historical Service Perspective	Today's Challenge

Technical Responsibilities

"Focus on process"

Technical Responsibilities	People Responsibilities

"Requires a balance between
the process and human needs and feelings"

> People have not been conditioned or encouraged to treat people inside their own organization as well as they treat customers.
>
> People often don't realize that working hard is not the same as delighting customers.

- Why should you be spending your valuable time learning about our brand promise?

Possible answers:

We want to improve.
Service is our job.
I feel better when "it goes well;" less stress.
Cost savings $. *(Better service actually costs less)*
To build relationships, not just transactions.
To progress from good to better to best.
We're proud of our brand.

Components of Service

- Explain the basics of every customer transaction. Looking at a service offering from behind the eyes of the customer is key to delighting the customer. Three components make up every service transaction:

Human
The experience the customers have with our brand's representatives as they go through the *process* component to access the *information* component.

Information
The product, information, or help the customer explicitly wants.

Process
The activities the customer must engage in to access the *information* component.

Principles of a Successful Brand Experience

- Reduce uncertainty
- Make it easy for the customer
- Make the customer feel special

Discuss: How do we accomplish each of these?

_____

_____

_____

_____

_____

_____

Trading Places with the Customer

Think of a situation where you were a customer and you needed someone's assistance. Take a few moments by yourself to recall these kinds of experiences:

- A situation where you received caring service and felt satisfied.
- A situation where you were dissatisfied with the assistance you received (What happened that made you feel dissatisfied?)
- Describe how an excellent service employee or associate makes you feel.
- Those who deal with customers are often placed in stressful situations. It's important to learn to deal with stress constructively in order to maintain a high level of personal satisfaction and service to others. The key is to take things professionally, not personally.
- It's important to *affirm* the person and *confront* the issues, not the reverse!

Good Service Traits

- Knowledgeable
- Not hurried
- Did not pass the buck
- Thank you
- Quick service
- Considerate of customer's time
- Pleasant and smiling
- Genuinely friendly
- Make the customer feel important

Face-to-Face Communication

Face-to-face communication is 60 percent body language, 33 percent tone of voice, and 7 percent words.
Actions do speak louder than words!

In films shown for $\frac{3}{24}$ of a second, most people could accurately interpret the body language that was being demonstrated! We use body language to read each other. It is a powerful tool.

Body language can be used to interpret both what customers are saying and what they are not saying. Managing your own body language helps you to communicate your interest and willingness to help.

Understanding body language involves interpreting many kinds of body gestures. The possibilities for interpretation are endless. We make sense of body language by looking at clusters of gestures, not any one gesture separately.

Nonverbal communication determines the meaning of the message!

Nonverbal Communication "Facts"

- The most powerful nonverbal signal is eye contact, and eye contact is culturally learned; that is, it differs from culture to culture.
- The only universally positive nonverbal signal is a *smile*.
- Because we process information four times faster than we can speak, we receive nonverbal messages first.
- We believe the nonverbal signals over the verbal ones.

Interpreting and Communicating Body Language

The following are several of the most useful clusters of gestures for interpreting a customer interaction or communicating and evaluating our signals to customers:

Enthusiasm
- Small upward or inner smile
- Erect body stance
- Hands open, arms extended
- Eyes wide and alert
- Lively and bouncy

Openness (willingness to reach a solution)
- Open hands
- Moving closer
- Leaning forward in chair
- Uncrossed legs
- Arms gently and loosely crossing lower body

Analysis (listening intently to ideas and input in order to judge their merit)
- Sitting in the front portion of the chair with upper torso projected forward
- Slightly tilted head
- When possible, taking notes

Confidence and Authority
- Steepling (the higher the hands are held, the greater the confidence)
- Proud, erect body stance with shoulders squared
- Continuing eye contact with little blinking

Defensiveness
- Rigid body
- Arms or legs crossed tightly in protective posture
- Minimal eye contact or sideways or darting glances
- Pursed lips
- Head down with chin depressed toward the chest
- Leaning back in the chair
- Moving away

Anger
- Body rigid
- Fists clenched
- Lips closed and held in tight, thin line
- Continuous eye contact with dilation of pupils

Frustration
- Tightly clenched hands or shaking fists
- Hand-wringing
- Rubbing back of neck
- Controlled, short breathing
- Blind staring
- Running hands through the hair
- Tightly closed lips
- Stamping a foot
- Pacing

When We're Not Face-to-Face

> Non-face-to-face communication is 60 percent tone, pace, and pitch and 40 percent words.
> **Vocal delivery impacts the message!**

When we engage in non-face-to-face interactions, such as talking on the telephone, the vocal delivery (tone, pace, and pitch) contributes 60 percent to the impact of the communication, while the words contribute only 40 percent.

Thus, tone of voice and other vocal delivery factors convey much of the message.

To be more effective...

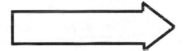

Call predetermined phone numbers and discuss with participants how they rate the:

- Tone of conversation
- Pitch of the person's voice
- Overall experience and feeling after the call

Pointers for Phone Proficiency

Answer Helpfully:

1. Answer promptly (two rings if possible)
2. Greet the caller
3. Introduce yourself
4. Offer your help

Telephone Answering and Closing:

- "Good (morning, afternoon, evening), thank you for calling Friendly Foods. This is Joe (name optional). How may I help you?"
- When directing a call to another department or person, be sure they have answered it.
- End of phone call: "Thank you; have a great day."

When You Need to Put Someone on Hold:

Action	Sounds like...
Apologize	"I'm sorry...."
Give them a choice	"May I put you on hold while I find the answer?" or "Would you please hold while I research the answer?" or "May I call you back in the next hour with the answer?"
Return to them every minute (60 seconds) to let them know you haven't forgotten them.	"I'm sorry, please keep holding and I will be with you in a moment."

How to Deal Effectively with a Difficult or Angry Customer

- Take a deep breath
- Prepare yourself:

  Check your body language.
  Get paper and pen.
  Remind yourself: "It's not me."

- Put a smile on your face:

  Smile as you greet a customer or answer a call; your voice will sound friendlier.
  Make eye contact by looking at the person or at the phone during the call.

- If you feel significant tension, excuse yourself for a couple of minutes to relax or put the caller on hold while you regain your composure.
- Techniques for keeping the spotlight on the issue:

Customer makes you feel like:	Ask customer:
You and your company are idiots	How can we help you? What can I do to make you happy?
You're making a mistake	How can we solve this situation?
It's your fault	Please tell me what needs to be done.
The brand has bad service	This isn't the kind of service we want to provide. What can we do to correct this situation?

- Options for handling difficult situations:

Let the customer vent.
Ask for their name,
Hang up, with a preset procedure.
Transfer to manager (person in charge).
Talk slowly and low.
Employ an emergency procedure, if threatened.

Living the Brand's Promise

- 200% guarantee; empowered only to say yes! Only the manager can say no.
- Always be "service-ready" and "user-friendly."

Apologize, or thank, a customer for waiting, even if the delay is caused by working with other customers. Example: "I'm sorry for keeping you waiting. How may I help you?" or "I appreciate your patience. How may I help you?"

- Ask customers open, not closed, questions.

Example: "How can I help you?" (open); as opposed to, "Do you need help?" (closed)

- The customer is never told he or she is wrong. Customers do not have problems!
- Provide expertise:

  Know the merchandise and services:
    - Characteristics
    - Uses
    - Comparisons among brands
    - Availability of alternative sources to meet customer needs

  Know the store and property:

    - Location of merchandise and services
    - Policies and their rationale
    - Procedures and their time frames

- Care for customers as though they are welcome guests in your own home.

Choose Positive Words:

- Positive words create a "can-do" image.
- Positive words are easier to understand.
- Positive words reduce uncertainty.

How to Change Weak Statements into Positive Brand Experiences

Not This	But This
"...I can't take care of this until I hear from my supervisor."	"I will ask my team leader about this and take care of it this afternoon, as soon as my team leader calls in." (If possible, include a time frame for when you expect to hear from the field.)
"I'll try to handle this today."	"I will handle this today." Or, "I will handle this no later than close of business tomorrow."
"You need to have your receipt and fill out this form."	(Discuss best answer with participants.)
"I'm really not too sure about that."	(Discuss best answer with participants.)
"I'm really busy."	(Discuss best answer with participants.)
"The person with that answer is not here right now."	(Discuss best answer with participants.)
"I'll have to ask someone about that."	(Discuss best answer with participants.)
"You have to; it's our policy."	(Discuss best answer with participants.)

Remember: It's better to underpromise and overdeliver!

The Power of Yes

- Indicate willingness to solve the problem. (Demonstrate effective listening skills.)
- Recognize the importance of the request to the customer. (Communicate to the customer that you understand the request is important to her or him.)
- Find the element of the request that can be responded to positively and, if possible, immediately.
- Look beyond the *action* to the *timing* and *purpose* to find alternatives.

Skillful Listening

There are five ways to become a better listener:

- Stop talking.
- Avoid distractions.
- Concentrate on what the customer is saying.
- Look for the "real" meaning and solution.
- Provide feedback to the customer.

Responding Nondefensively

- **"And" versus "But."**
  "That's a good point, **and** we'll need further information to act on your suggestion."
  Not, "That's a good point, **but** we'll need further information to act on your suggestion."

- **Use "I" or "me" statements.**
  "I'm confused about..." or, "Could you explain this to **me**?"
  Not, "You're so confusing."

- **Use "why" questions very carefully.**
  "I couldn't book the requested rooms because the required information didn't arrive."
  Not, "Why didn't you send the form to me?"

- **Avoid "always" and "never."**
  "We realize it's sometimes difficult to get your requests in on time."
  Not, "Everyone from your office always has last minute requests."

- **Don't get hooked into arguing.**
  "I understand you're angry; I will do my best to help."
  Not, "Don't yell at me. It's not my fault."

Building Brand Trust and Rapport

> Research indicates that only a small percentage of
> dissatisfied customers actually complain, whereas
> more than one-third switch brands.

- Remember to use the customer's name.
- Project an image of confidence in yourself and interest in the customer.
- Actively evaluate the customer's personal style.
- Identify and respond to the customer's personal style.
- Don't overpromise and underdeliver.
- Be honest with your customers; admit it if you or your company has made a mistake.
- Follow through on everything you say you'll do.

Fulfill the brand's promise.

Living Our Brand Promise

The success of your brand will depend on whether you and your team members can actually create positive relationships with every single customer that walks in the door. Engaging every customer that comes within 10 feet of you is the key! Do you want to engage every customer within 10 feet of you? Will you work at developing the habit of doing so?

The following concepts were presented in this session:

- The importance of the brand's promise
- Understanding the customer's needs
- Face-to-face communication skills
- Telephone communication tips
- Problem-solving methods
- The importance of listening
- Skills for responding nondefensively
- The power of *yes* and a positive approach

Please think about how you will apply these skills as you develop the "10-foot" habit for yourself. What is your action plan to integrate these skills into your life?

Personal Action Plan:

_____

_____

_____

_____

_____

_____

INTERNET BRAND EVALUATION MATRIX

(5 = Excellent   4 = Good   3 = Just Okay   2 = Poor   1 = Unacceptable
Blank = Not Applicable or Unknown)

		Website 1	Website 2	Website 3	Website 4
C O N T E N T	Opening				
	Purpose				
	Target				
	Copy				
	Links				
	Updates				
	Customer service				
	Entertaining				
	Atmosphere				
	Consistency				
	Online Shopping				
Visual Appeal	Engaging				
	Useful				
N A V I G A T I O N	Speed				
	Site map				
	3-click rule				
	Descriptive links				
	Links to *home*				
	Platform independence				
Overall	Finding site				
	Brand expectations				
Average Score					
Summary Comments for Each Brand					

THE BRAND DOCTRINE REPORT
(A Sample of the Written Document)

I.   The Brand's Promise

The brand's promise is a concise statement or description of the core benefits that our company offers current and potential customers. The fundamentals of creating the value proposition concept for our business includes answering the following questions:

- What business is our brand in?
- What differentiates our products and services from the competition?
- How do we offer superior value to our customers?

Friendly's Supermarket
Our Promise

Only Friendly's combines the freshest foods
available and special values every day in stores that are as clean
as Disneyland.
We are dedicated to our customers' enjoyment of fine food.
Our customers appreciate our engaging, knowledgeable
associates, who are fast and friendly.

Our Values

Freshest	Freshest food in town
Fastest	5 minutes or less
Cleanest	A delight to all the senses
Quality	Nothing but the best
Value	Our customers decide what is on sale

II. Brand Doctrine Principles *(Examples)*

- *Expertise and Credibility*. Every customer/client interaction and external and internal communication, will reinforce customers' perception of our brand's expertise.

- *Service versus Products*. We differentiate our offering from the competition through an examination of every aspect of the business and transactions with our customers by asking the question: How can our brand be perceived as providing superior service with each product or service we offer?

- *Maximize Brand Identity*. Each communication, letter, software screen, product, promotion, etc., will consistently and accurately communicate our brand architecture. A comprehensive graphics standards manual will be developed to aid in the management of the brand image.

- *Sales, Advertising, Promotion, and Public Relations*. All promotions, speeches, advertising, and sales efforts will be customer-driven to reinforce our promise.

- *Growth: Exceeding Customer / Client Expectations*. Controlled successful growth will be focused on the commitment to delight our customers and provide the highest levels of customer service—in other words, to exceed their expectations.

- *Customer / Client Partnership*. The *modus operandi* will be to "reality-check" all proposed brand executions (public relations, promotion, correspondence, etc.) in advance with current or potential customers. We will view our business as one of *relationship,* as opposed to a "transaction" mentality.

- *Strategic Alliances*. These will be utilized extensively to facilitate our growth strategy and leverage our brand's success.

III.   Market Analysis *(Examples)*

A partial listing of information that should be researched and analyzed includes:

Business Conditions

[Insert a brief executive summary of the overall business and economic situation facing the brand. (For an example, see Exhibit 1 that follows report.)]

- Consumer trends
- Products and services (with charts and graphs to support short narrative)
- Consolidation trends
- General economic forecast
- Technological impacts
- Forecast for specific business segments, markets, etc.

Competitive Environment

(Insert a brief executive summary of the overall competitive situation and landscape.) Prepare similar, detailed analyses of each competitor and attach as exhibits. Each analysis should address the following:

- Introduction to competitive set (types of products and services, related businesses, etc.)
- Summary paragraph describing each key competitor's overall situation, business trends, profitability, etc.
- Mission, vision, promise, etc.
- Location, relative size (employees, sales, customers)
- Strengths, weaknesses
- Growth strategy
- Future plans
- Financial performance
- Leadership (CEO and executive team's background, etc.)

IV. Business Profile *(Examples)*

The Company

Friendly's Supermarket, Inc. is a privately held company whose major shareholder is Big Bucks, Inc., America's premier venture capital firm. Big Bucks has launched many of America's retail successes, including ABC Retail, XYZ Wholesale, web u.s., etc.

Friendly's knows it takes more than money to build a successful brand; it takes the right people. Friendly's executive team has over 195 years combined leadership experience in developing new retail concepts and successful restaurants.

Strategic Partnerships

Friendly's expertise and capabilities are enhanced by several brand alliances, including:

(List brand alliances here)

Corporate Commitment

We make our customers happy, one at a time!

V. Brand Doctrine Action Plan *(update annually, consistent with budget process)*

(Examples)

A Brand Doctrine's purpose is to maximize the organization's brand equity. It is designed to achieve the following objectives:

- Increase real sales and profits.
- Maximize the perception of differentiation and value of the company's products and services in the market.
- Remove barriers for successfully converting new sales.
- Increase the perceived value of the brand's products and services.
- Occupy a "position of privilege" in the marketplace by creating sustainable competitive advantages.
- Increase brand equity and awareness.

Success is measured by monitoring the following indicators monthly or quarterly:

- Customer/client satisfaction (as appropriate)
- Profits and growth
- System performance (as appropriate, for franchising or agency-related organizations)
- Employee excitement
- Overall brand equity

Objectives will be achieved by focusing on the following key areas:

1. Perceived quality
2. Brand loyalty
3. Brand awareness
4. Brand associations and proprietary brand assets

1. Perceived Quality *(Examples)*

Perceived quality is defined as our customers' perception of the overall superiority of our brand's products and services compared to our competitors. The tactics to be used to build this perception are the following:

[Note: *The target date for the completion and executive responsibility for each action step should be added to each task listed below*.]

- Promote our quality perception by creating a family of distinctive subbrands—similar to the successful coffee company which, instead of just offering coffee from Colombia, created 17 coffee varietal brands, even a "Christmas Blend."
- Every display of our products will reflect our uniqueness and quality orientation as well as tell our story.
- Each and every product and service we offer will be truly distinctive.
- We eagerly offer and stand behind our money-back, absolute guarantee of satisfaction.

- We view every interaction with customers, consumers, or prospects as another opportunity to reinforce our relationship and quality perception.
- We will create a "conversation guide" for each type of customer interaction to ensure delivery of our brand's promise. We will answer all inquiries within one week and strive to respond the next business day.

Website
Telephone calls/voicemail
Correspondence

2.   Brand Loyalty *(Examples)*

Brand loyalty is the measure of commitment our customers and clients have to the brand as well as the feelings or perceptions of prospective customers and clients. All of our activities, promotions, presentations, public relations, etc., will strengthen this attachment and build our brand equity by reinforcing our customers' and clients' confidence that they have made the right choice when selecting our products and services.

[Note: *The target date for the completion and executive responsibility for each action step should be added to each task listed below.*]

- We will create a list of customer endorsements by third parties to enhance our position of privilege, and these will be utilized, as appropriate, in everything we do.
- A comprehensive continuing-improvement strategy will be implemented. This will involve quality measurement, policies and procedures, and training.
- Standard answers to the 20 most frequently asked questions will be provided to all appropriate employees, associates, members, etc.
- A 100–200% guarantee on all products and services will be established.

3.   Brand Awareness *(Examples)*

Every activity that our organization engages in to help potential customers become aware of our products and services should be consistent with our desired brand image.

[Note: *The target date for the completion and executive responsibility for each action step should be added to each task listed below.*]

- Develop nontraditional programs that optimize awareness of the company's distinctiveness.
- An internal communications plan and training/development strategy will be developed to educate all of the organization's associates and to inculcate the value proposition.
- Public relations play a key role in our brand awareness campaign. A plan will be completed in order to position the brand in the marketplace so that it occupies a position of expertise. In addition, a "disaster recovery plan" will be developed.
- The brand story will be created, revised, and printed, as appropriate.
- An external communication plan will be prepared for presentation to all brand alliances, strategic partners, vendors, and marketing relationships.
- A "sales lap deck" will be prepared for all representatives to use in meetings with influencers, customers, and prospects.
- A sales plan has been completed and approved on _____ .
- A statement will be created and approved that will be incorporated into all correspondence as the company's standard reference to our promise.
- A speech and public appearance plan will be created including presentations at _____ .
- A premier client program has been completed that will result in 10 premier orders being placed by _____ . (Add others as appropriate.)
- A guest service representative will answer the guest phone line. The representative will be responsible for tabulating guest surveys, comment cards, and phone calls to provide actionable information for improvement in guest services.

4.   Brand Associations and Proprietary Brand Assets *(Examples)*

Brand associations consist of anything that is "linked" to our products and services in the minds of our customers. Our brand assets include our trademarks, design, standards and specifications, vendor and development relationships, and our people.

[Note: *The target date for the completion and executive responsibility for each action step should be added to each task listed below.*]

- Create a new brand identity and refined logo that enhances the organization's position for segment dominance.
- A focused, relationship-building strategy will be implemented with current and potential industry influencers. This will include regularly providing them with stories about our successes, especially brand-building, public relations, and advertising.
- A business plan will be written to maximize sales in each appropriate channel.
- All merchandising and print material will reinforce our emotional brand association.
- We will develop a comprehensive legal description of our "trade dress."
- A design standards book will be developed and published for each product and service.
- All printed materials will focus on the image and tone of what is unique about our products and services. The brand's promise will serve as the guide.
- Proprietary, cobranded products and services will be introduced to support and reinforce the brand's values.
- In addition to our existing brand alliances, we will explore possible alliances with _____, _____, and _____.

- A database of customers' names and other pertinent information will be established. It will be used to reinforce brand loyalty. We will focus on relationships, as opposed to transactions.

- A series of high-quality, branded retail items will be made available for sale by mail order.
- A newsletter, *Brand News*, will be published regularly and distributed throughout the organization. It will contain such items of interest as sales, customer service, and brand-building ideas as well as success stories.
- All merchandising messages will be tailored to suit each channel of distribution.
- All key indicators (aided and unaided awareness, penetration levels, guest satisfaction rates, etc.) will be benchmarked and measured at least quarterly.

EXHIBIT 1

EXAMPLE OF A MARKET ANALYSIS REPORT *(EXAMPLES)*

BUSINESS CONDITIONS

The overall economy has been strong for at least three years, with high consumer confidence and a low unemployment rate. Consumer confidence is closely linked to the continued strong performance of the equity markets. The economy is stronger today than a year ago but is still vulnerable to many global economic problems.

CONSUMER TRENDS

Today's customers want:

- Stress reduction
- Convenience
- Innovations
- Good service
- Fun

Customers want "meal solutions" when they shop supermarkets. When they go out for dinner, they want restaurants that are fun and stimulating and where the food is tasty and the staff attentive.

Changing Supermarket Trends

What's In	What's Out
Meal solutions	Deli
Quick quality Casual food	Fast food
Guests	Customers
Prepared food	Ingredients
Hospitality	Food service
Call ahead and pick up	Wait in line to order

Consumers have a "grab and go" mindset today; consider these facts:

- Over the last 20 years, American cooking skills have declined due to time pressure and especially due to the microwave.
- Typical supermarket advertising focuses primarily on ingredients, not meals!

- When customers take food home, they expect it to be simple and to include condiments, napkins, flatware, plates, cups, etc.
- Supermarkets should examine their fast-food restaurant competitors and select the best ideas in order to win.
- Generic supermarket food is not the meal solutions customers want. Customers want the assurance of taste and quality they get from a known brand. Grocery stores need to think more like restaurants.

CONSUMER CHOICES

Health and fitness are still important to consumers. Consumers continue to garden more, with significant expenditures (up 16 percent last year) for flower seeds, vegetable seeds, and starter plants, and other potted plants. The popularity of and the interest in home dining and entertaining has increased sales of records, tapes, CDs, and audio equipment. Kitchen and household appliance sales grew by 4.3 percent. Exercise-related equipment sales have shown signs of slowing; however, this still seems to be an important area for consumers.

Specialty and warehouse stores also continue to be quite popular with consumers, with such popular choices as Barnes & Noble and Costco. Consumers are attracted to the new "experience" stores, such as The Discovery Channel Store in Washington D.C., which features interactive presentations, educational displays, and museum-quality exhibits.

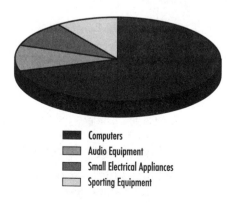

The Largest Growing Consumer Purchase Categories for the Last 5 Years

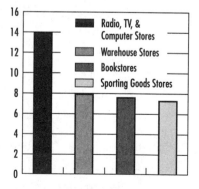

The Largest Growing Store Types by Annual Sales Growth Rates

DIGITAL AGE

The electronic age is with us. Consumer interest in computers and computer services has increased dramatically in the past three years. Computers and related products have been the fastest-growing consumer purchase category for that three-year period. And with the increased interest in the new technology, consumers are changing the face of the retail market by shopping more on the Internet. Consumers continue to want more for less, and in opting for the convenience of electronic shopping, that category will become an even more important factor in the future. With the new technology comes new competitors, such as Amazon.com, Webpages, and Internet shopping services. Retail stores are now finding that shopping on the Internet is becoming a bigger retail factor, and many have developed their own Websites for consumers' convenience.

What once was a commute to the local retail store is now just a touch of a few buttons.

The Internet provides a new world of convenience for the consumer, from booking an entire vacation, ordering flowers, and purchasing insurance to taking college courses.

As the computer age continues to boom, technology will continue to grow, and the retail world will integrate the new technology to offer consumers the quality, convenience, and variety they long for.

[Brand Teams: Insert forecast for the brand's specific business segment here]

NOTES

BRANDICTIONARY™

1. David A. Aaker, *Managing Brand Equity: Capitalizing on the Value of a Brand Name*, The Free Press, 1991.

CHAPTER 1

1. Henry Elrich, *The Wiley Book of Business Quotations*, John Wiley & Sons, New York, 1998, p. 7.
2. Kevin Clancy and Robert Shulman, *Marketing Myths That Are Killing Business*, McGraw-Hill, New York, 1994, p. 3.
3. John Bissell, "High-Tech's Future Lies with Consumers," *BrandWeek*, January 25, 1999, p. 24.
4. T. Scott Gross, "Guilt-Free Selling," *Design Forum / Ideations*, Fall 1998, p. 3.
5. Young & Rubicam, "The Story of the Y&R BrandAsset® Valuator Investigation," http://yr.com/bav.
6. Erich Joachimsthaler and David A. Aaker, "Building Brands Without Mass Media," *Harvard Business Review*, January–February 1997, p. 38.

CHAPTER 2

1. Bissell, op. cit., p. 24.

CHAPTER 4

1. Emil Dickstein, M.D., Jonathon Erlen, Ph.D., and Judith A. Erlen, Ph.D., R.N., "Ethical Principles Contained in Currently Professed Medical Oaths," *Academic Medicine*, vol. 66, No. 10, 1991, pp. 622–624.

CHAPTER 5

1. David Kiley, "Steve Wilhite, Finding the Soul of a Brand," *BrandWeek,* October 12, 1998, pp. 9–16.

2. "Coat of Arms," *The Random House Webster's Unabridged Dictionary*, Random House, 1998, p. 394.

3. "Does a Rose Really Smell as Sweet?" *Business Wire*, December 14, 1997.

4. Al Ries and Jack Trout, *Positioning: The Battle for Your Mind,* McGraw-Hill, New York, 1986, pp. 19–21.

5. Chuck Pettis, *TechnoBrands,* New York, American Management Association, 1995, pp. 19–21.

6. David A. Aaker, *Managing Brand Equity,* The Free Press, New York, 1991, pp. 242–262.

7. Tom Peters, *The Circle of Innovation*, Alfred A. Knopf, New York, 1997, p. 337.

CHAPTER 6

1. Russ Banham, "Making Your Mark," *CFO Magazine*, vol. 14, no. 3, March 1998, pp. 35–44.

2. D. Lee Carpenter, "Chairman's Commentary," *Design Forum / Ideations*, Fall 1998.

3. Ronal B. Lieber, "Now Are You Satisfied?" *Fortune Online,* www.fortune.com, February 16, 1998, p. 1.

4. Ibid.

5. Justin Martin, "As Customers Go, so Goes the Dow," *Fortune Online,* www.fortune.com, February 16, 1998, p. 2.

6. Gross, op. cit., p. 3.

7. Ibid., p. 3.

8. Michael Treacy and Fred Wiersema, *The Discipline of Market Leaders,* Addison-Wesley, Reading, 1995, pp. xiv–xvi.

9. Marilyn Adams, "Humor Goes a Long Way," *USA Today*, September 22, 1998, p. 2E.

10. American Society for Quality, "Customer Satisfaction Shows Upturn—Finally," *American Society for Quality Online,* www.asq.org/articles, accessed October, 9, 1998, p. 2.

11. Ibid., p. 2.

12. Sara Nathan, "Microsoft to Refocus on Users, Internet," *USA Today,* February, 8, 1999, p. 8.

13. Kelly Barron, "The Sam Walton of Supermarkets?" *Forbes,* October 19, 1998, p. 66.

14. Kirstin Downy Grimsley, "At Safeway, It's Service with a Smile— or Else," *The Seattle Times*, October 25, 1998, p. G1.

15. John R. Graham, "27 Ways to Strengthen Customer Loyalty," *Smartbiz Online*, www.smartbiz.com, September 4, 1998, p. 1.

16. Robert Spector and Patrick McCarthy, *The Nordstrom Way, Inside America's #1 Customer Service Company*, John Wiley & Sons, New York, 1995, p. 152.

17. Ibid., p. 13.

18. Kate Kane, "L.L. Bean Delivers the Goods," *Fast Company*, August–September 1997, p. 104.

19. Daniel J. Burrus, with Roger Gittines, *TechnoTrends, 24 Technologies That Will Revolutionize Our Lives,* HarperBusiness, New York, 1993, p. 354.

20. Reprinted by permission from GMA Research Corporation.

CHAPTER 7

1. Susan Zimmerman, "The Millennium Series—Store Brands: A Rosy Future," *Progressive Grocer*, November 1998, pp. 45–52.

2. Ibid., pp. 45–52.

3. Len Lewis, "Hanging Up the Gloves? A New Age of Collaboration," *Progressive Grocer,* October 1998, p. 28.

4. Ibid., p. 28.

5. Burrus, with Gittines, op. cit., pp. xviii–xx.

6. Michael Eisner, with Tony Schwartz, *Work in Progress*, Random House, New York, 1998, p. 398.

7. Ibid., p. 398.

8. Evan Schwartz, *Webonomics,* Broadway Books, New York, 1997, p. 173.

INDEX

ABOUT THE AUTHOR

Duane Knapp is president of BrandStrategy™, Inc., and advises leading brands worldwide and lectures frequently at universities and graduate schools. He has held senior executive positions with Westin Hotels, Holiday Corporation (Holiday Inn, Holiday Clubs, Residence Inn, Perkins Family Restaurants), The Promus Companies (Embassy Suites, Hampton Inn, Homewood Suites, Harrah's Casinos), and Cinnabon World Famous Cinnamon Rolls and has been a member of the Board of Directors of many organizations. His articles have appeared in *BrandWeek, Washington CEO, Risk Management,* and *The Journal of Commerce*. He lives in the San Juan Islands, near Seattle, Washington, and can be contacted at www.brandstrategy.com.